VOICES AND INSTRUMENTS

IN

CHRISTIAN WORSHIP

VOICES AND INSTRUMENTS

IN

CHRISTIAN WORSHIP

Principles, Laws, Applications

by

REV. JOSEPH GELINEAU, S.J

translated by

REV. CLIFFORD HOWELL, S.J.

THE LITURGICAL PRESS

COLLEGEVILLE, MINNESOTA

TRANSLATOR'S NOTE

Not infrequently the author quotes from Holy Scripture and from papal documents of which English translations already exist. Some of these are listed below, together with abbreviations (when used) and the English version which has been followed.

Holy Scripture (except for the psalms) is quoted from the Knox version.

Psalms are quoted from the Grail version published by Collins, London, England, as a "Fontana Book" entitled *The Psalms, A New Translation.*

Tra le sollecitudini (TLS), *motu proprio* of Pius X, Nov. 22, 1903, is quoted from the version of the Society of St. Gregory, Fowler Wright Books, Tenbury Wells, Worcs., England.

Divini cultus (DC), apostolic constitution of Pius XI, Dec. 20, 1928, is quoted from the version of the Society of St. Gregory.

Mediator Dei (MD), encyclical of Pius XII, Nov. 20, 1947, is quoted from the version of the Catholic Truth Society, London, England.

Musicae sacrae disciplina (MSD), encyclical of Pius XII, Dec. 25, 1955, is quoted from the version of the Society of St. Gregory.

Instructio de musica sacra et sacra liturgia (IMS) from the Sacred Congregation of Rites, Sept. 3, 1958, is quoted from the version by Clifford Howell, S.J., issued by B. Herder Publications, London .

Constitution on the Sacred Liturgy (CL) issued by the Second Vatican Council, Dec. 4, 1963, translation published by The Liturgical Press, Collegeville, Minn.

Sincere thanks are due to Dom A. Gregory Murray, O.S.B., of Downside Abbey, Bath, England, who kindly worked through the manuscript; he has not only ensured the accuracy of technical musical terms but has also improved the translation by many valuable suggestions.

Voices and Instruments in Christian Worship is the authorized English translation of *Chant et Musique dans le Culte Chrétien* by Joseph Gelineau, S.J., published by Éditions Fleurus, Paris, France.

Imprimi potest: John Coventry, S.J., Provincial of the English Province. *Nihil obstat*: John Eidenschink, O.S.B., J.C.D., *Censor deputatus*. *Imprimatur*: ✠ Peter W. Bartholome, D.D., Bishop of St. Cloud. June 10, 1964.

SELECTED READINGS

Actes du troisième Congrès international de Musique sacrée (Paris, 1957). Paris: 1959.

Aigrain, R. *La musique religieuse* (Bibliothèque catholique des sciences religieuses). Paris: Bloud et Gay, 1929.

Atti del Congresso internationale di Musica Sacra (Rome, 1950). Tournai: Desclée et Cie., 1952.

Baumstark, A. "Psalmenvortrag und Kirchendichtung des Orients," *Gottesminne,* 7 (1913).

————. *Nocturna Laus* (Liturgiewissenschaftliche Quellen und Forschungen, 32). Münster: 1957.

Bugnini, A. *Liturgia viva.* Milan: Ancora, 1962.

Cocheril, M. "Hymne," "Psalmodie," "Tropaire," etc., *Encyclopédie de la musique.*

Corbin, S. *L'Église à la conquête de sa musique* (Pour la musique). Paris: Gallimard, 1960.

————. "Centon," "Grégorien," "Répons," etc., *Encyclopédie de la musique.*

DACL: *Dictionnaire d'Archéologie chrétienne et de Liturgie,* published under the direction of F. Cabrol, H. Leclercq, and H. Marrou. Paris: Letouzey et Ané.

Davenson, H. *Petit traité de la musique selon saint Augustin* (Cahiers du Rhône). Neuchatel.

Encyclopédie de la musique, published under the direction of F. Michel, F. Lesure, V. Fédorov. 3 vols. Paris: Fasquelle, 1958-1961.

Études grégoriennes. 4 vols. Solesmes: 1954ff.

Froger, J. *Les chants de la messe aux VIIIᵉ et IXᵉ siècles.* Tournai: Desclée et Cie., 1950.

Gastoué, A. *Les origines du chant romain.* Paris: Picard, 1907.

————. *L'Église et la musique* (La vie chrétienne). Paris: Grasset, 1936.

————. *Le cantique populaire en France.* Lyons: Janon, 1924.

Gelineau, J. "Fonction et signification des principaux chants de la liturgie," *Église qui chante* (9 articles), 1959-1961.

————. "Les rôles dans l'assemblée qui chante," *Église qui chante* (6 articles), 1958-1959.

————. *Antiphona: Recherches sur les formes liturgiques de la psalmodie aux premiers siècles* (in preparation).

Gerbert, M. *De cantu et musica sacra.* 2 vols. Saint-Blaise: 1774.

————. *Scriptores ecclesiastici de musica sacra potissimum.* 3 vols. Saint-Blaise: 1784.

Gérold, Th. *Les Pères de l'Église et la musique* (Études d'histoire et de philosophie religieuse, 25). Paris: Alcan, 1931.

Gevaert, F. A. *La mélopée antique dans le chant de l'Église latine.* Ghent: 1895.

Handschin, J. "Gesungene Apologetik," *Mélanges Mohlberg.* Rome: 1949.

Hanin, A. *La législation ecclésiastique en matière de musique religieuse.* Tournai: Desclée et Cie., 1953.

Hesbert, J. *Antiphonale missarum sextuplex.* Brussels: Vromant, 1935.

Hucke, H. "Cantus gregorianus," in H. Schmidt, *Hebdomada sancta,* II. Rome: Herder, 1957.

Huot-Pleuroux, P. *Histoire de la musique religieuse.* Paris: P.U.F., 1957.

Jungmann, J. A. *The Mass of the Roman Rite: Its Origins and Development.* 2 vols. Trans. by F. A. Brunner. New York: Benziger Bros., 1950-1955. Rev. by Charles K. Riepe, 1 vol., without notes, 1959.

———. *Des lois de la célébration du culte liturgique.* Trans. by M. Zemb. Paris: Éditions du Cerf, 1956.

Kressmann, E. *De la musique religieuse.* Paris: "Je Sers," 1844.

Liturgy, The. Translation of *Les Enseignements pontificaux: La liturgie* by the monks of Solesmes. Boston: St. Paul Editions, 1962.

Mansi, J. D. *Sacrorum conciliorum nova et amplissima collectio.* 31 vols. Florence-Venice: 1757-1790.

Martimort, A. G.–Picard F. *Liturgie et musique* (Lex Orandi, 28). Paris: Éditions du Cerf, 1959.

Martimort, A. G. *L'Église en prière: Introduction à la liturgie.* Paris: Desclée et Cie., 1961.

MGG: *Die Musik in Geschichte und Gegenwart.* Ed. F. Blume. Kassel: Bärenreiter, 1949ff.

Mueller, K. F.–Blankenburg, W. *Die Musik des evangelischen Gottesdienstes* (Leiturgia, 4). Kassel: Stauda, 1961.

PG: J. P. Migne. *Patrologiae cursus completus — Series graeca.* 161 vols. Paris-Montrouge: 1857-1866.

PL: J. P. Migne. *Patrologiae cursus completus — Series latina.* 221 vols. Paris-Montrouge: 1844-1864.

Quacquarelli, A. *Retorica e liturgia antenicena.* Rome: Desclée, 1960.

Quasten, J. *Musik und Gesang in der Kulten der heidnischen Antike und christlichen Frühzeit* (Liturgiewissenschaftliche Quellen und Forschungen, 22). Münster: 1930.

Roland-Manuel. *Histoire de la musique,* I (Encyclopédie de la Pléiade). Paris: Gallimard, 1960.

Romita, F. *Jus musicae liturgicae.* Rome: Edizioni Liturgiche, 1947.

Samson, J. *Musique et chant sacrés* (Pour la musique). Paris: Gallimard, 1957.

Schmidt, H. *Introductio in liturgiam occidentalem.* Rome: Herder, 1960.

Sesini, H. *Poesia e musica nella latinità cristiana dal III° al X° secolo.* Turin: Societa Ed. Internazionale, 1949.

Staeblein, B. "Frühchristliche Musik," "Litanei," "Kyrie," *Die Musik in Geschichte und Gegenwart.*

Ursprung, O. *Die katholische Kirchenmusik* (Handbuch der Musikwissenschaft). Potsdam: 1931.

Valois, J. de. "Alléluia," "Antienne," "Psalmodie," etc., *Larousse de la musique.* 2 vols. Paris: 1957.

Wagner, P. *Origine et développement du chant liturgique jusqu'à la fin du moyen âge.* Tr. Bour. Tournai: Desclée et Cie., 1904.

Wellesz, E. *A History of Byzantine Music and Hymnography.* 2nd ed. Oxford: Clarendon Press, 1961.

Werner, E. *The Sacred Bridge.* New York: Columbia University Press, 1959.

Zweiter internationaler Kongress für katholische Kirchenmusik (Vienna, 1954). Vienna: 1955.

TABLE OF CONTENTS

INTRODUCTION

As aids to her official worship of God, the Church has accepted, and continues to accept, musical compositions which differ enormously from one another in their origin, date, type, style, purpose and employment. Some of them have come down to us by oral tradition from early Christian times; but we have inherited others from every succeeding age, and hardly a day goes by without the birth of some new composition. We can trace some to ancient Jewish and Mediterranean sources dating back to the first Christian centuries; others, belonging to the Middle Ages, are of Latin or Syrian provenance; and then we have the contribution of all the subsequent composers who have written for the Church, from Perotinus to Stravinsky, remembered by name or forgotten. Of these many works, some are just a single melodic line, others are polyphonic, and yet others are instrumental. Some utilize only three or four notes of the musical scale, while others call upon the utmost resources of the human voice and instruments. Simple popular airs can be contrasted with sophisticated compositions; there are works intended for soloists, for choirs and for congregations.

For use in the solemn celebration of her liturgy the Church prescribes certain melodies, recommends others, permits yet others, or relegates them to non-liturgical worship. Immortal masterpieces survive the passage of centuries, works of no merit are forgotten. There are compositions for special occasions and those which form the ordinary repertoire of parishes; items traditional among the people of one nation or region, and those universally accepted throughout the Roman rite, and so on. Faced with this luxuriant growth so astonishingly varied in nature, how is one to assess the qualities which make a particular musical composition more or less suitable for use in Christian worship?

The basic question which Christians have to consider as regards music intended for worship is not on the historical or esthetic plane, nor even on

9

the technical or sociological plane. It is a religious question. In the celebration of the Church's worship the point at issue is not "music-making," but entry, by means of the art of music, into the salvific mystery. Although, to the eye of faith, everything may have some significance, not all signs are equally meaningful. And though all true music can be turned into prayer, not every musical composition introduces Christians with equal effectiveness into the prayer of the Church. What, then, are the criteria for judgment?

The first criterion is provided for us in the *praxis Ecclesiae*, and in the Church's laws, or customs having the force of law, which express her practice. For a long time ecclesiastical legislation on the subject of sacred music was but implicit and fragmentary. Only in the twentieth century did it assume explicit form and acquire precision in the pronouncements of Pius X (*motu proprio, Tra le sollecitudini*, 1903), Pius XI (apostolic constitution *Divini cultus*, 1928), and Pius XII (encyclicals *Mediator Dei*, 1947, and *Musicae sacrae disciplina*, 1955; Instruction of the Sacred Congregation of Rites, September 3, 1958). But there does exist nowadays a code of law concerning sacred music which pastors, musicians and composers can and ought to consult.[1]

But even when there are such things as prescriptions, prohibitions and directives expressed in written laws, there still remains the question of the best way to apply them in each concrete case. At next Sunday's high Mass in a given parish, should the *Kyrie* be sung in Gregorian chant or in polyphony? And to which setting? Which Mass should be chosen out of the *Kyriale*? Or is there any reason for preferring Josquin Deprès to Perosi, or conversely?

A second criterion is the artistic worth of a composition. For it is only by its beauty that music can signify the sacred. Moreover, within the limits set by positive law, the choice of music to be performed at any ceremony is normally decided on esthetic grounds. Anyone is at liberty to go to a library, consult some of the numerous books which list the settings of any particular liturgical text, and then make a decision according to his taste.

[1] A recent addition to these documents is the Constitution *De Sacra Liturgia* promulgated by the Second Vatican Council; chapter VI of this Constitution treats of sacred music. It is a document of the highest importance which will henceforth determine the interpretation to be put upon all points discussed in previous documents concerned with the liturgy. Nevertheless, the Constitution itself formulates only the *altiora principia*. Chapter VI, in particular, is not to be taken as a new code of legislation for sacred music; it presupposes all the previous norms, and does but lay down that the manner in which they are to be implemented in the future is to conform to the principles expounded in the Constitution.

(This English translation of Père Gelineau's book was completed before the Second Vatican Council had promulgated its Constitution on liturgy. The conclusions put forth in the book have by no means been weakened; on the contrary, they acquire added strength in the light of the Council's teaching. At a time when liturgical life and sacred music in all countries should be deriving new vigor from the Council, the publication of this book is particularly opportune. The author has not felt any need to modify his text in any way, but has thought it worthwhile to add, in the footnotes, references to articles of the Constitution (CL) which vindicate or strengthen the views he has expressed or are helpful in rendering them more specific.)

But music is only one constituent of a liturgical rite. More important than the performance of a work of art is the celebration of whatever mystery of salvation is presented by that rite to those who take part in it. And so the esthetic criterion is not decisive for judging the appropriateness of a piece of music for a particular celebration. One must first know what the Church intends as regards each item designed to be sung as part of her ritual, even when her written law specifies no details. One has to make sure that every sung item is performed in such a way that it will procure the active and intelligent participation of the assembled faithful required by Pius XII.[1a]

Hence one cannot give a sufficient answer to these last two preliminary questions just by assessing the musical worth of a repertoire. And yet a study of the books so far written about sacred music shows that most of them are concerned only with the compositions considered in themselves. They treat the subject from the point of view of the historian, inquiring into the origin, date, characteristics and esthetic value of each work, whether it be Gregorian chant, classical polyphony or a modern composition.[2] Among these books there are a few which deal with the Church's legislation.[3] Some of them give a rather general assessment of the religious and spiritual worth of instrumental and vocal music.[4] But hardly any of them have taken as their starting-point a study of the liturgical rites and their celebration; they make no attempt to establish, in the light of these, how music ought always to be a help to the liturgical rite being celebrated, and how it should profit those who are taking part in it.[5]

In our own day this lacuna is making itself felt in a very marked way. For a number of liturgical reforms have been undertaken by the Church recently; they were prepared and fostered by many efforts made during several past decades to make the liturgy become once again the "primary and indispensable source of the true Christian spirit" (St. Pius X); and all

[1a] Address to the members of the Assisi Congress, 1956, in *The Assisi Papers* (Collegeville, Minn.: The Liturgical Press, 1957). Cf. CL 14. Participation is to be "full, conscious and active."

[2] Among French books, this is so of R. Aigrain, *La musique religieuse* (Paris, 1929); P. Huot-Pleuroux, *Histoire de la musique religieuse* (Paris, 1957). To these must be added a great many particular studies and monographs.

[3] For example: A. Hanin, *La législation ecclésiastique en matière de musique religieuse* (Tournai, 1953); F. Romita, *Jus musicae liturgicae* (Rome, 1947); A. Pons, *Droit ecclésiastique et musique sacrée* (Saint-Maurice, 1959).

[4] For example: Th. Gérold, *Les Pères de l'Église et la musique* (Paris, 1931); H. Davenson, *Petit traité de la musique selon saint Augustin*, "Cahiers du Rhône," Neuchatel; J. Samson. *Musique et chant sacrés* (Paris, 1957), etc.

[5] It is worth noting that a recent textbook on liturgy (A. G. Martimort, *L'Église en prière*, Paris, 1961) which gives a very carefully compiled bibliography after each article, does not cite a single work dealing expressly with the relationship of music to liturgical celebrations. On the other hand, this question has been discussed quite often in Protestant writings; for example: R. Will, *Le culte* (Paris, 1925); E. Kressmann, *De la musique religieuse* (Paris, 1944); and above all K. F. Mueller, "Die Musik des evangelischen," *Leiturgia*, IV (Kassel, 1961). See also A. Bugnini, *Liturgia viva*, a commentary on the Instruction of September 3, 1958, which was published in Milan (Ancora, 1962) since this book was written.

these things have made both priests and people become far more sensitive than formerly, not only to the quality of the ceremonies considered as a whole, but also to the particular meaning and specific graces latent in each of their several parts. This refinement of liturgical perception on the part of the faithful, and the reforms promulgated by the hierarchy, have already produced considerable fruit in various fields: the content of celebrations and the meaning of the rites involved in them have become much clearer, and the architectural and artistic setting for the liturgy has been improved. Can we say that music has applied or even followed this renewal to an equal extent?

Many Church musicians are extremely conscientious about the canonical and esthetic requirements bound up with the art of sacred music, and there can be no question of departing from these. But few of them have become sufficiently well informed liturgically and pastorally to be able to collaborate intimately in the present-day deepening of liturgical life. And yet this imperatively demands the combined help of technical knowledge, art and piety. It is true that among the historical and theological works written by modern liturgists any treatment of the subject of liturgical music occupies a very subordinate place.[6] And so nowadays pastors and musicians can learn nothing about all this except from sources that are both fragmentary and dispersed.

The aim of this present work is to probe into the relations between music and Christian worship, taking as a starting-point the life and laws of the Church, together with the sciences of liturgy, history and pastoral practice. But although it will be based wholly and exclusively on present legislation, it does not aim to handle the subject from the juridic standpoint; and while making constant references to history, it likewise repudiates any claim to be a history of Christian music. Furthermore, though frequently appealing to comparative liturgy in order to elucidate important or obscure points, it professes to deal only with the Roman rite as it actually exists at the present moment, and the liturgical ceremonies and public devotions here and now in use within that rite. Finally, although it will utilize technical, sociological and anthropological data which condition the practice both of music and of pastoral work, it makes no pretensions to be a practical textbook of sacred music.

In many countries of Western civilization, and in almost every mission country, music is today confronting pastoral liturgy with a series of relatively new problems to which neither liturgists nor musicians can provide

[6] Of course, all the important works about liturgy, whether concerned with its history or theory, do give some treatment to the question of music, and the reflections one can find in such books are of considerable value. But there is often a contrast between the standard of specifically liturgical research, and the lack of technical competence in the sphere of music, or dependence at second hand on work previously done by others. For example, the great work of J. A. Jungmann, *The Mass of the Roman Rite*, 2 vols. (New York: Benziger Bros., 1950–55) relies, as regards matters musical, on P. Wagner, *Einführung in die gregorianischen Melodien* (Leipzig, 1911–1912), or on O. Ursprung, *Die katholische Kirchenmusik* (Potsdam, 1931).

cut-and-dried answers. For this reason it seems best to attempt here a general treatment of the inner meaning and function of music within Christian worship.

The first part of this book sets out to answer three general questions: Why should there be singing in Christian worship? How should music be coordinated with ritual action? What function does it fulfill therein? From these questions certain fundamental principles emerge: the act of singing is a mystery;[7] singing is a ritual form of expression; music is the handmaid of the sacred text.

The second part of the book will then try to explain the ritual function of music as deduced from the rite celebrated according to the mind of the Church. Here we shall meet a series of laws of function, laws which vary according to the more or less official character of the rites being celebrated, according to their intrinsically significant nature, according to the persons responsible for their performance, according to the literary texts which are to be sung and to the music which of its nature is suited to them.

But celebration according to the mind of the Church is itself relative to those who take part in the celebration. In the very performance of items which are to be sung conformably to their functional laws, one has to take into account both the capabilities and the taste of those who are to sing them. Hence there arise questions concerning the type and style of music to be adopted for a given assembly, and the extent to which polyphony and musical instruments are to be employed.

Only after establishing the conditions determined by the rite itself and by those who perform it does it become possible to apply them to each of the items which are to be sung at Mass or in the other offices of the Church. And then one can attempt to assess objectively repertoires or individual works, whether ancient or modern, as regards their fittingness for liturgical use.

May these pages help both performers and composers of sacred music to a better understanding of, and love for, the world of music used by the Church to surround her worship for the greater glory of the true God.

[7] Here we use the word "mystery" as meaning that which the Fathers of the Church expressed by the word *sacramentum*, that is, a sacred sign, perceptible by the senses, which reveals and communicates an invisible reality of the order of grace, a reality which has, towards the perceptible thing which signifies it, a symbolic relationship derived from the nature of things or prophetic events drawn from the history of salvation. Later on the word "sacrament" was reserved for those seven signs which are fully causative of the grace of Christ; and the word "sacramental" has also been given a much restricted meaning. It is therefore the word "mystery" which seems most suited nowadays to designate that "complexus of the efficacious signs of the Church's sanctification and her worship" (C. Vagaggini, *Theological Dimensions of the Liturgy* [Collegeville, Minn.: The Liturgical Press, 1959], I, p. 17) of which the liturgy is made up. Cf. CL 33, 59–60.

1 SINGING

AS A MYSTERY

It has been said that music is something divine, and that melody is the daughter of God. Are such sayings without foundation? However familiar the song of a bird or the sighing of the wind, however human the lilt of a song or the tune of a reed-pipe, neither nature nor art can be, for one who believes in an invisible world, a goal where his spirit can rest. The passing sounds of this world stimulate him as much as they soothe him, like the call of a voice from the beyond, whose echo they might well be. For every upright man has a presentiment and partial understanding of the sacred word which the sounds of this world bring to his ear and yet, at the same time, prevent him from hearing. But when Christ's *Ephpheta* has opened the ears of his faith, the whole of creation begins to sing for him the glory of the Creator. Then he hears the harmony of the universe, like a summons to the new world into which the Savior wills that all flesh should enter. And when at last, surrounded by the hymns of the Church, the neophyte goes forward to his meeting with the living God, the voice which comes to his ears is that of the Word of God; the prayers which rise to his lips are the inexpressible groanings of the Spirit which says "*Abba*, Father."

How, then, can a song which is heard signify a reality which is not heard? How can sound coming from a human mouth convey the truth of the Spirit of God? How, in a word, can singing be a mystery?[7a]

[7a] Read once more the last footnote in the Introduction.

14

To understand this we must first recall the natural significance of song in human life. We know from Christian revelation that grace does not take the place of nature, but completes and fulfills it. Nothing can be a sign of God unless it has some meaning for men. However, though nature can give some presentiment of the divine, she cannot impart it; only God can communicate what is divine. And so, in the history of salvation, song takes on a significance deeper than the merely natural; in the voice of Israel, and especially in the psalms, the cry from the human heart is spiritualized, and within it there sounds forth an echo as from the surface of a new world which draws near. In the Word-made-flesh, the only Word of the Father and the perfect praise ascending from creation to the Creator, the full truth of human song is revealed. It is this truth which ever continues to resound under the influence of the Spirit of Pentecost, like the strings of a harp under the fingers of the harpist, in the songs of the Christian liturgy, which is the unceasing and harmonious dialogue between the Bridegroom and His Bride, between the Lord and His Church.[7b] These songs are the image and presage of the celestial praise wherein music, eternally living, will have stripped away the externals of the art of sound to allow its inner rhythm to develop.

Human speech transformed into music holds such rich possibilities that we have to choose among the various avenues to the world above which it opens to us. But whether we explore man's cry for help or his paean of praise, his personal meditations or his communal song, we shall always find that the way we follow leads us towards the one single truth which is the love of Christ.

1. From the Call for Help to the Prayer of Supplication

A child is afraid: he utters a cry. He is hungry: he weeps. A man is in danger: he shouts for help; when he is suffering he groans. These vocal expressions of fear or pain are anterior in nature to any words, and yet their meaning is quite startling. It is the sudden arousing of the will to live; it is a denial of the need to die. For the one facing the crisis, it is a refusal of despair. Whether he is conscious of it or not, in uttering his cry he is sending out an appeal. He is affirming that there does exist someone to hear and to bring help: "If I can make myself heard I shall be saved."

But if he is a prey to doubt, or if his cry is too feeble, he repeats it: "Help, help, help!" To make his voice carry further he prolongs the sound, gives it inflections which approximate those of a spontaneous melody charged with emotion. Mourners wailing around a funeral bier are not expounding in words the nature of death; but their long lamentations give eloquent testimony of its fearful power. For the man of faith the prayer of supplication

[7b] Cf. CL 83.

has a similar genesis. "Save me, O God!" This is the origin in worship of the prayer-form known as the litany: *Kyrie eleison, Kyrie eleison, Kyrie eleison!*

In view of all this, we should not find it surprising that, among the people to whom the true God chose to reveal Himself, the majority of their prayers were those of supplication, and most of these were in the form of urgent appeal. In the very process of learning to know Yahweh, Israel realized that she was nothing without her Savior and was powerless without her Protector. In her alliance with the God of fidelity she learned of her own infidelity and sinfulness. And thus the first collection of human prayers that were inspired by God, the book of Psalms, is filled with cries of appeal in the face of death, suffering and sin, and with lamentations before injustice, persecution and defeat. "Have mercy on me! Save me! Deliver me! Hasten to my aid! How long, O Lord, how long? Hear my prayer! Lend me your ear! Listen to the cry of my appeal!"

The sinner calls out for grace. The poor man demands justice. The people appeal for help. Is not Yahweh Himself Pity and Pardon, Love and Truth, Salvation and Justice?

> Out of the depths I cry to you, O Lord;
>   Lord, hear my voice!
> Oh, let your ears be attentive
>   to the voice of my pleading!
>
> Because with the Lord there is mercy
>   and fulness of redemption;
> Israel indeed he will redeem
>   from all its iniquity (Ps. 129:1-2, 7-8).

No matter what melodies may have been used to sing these words, they were the vehicle for the primitive cry of the man of faith expressing himself in sacred music; this cry was the origin of the sung prayer of mankind.

When the Son of Man came, poor among the poor, persecuted to death, "made sin" for the sake of sinners, He made His own and Himself uttered the cry of appeal of all humanity in distress. "Christ, during his earthly life, offered prayer and entreaty to the God who could save him from death, not without a piercing cry, not without tears, yet with such piety as won him a hearing. Son of God though he was, he learned obedience in the school of suffering" (Heb. 5:7-9). And what did the soldiers who guarded the Cross make of the final appeal of our Lord, "*Eli, Eli, lamma sabachtani?*," which came from a psalm (21:2; Matt. 27:46)?

What does it matter, in view of the fact that for the first time a human cry, in the form of this song, was eloquent enough to rend the heavens and the heart of the Father, and that once and for all an appeal from the earth was heard:

> And my soul shall live for him,
>   my children serve him.
> They shall tell of the Lord to generations yet to come,
>   declare his faithfulness to people yet unborn:
>   "These things the Lord has done" (Ps. 21:31-32).

That is why the Church knows that she is already heard every time she appeals to her Savior in the liturgy, whether she does it in short, powerful phrases or in long recitatives. *"Kyrie eleison! Miserere nobis! Libera nos, Domine! Te rogamus, audi nos!"* When the Spirit and the Spouse say "Come," the Lord is there, and the man of desire receives the water of life (Apoc. 22:17).

Let man send up the song of Christian prayer from his burdened heart and his parched lips. Then his breath will expand under the influence of the liberating Spirit, and his mouth will be grace-filled as with dew.

2. From the Cry of Admiration to the Prayer of Thanksgiving

The contented infant prattles; the child who is given his birthday presents dances and shouts with glee; the lover on his way to meet his beloved whistles or hums a song; a victorious nation thunders forth its national anthem. For the expression of a powerful sentiment of exultation mere words are not enough; music comes to the rescue of words by adorning or prolonging them.

If someone spontaneously breaks into song, we say that he is happy, for song is a sign of joy. But whence comes this joy which breaks forth in song? It originates in a sense of well-being, of euphoria, which is able to overflow without constraint. Song, therefore, is also a sign of health and of liberty. And what are life and liberty for a man if not the power to develop and communicate himself? In singing, a man becomes, as it were, a pouring-out and a gift, because song, compounded of the breath which he breathes out from his inmost self and of the sound of his voice which cannot be held or imprisoned, is the free expression of himself, the manifestation of his interior being and the gratuitous giving of his personality. Brought face to face with entrancing beauty, man lifts up his heart in a cry of admiration; he comes forth from himself in the sound of his voice that he may be carried towards the object of his praise. Finally, song is the living portrayal of spiritual self-giving. It is the gift of love whereby a man sets himself free in a joyous abandonment and complete affirmation, knowing that precisely there, where he seems to lose himself, is in fact where he finds and expresses himself to the full. His very being gushes forth under the impulse or attraction of love which his heart, overflowing or vanquished, is no longer able to contain: *Amantis est cantare.*

The man of faith, overwhelmed with reverence before the divine majesty, confident that he is protected or filled with God's power, breaks forth into praise. The holiness of God, even though it fills him with awe, at the same time fascinates and attracts him; it evokes from his lips a hymn of adoration. And when he has experienced God's bounty he is moved to thanksgiving.

What Yahweh gave to Israel was first of all life and liberty. When He freed Israel from the slavery of Egypt, when He delivered her from the Amalekites or the Philistines, from Moab or Edom, when He opened the way of return to the captives of Babylon, what He gave was victory and assurance of a free life. When He vindicated the poor man oppressed by tyrants, when He pardoned sins and blotted out faults, when He rescued the condemned or the sick from the portals of death, He was always conferring life and liberty. Security, peace, abundance, happiness, rest, strength —these are what prompted the cries of joy which form the warp and woof of the psalms of praise: "You have saved me! You have lifted me up! You have set me at liberty! Happy the man who . . . Happy the people who . . . Cry out with joy, exult, praise, play instruments!"

> Ring out your joy to God our strength,
>   shout in triumph to the God of Jacob.
> Raise a song and sound the timbrel,
>   the sweet-sounding harp and the lute,
> Blow the trumpet . . . (Ps. 80:2-4).

Cries of misery have their origin in man himself, by reason of his sins. By contrast, the joy of which the psalms sing is not regarded as originating on earth—it is always a gift from God. That is why Israel's praise is so constantly in the form of a "confession" to Yahweh, Savior. It is He who is extolled, blessed, praised and adored for His holiness, His greatness, His justice, His valiance and His power as these attributes are manifested in His works. It is a "new song" which belongs only to the people to whom God has revealed His judgments (Pss. 147-149). "Happy the people who acclaim such a king" (Ps. 88:16).

One word indicates the characteristic of this song: *Thanks!* This thanksgiving is more than just admiring praise, and something other than gratitude for benefits received.[8] It is a solemn attestation or public acknowledgment that Yahweh is the only true God, the only Lord and Savior. This praise is at the same time an expression of faith, trustful adoration and gratitude for God's faithful love:

[8] The English words "thank" and "thanksgiving" are a somewhat inadequate translation of the Hebrew words *yadah* and *todah*. While being stronger than mere simple praise (*hll, rnn*), these are not exactly the same as "giving thanks." The Vulgate comes nearer to the original sense with *confiteri* and *confessio*. One can justify "thanksgiving" by the fact that the *eucharistia* of the New Testament is related to the *todah* of the Old Testament. It seems that the basis for this word is the gesture of raising the hand (*yad*) in public testimony of that which is asserted.

> Give thanks to the Lord for he is good,
> for his love has no end!
> Let the sons of Israel say:
> "His love has no end" (Ps. 117:1-2).

There is one acclamation which sums up all this praise: *Alleluia*—Praise the Lord! It is the cry of victory and salvation, the cry of admiration and joy, of faith and love, the cry of thanksgiving of the people saved for eternity (Apoc. 19:1-3).

But the genuine paschal *Alleluia* of redeemed man was not fully and definitively sung until Christ, the conqueror of death, uttered it on the morning of His resurrection. The perfect rendering of thanks is the sacrifice which Christ offered to His Father. Before singing the *Hallel* psalms for the last time under the Old Alliance (Matt. 26:30), our Lord showed us how we were to celebrate ritually His paschal sacrifice—and this was during a thanksgiving meal. Taking bread He "blessed it" (eulogēsas, Mark 14:22), and taking the cup He "offered thanks" (eucharistēsas, Mark 14:23), saying: "This is My Blood of the New Testament shed for many." It was customary among the Jews always to sing this blessing: "Let us give thanks to the Lord our God." [9]

It is no accident that the celebration par excellence of Christian worship carries the name *Eucharist*. For this word expresses both a sung thanksgiving expressed in the rites of the Mass, and also the sacrifice of our Savior who died and rose again. This enables us to understand better why the eucharistic prayer of the Mass finds its supreme lyrical expression in the singing of the Preface. And one can grasp its inner meaning: in the testimony and praise of the priest, to which all the people respond, the Church gives thanks (*gratias agit*) for the graces (*gratias*) of salvation. Her song is none other than that uttered by the whole Christ to His Father, to "manifest God's glory" (Eph. 1:14).

Formerly men rendered thanks to God by offering to Him victims immolated with bloodshed; but for this there was substituted, after the Passover of Christ, "through whom we must offer to God a continual sacrifice of praise, the tribute of lips that give thanks to his name" (Heb. 13:15). And so for us song has become a special sign of spiritual sacrifice.

3. From Recitation to Meditation

According to the universal consensus of opinion, often expressed by early writers, right thinking, right speaking and right acting in man are but three inseparable branches from the trunk of the same tree: the tree of wis-

[9] G. Dix, *The Shape of the Liturgy* (London, 1954). Cf. L. Bouyer, "L'Eucharistie dans la dernière Cène," *La Maison Dieu*, 18 (1949), pp. 34-47.

dom.[10] He who can formulate beautifully what his mind has conceived possesses intelligence and wisdom. That is why, in every culture and every language, the wisdom of the nations has found expression in proverbs and sayings cast in phrases whose very euphony indicates the worth of the thought they contain. If the verses of a poet preserve the vitality of some idea or sentiment which would have perished if expressed only in a banal way, this can only be because of their construction. In like manner, the rhythmic recitation of proverbs, "wise sayings," imparts to the reciter an appreciation of order, a demand for justice, a love for a harmonious way of life. *Bene dicere non possit nisi bonus* (Quintillian).

Now it is well known that in ancient cultures, as also in that of the West up to the Renaissance, a poetic or sapiential literature was always considered to require a lyrical style of recitation. Corresponding with the ancient trilogy of poetry-music-dance, any time that the words of a literary work of art were pronounced, they were uttered in the form of a recitative having both rhythm and melody. The melody is normally no more than a few notes, and the rhythm no more than the balancing of accents or of feet within the verse. But by this kind of recitation the speaker-singer is identifying himself with what he utters. He is nourishing himself upon the very marrow of the thought which the words contain; by means of number,[11] he grasps its fugitive duration and inserts it into a freely ordered sequence which he subordinates to wisdom; by means of melos[12] he lets the words take on the colors of the prism of sentiments which illuminates them.

"To speak" here means much more than to enunciate an idea; it implies that one savors and derives nourishment from the idea; it is to become the truth which is spoken. We must not be surprised, therefore, that the man who believes, when he is reciting a ritual prayer (or a magic formula), feels the need to clothe it in number and melos. For by his recitation he is seeking to identify himself with the divine text.

It is characteristic of the Bible to clothe sapiential sayings in a poetic and lyrical form, by the recurrence of accents, by parallelism of phrases and melodic recitation. The basis of all sapiential literature, as also of the psalms,

[10] A. Quacquarelli, *Retorica e liturgia antenicena* (Rome, 1960), pp. 1ff. R. Schwab, "Porche oriental," in *Histoire des littératures*, I, Encyclopédie de la Pléiade (Paris, 1956). On the subjects of rhythm and melody, see M. Jousse, *Rythmo-mélodisme et rythmo-typographisme pour le style oral palestinien* (Paris, 1952).

[11] By "number" (*numerus*) we mean a certain rational ordering of verbal flow and musical movement. Number always includes a grasping of duration by the mind. It is different from rhythm, which has a broader connotation, and from measure (in the sense of modern solfeggio), which is narrower (see ch. 8, pp. 112ff., and especially note 253).

[12] In the absence of any appropriate English word, we use the word "melos" to mean the melodic element (sound) taken in the strict sense, as opposed to the agogic element (movement) of the music. The term "melody" is equivocal because it often implies either one or the other of these elements.

is *mashal,* or rhythmo-melodic proverb. And it is just as fundamental that this "wisdom" should be *in actu.* For the art of speaking is already action, just as the Hebrew word *dabar* means equally "word" and "deed."

For the Law, the song of the Alliance, condensed into words of wisdom, is meant to be obeyed. And who is to obey it? First of all the man who "meditates" on it. Let us be clear on this: he who psalmodizes the Law, utters it, scans it, repeats it, examines it, ponders it, is "murmuring it day and night" (Ps. 1:2). For there is music in this process. The devotee of the Law savors it in his mouth like honey (Ps. 18:11); it strengthens his soul, gladdens his heart, enlightens his eyes so that he behaves without blame (Ps. 118) and brings forth in season his due fruit of life and of justice. Has he not reduced to order his breath, his nerves, his blood, his members, his "heart" with its thoughts, his "loins" together with his will and his desires? The one who loves the Law never says, "Enough of words, let us proceed to action!," because for him, to speak is to become. Just as a child will tirelessly repeat what it wants until its desire has become fact, so the man of faith, singing the word of God, transforms himself into that supreme activity which is divine wisdom.

Man, however, is of flesh. Is it possible for him really to become Word and Wisdom of God? Yes, on condition that the Word of God could become flesh. He of whom it was said, "No man ever spoke as this man speaks" (John 7:46), came to speak within us the Wisdom of the Father. It was He who first taught us the truth of the Kingdom. And it was He who formulated the charter of the New Alliance in the form of *mashal* to be repeated until He comes again:

> Blessed are you who are poor,
> the kingdom of God is yours.
> Blessed are you who are hungry now,
> you will have your fill . . . (Luke 6:20-21).

And He has told us to recite without ceasing, in the manner of a psalm: "Our Father, who art in heaven, hallowed be Thy name, Thy kingdom come Thy will be done . . ." (Matt 6:9-10).

But in order that our singing may not be wasted breath or hollow word, He has communicated to us the Spirit of the Son raised up by the Father, so that this Spirit may Himself say within us, "*Abba,* Father!" God willed that the word of Christ should remain with us in abundance, that we should instruct each other in all wisdom by singing to each other and to God in psalms, hymns, and spiritual music (Col. 3:16).

For the Word of God is already a living Bread which has come down from heaven to give life to the world (John 6:32). At her festive table the Church first provides for her children the nourishment of Truth under the appear-

ance of word, cadence and sound as a prelude to the more perfect sacrament
to follow.[12a]

4. From Choral Singing to Community of Love

Union of voices expresses union of hearts. No meaning attached to song is
more universally acknowledged than this, or more vividly realized by those
who sing together. It is singing together which both manifests and constitutes a community. It controls the steps of those who advance in pilgrimage
or procession; it coordinates the movements of rowers or reapers; it unites
the hearts of a people in a hymn of victory; it strengthens the bonds of friend-
ship among those who attend a marriage feast. In fact, it is impossible, without insincerity, to sing with other people and yet to hate them. How can
members of the same chorus ignore one another? The more any culture is
endowed with a sense of solidarity, the more will community singing find
place in it.

Song in common signifies the community so well because it affords man
an opportunity to express himself in a way that is at once fully personal
and yet essentially social. We have already discussed how song is a complete
expression of the person, coming from within him, involving all his powers
of desire and development, filled with life because of its rhythm, with meaning because of its words, and with emotion because of its melos, springing
forth toward another in a cry of appeal or exclamation of loving admiration.
But this "other" who is sought by the voice expressing the soul is not, in
this instance, merely an addressee; the voice seeks him as one who responds
and shares. He who delivers and loses himself in singing expects to find
himself in the voices of those who have joined him in unison. By means of
rhythm, all these individuals become unified in order to share a common
experience; these same words on many lips make up one single cry of desire
or of admiration. By means of melody all these different voices come together harmoniously so that there is but one single music.

Every form of public worship, precisely because it is the expression of a
community with a common faith, has made use of community singing. But
such singing came to have an added meaning in the Judeo-Christian revelation. For salvation, in very truth, was sent by God, not to each man in
isolation, but to a people, to Israel, to the posterity of Abraham, community
of the Covenant, a chosen race, a royal priesthood. That is why Jewish cult
is that of a nation, of a community. The prayer and thanksgiving of Israel
are those of all her faithful, priests and people, of Levites and all the tribes,
of king and poor, of Jews and proselytes, praying and confessing together
their one Savior:

[12a] Cf. CL 112. The first effect of sacred music is to "add delight to prayer."

> Sons of Israel, bless the Lord,
>   sons of Aaron, bless the Lord,
> Sons of Levi, bless the Lord,
>   you who fear him, bless the Lord (Ps. 134:19-20).

Furthermore, the knowledge of the true God given first to Israel was not for her alone; it was the mission of this priestly nation to make God's name known to all pagan nations so that these too might enter into the song of praise:

> Cry out with joy to God, all the earth,
>   Oh sing to the glory of his name;
> O peoples, bless our God,
>   let the voice of his praise resound (Ps. 65:1, 2, 8).

Every people is to acclaim Sion as mother of salvation; in Sion every nation is to sing and dance:

> And while they dance they will sing:
> "In you all find their home" (Ps. 86:7).

Nevertheless, it was only in a prophetic way that Israel could proclaim the great unison of all redeemed peoples. Ever since sin had introduced dissonance and satanic din into this world, ever since Babel had symbolized, by the confusion of tongues, the essential discord between man and God and between man and man, no one had been able to intone in this world that pure and true note capable of initiating the universal concert as a spark can initiate a fire.

So God chose out one faultless voice, the *fiat* of the Virgin Mary. Filling her with the divine Breath, He entrusted to her the divine Word so that from this unique and pure note there might begin the Song of the Father. And humanity could hear, coming from on high, its epithalamium: the voice of the Bridegroom who was righteous with the righteousness of God. This voice called men together, consoled them and exhorted them. But men, deafened by the cacophony of their sins, did not recognize this music; and in their discord, they did not come to dance in chorus when the flute of the nuptials sounded in the market place. They preferred to howl: "To death with Him! Let Him be crucified!" Then, with a great cry, the Word of God expired. But in His very death He had resolved the discord.[13]

This voice is raised anew on Easter morning. It intones an unknown *Alleluia.* Sweet and penetrating, it calls together once more those who had believed in it, and the first Christian chorus was formed. The voice returns

---

[13] "The first one who intoned the concert of life was the sweet Word of love when, having taken your humanity to join it to His divinity, He caused to be heard from the Cross a song so sweet that it attracted to Himself the whole human race and subjugated the demon" (*Dialogue* of St. Catherine of Sienna, *La Providence* [Paris, 1913], III, p. 217).

with power on the day of Pentecost, carried upon a mighty wind. It pierced the walls of the Cenacle, filled the mouth of Peter in the market place, rejoiced in the diversity of tongues and invaded many hearts. Three thousand voices were lifted to reply to the *Alleluia* of the risen Christ. But there was among them only one heart and one mind, one faith, one baptism, and one single praise in the Church. The Bride had at last learned the wedding music and joined her song with that of the Bridegroom in the single voice of the one Body.[14]

The future will never lack faithful who reply to the Word of God. Their song has become a sacred sign of their communion in the charity of Christ.[14a] It fills the hall of the marriage feast where the guests give thanks as they break the bread of unity. For the choruses of the Church are not just the sum-total of the voices of the baptized, nor mere human music, but the praise which ascends to the Father from the Son in the Spirit. St. John has given us a picture of it, once for all, in the hymn of those who came ransomed from the earth and who follow the Lamb wheresoever He goes:

> I heard a sound from heaven louder than water in full flood or heavy thunder. This sound which I heard seemed to come from harpers, playing on their harps, as they sang a new song, there before the throne, and the living figures, and the elders. It was a song none else might learn to sing but the hundred and forty-four thousand that came ransomed from the earth (Apoc. 14:2-3).

5. The Chanting of Holy Scripture

The song which rises from the mouth and heart of man as he endeavors to raise himself up towards God in supplication or thanksgiving is, in reality, a reply. Prayer can ascend to the true God only because He has first made Himself known to man. In revealed religion the call of God precedes and prompts the return-call from the Church. Worship presupposes the prophetic ministry.

Now the proclamation of God's word itself stands in need of song to express its own mystery, a type of song proper to itself. Every sacred word is a word of power and efficacy. When God speaks,

> He speaks, and it comes to be.
> He commands, and it springs into being (Ps. 32:9).

The phrase "word of God" is used not only to designate an invisible act of God, but refers also to the human language which God has used to speak

---

[14] "The Spirit came down on the disciples at Pentecost, for it is He who has the power over all nations to introduce them to life and to open to them the New Testament. That is why they sang to God in a unison of all languages — the Spirit gathering into unity all the distant races, and offering to the Father the first fruits from all nations" (St. Irenaeus, *Adv. Haer.*, III, 17, 2; PG 7, 929-930).

[14a] Cf. CL 112: "fosters unity of minds."

to us. Hence the form of that language is inseparable from God's act in speaking and from the message which it conveys. So it is quite natural that the prophet has recourse to those human means which are appropriate to the word of power and signify its efficacy.

In contrast with prayer, which has a tendency to be repetitive, an order given by one who has authority is usually brief and promulgated but once.[15] Conciseness of language is one of the main signs of authority. But the effect is heightened if the words are clothed in number and melos. Admonitory speech calls primarily on number, for, in order to procure obedience, it must eliminate in the hearer a tendency to independence and liberty incompatible with itself. Through balance of phrases or poetic meters, rhythmic speech reduces haphazard durations into order, and through the use of cadence it endows the words with finality. The art of the speaker, in fine, involves the use of interruption and balancing of phrases by means of the caesura which signifies the sacred.[16] The word of power, on the other hand, uses chiefly melos in order to persuade. The very music of the words renders them more penetrating, carries them into the heart. Because it has to overcome the noise of the world in order to be heard, the word is able to cut through indeterminate sounds by reason of its definite pitch. In borrowing from the art of sound, it sets itself apart from ordinary conversation and surpasses simple speech. He who recites Scripture without "chanting" it, says the Mishnah, is an idolater.[17] Why so, unless it is because he is dragging it down to the level of merely human speech? He profanes it by stripping it of its musical adornment, a symbol of respect by which the believer knows that it is the word of God.

6. The Language of Pure Music

Whether as a vehicle of the revealing word addressed by God to man or of the appealing and thanking word sent up by man to God, music integrated into the Christian cult mystery has so far appeared to us only in the guise of song. Does that mean that there is no place in this economy for music without words, pure music such as a wordless *iubilus* or an instrumental melody? Has such music no right to be called mystery? Were that so, we could not but regret it. For, indeed, music which is set free from all verbal restraint would seem to be more perfect. Is it not pure music which has given us the greatest of the immortal masterpieces achieved by the musical genius of men? How could such pure praise from man's mind and heart

---

[15] Development, as opposed to conciseness, pertains rather to the oratorical aspect of language; the orator tries to persuade precisely because he is not assured of the efficacy of his word. Compare the homily and exhortation which follow the proclamation of the inspired Word.

[16] See chapter 2, pp. 29ff.

[17] "Chanting" here means a sing-song recitation of the biblical texts that was used in the worship of the synagogue, or the rhythmo-melodic declamation used in the study of the Talmud. Christian worship has retained it for use in scriptural readings and solemn prayers, as also in recitative psalmody. Cf. S. Corbin, *L'Église à la conquête de sa musique* (Paris, 1960), pp. 62ff.

be excluded from the symphony which redeemed humanity offers through Christ to the Father?

We must not, of course, lose sight of the fact that the scale of values applied to art is very different from that applied to charity. Beauty perceptible by the senses can be a sign of grace, but never the source of grace. As we shall see later,[18] in this respect liturgical music and religious music stand on the same footing—they cannot be judged solely from the artistic point of view, and music without words cannot normally be ranked as liturgical music. Nevertheless, in those spheres of the Christian life which border on worship, pure music has a meaning very much like that of song. To the degree in which it arouses faith and love it can have a spiritual worth equal to, or even greater than, liturgical music.[19]

Of the religious mystery of the wordless *iubilus* no one has spoken more eloquently than St. Augustine in certain well-known pages. It should suffice here to give one excerpt:

> He who sings a *iubilus* does not pronounce any words; he utters a wordless sound of joy; it is the voice of his soul pouring forth happiness as intensely as possible, expressing what he feels without adverting to any particular meaning. To manifest his joy, the man does not use words that can be pronounced and understood, but he just allows his happiness to burst forth without any words; his voice then seems to express a joy so intense that he is incapable of formulating it.[20]

The perfection of pure music comes from the transparence of its message. It does not seem to convey anything except itself. Indeed, because it does not attempt to say anything to the discursive reason, it can say everything to the loving heart and contemplative spirit. For the lamentations of the wounded heart, for the exultations of the joyful spirit, the sorrow of the penitent, the faith of the contemplative soul, the hope of the steadfast or the charity of the soul ravished with love, pure music is constrained by no limits.

Though man may find in his own voice the musical instrument which is closest to his heart, for it ever accompanies him in all his joys and sorrows, he nevertheless has other means, even more powerful and subtle, for expressing himself in that world of sound which his own spirit has created. In nature, secretly in tune with himself, he found reeds more docile to his breath, strings more supple under his fingers, and shells more sensitive to

---

[18] See the next chapter: "Singing as Ritual Action."

[19] Two things must carefully be distinguished: (1) the sacred signs of the Christian mystery objectively considered, the laws of which are fixed by the Church's liturgy and to which she has attached great efficacy in the history of salvation; and (2) the greater or less meaning, considered subjectively, which those things of this world that are fitted to set a man on his way to God may have for him personally and for his own history of salvation.

[20] *Enar. in Ps.* 99, 4 (PL 37, 1272). And see other texts in Th. Gérold, *Les Pères de l'Église*, pp. 120-121.

his impacts. He has made such things even more human than himself, capable of weeping or laughing, of understanding or of loving, even of praying and adoring.[21] It is not merely his own flesh which groans in travail waiting for the sons of God to be made known, but the whole of creation with him; it is not only the redeemed who are to give thanks to God, but with them the whole universe, first fruits of the new heavens and the new earth.

> Let the heavens rejoice and the earth be glad,
>   let the sea and all within it thunder praise;
> let the land and all it bears rejoice,
>   all the trees of the wood shout for joy,
>   at the presence of the Lord, for he comes . . . (Ps. 95:11-13).

The mystery of music would remain incomplete if man's song failed to carry with it up to his Creator and Savior the hymn of creation which was made for the praise and glory of God. And the Holy Spirit would not have moved the psalmist to write the great doxology which crowns and completes the book of sacred songs:

> O praise him with sound of trumpet,
>   praise him with lute and harp.
> Praise him with timbrel and dance,
>   praise him with strings and pipes.
> O praise him with resounding cymbals,
>   praise him with clashing of cymbals.
> Let everything that lives and that breathes
>   give praise to the Lord! Alleluia (Ps. 150:3-6).

Music is indeed "God's daughter." He gave music to mankind that it might signify the suffering and glory, the sacrifice and love of His Son who dies and lives among His brethren. It is a mystery of faith. But because it is a sign it is not the reality itself. In fact, it still hides from us the loving praise which it reveals to us and which is sung by the elect in heaven.

Music can never reveal to us the whole of its mystery until it has become silent and no more sounds reach our ears. For the praise of heaven, pure love, will have no further need for the art of sound.[22] After this life the only

---

[21] On the role of instrumental music in Christian worship, see ch. 10, pp. 142ff.

[22] In heaven there will be no more "signs," such as sound, the "raw material" of our art of music. Even on earth, music is not reducible to mere sound, a physical phenomenon; it is a kind of spiritual language. That is why one cannot speak, in a strict sense, of transcendent and eternal music, of heavenly music. Nevertheless, when we make a definitive passage from the sensible sign to the reality which it signifies, we are bound in so doing to eliminate the sign. That is a law inherent in the symbolism of the transcendental. Just as for us divine Truth is both light and darkness, and just as our life in Christ is simultaneously life and death, so also "true" music or "heavenly" music is for us both "pure sound" and also "silence." We must not shy away from this contradiction between the concepts of "music" and "silence"; it is only by associating them that one can obtain any idea of the eternal-inaudible aspect of music, and thus distinguish it from its transitory aspects which alone are known to us here below.

music which will be able to satisfy the soul will be the music of silence! [23]
He who slakes his thirst from a material stream will inevitably thirst
again. He who sings with faith must never allow himself to be immersed in
the mere delight of musical sounds or yield himself to the euphony of cadence;
for through music he is searching for that which no ear has ever heard.
Rhythm and melos are like a pair of wings which carry him up to the point
where he will hear something else: the single note, anterior to all time, wherewith the Word of God praises the Father in the Spirit of love.

[23] On silent music, see the Platonic interpretation of H. Davenson, *Petit traité de la musique
selon saint Augustin,* and the pertinent reflections of E. Kressmann, *De la musique religieuse,*
pp. 137 ff. A good treatment may be found also in B. Morel, *Le signe sacré, essai sur le sacrament
comme signal et information de Dieu* (Paris, 1959), p. 218. On the dialectic symbolism of this
mystery, see G. Morel, *Le sens de l'existence selon saint Jean de la Croix* (Paris, 1960), especially Vol. III, Introduction: "Symbole et Description."
    One may refer also to the strophe of the "Spiritual Canticle" of St. John of the Cross, in
which he appeals to the contrast of antithetic ideas in order to signify this mystery:

> Before the dawn comes round
> Here is the night, dead-hushed with all its glamor,
> The music without sound,
> The solitude that clamors,
> The supper that revives us and enamors.

(Translated by Roy Campbell: St. John of the Cross, *Poems,* Penguin Classics, p. 35).

2 SINGING

AS A RITUAL ACTION

All true music is mystery for one who listens to it in the spirit of religion. And for anyone who believes in the incarnate Word it becomes a sign of the Kingdom of God.

But not all music is rite. People say sometimes that a concert is a kind of "rite," and that what takes place is a sort of "liturgy." Such a statement has a basis of truth in the fact that there is something common to art and to worship. There is, in fact, a relationship between them which we must explore. But, in speaking thus, we are using the terms "rite" and "liturgy" in a rather wide and figurative sense. Taken strictly, a rite is a formal act in religious worship. It is identified with the mystery in that it is a visible sign of an invisible reality; but it differs from the mystery in that it belongs to a series of ceremonies instituted by religious authority for cultual purposes. If the cult is public, as in Christianity, then the rite is liturgical.

In the Church, song used by the faithful to adore or praise the true God within the framework of revelation and in accordance with the Church's ceremonies is a rite. The singing which accompanies those sacred actions which the Church recognizes as her own official and public worship is liturgical.

In the various religions art has always occupied an important place in worship, and this is especially true of the art of music. This fact is too well known to stand in any need of demonstration; but it does give rise to the question of whether this conjunction of music with worship is something accidental, or whether there is not some natural foundation for it. There are some who maintain that all the arts originate in religion. Not a few myths represent music as being an art divinely revealed (Orpheus, Krishna, etc). In any case, no one can deny that we owe to the ancient religions the majority of those monuments which enable us to reconstruct the history of the different arts. Is art, therefore, a specially privileged means whereby man may grasp the divine? Or is it some form of magic? Is it compatible with Christian worship? And if it is, what place does the art of music hold in liturgical rites? These questions lead us to consider, first of all, the relationships between rite and art, and then those between music and liturgy.

A. RITUAL IS ART

a) *Ritual Gesture and Natural Gesture*

A man at prayer stands upright before his god with hands outstretched and palms turned towards heaven; or he turns toward Mecca and prostrates himself; a priest approaches an altar in procession and kisses the altar; a muezzin chants the *shahada* or a deacon chants the Gospel; a choir of monks sings psalms: in all these instances and in many others the behavior of a man at his worship differs markedly from that of his ordinary life. The ritual gesture, although it is a human gesture and has (at least in principle) a meaning for the one who makes it, is nevertheless not an absolutely "natural" gesture. The sacred minister in the temple does not walk, speak or dress precisely as he does in his own home or in the street. For he is "celebrating."

In ritualizing his gesture, a man always modifies the appearance of some spontaneous gesture; by transforming it thus he elevates or ennobles it in two ways. He removes it from the sphere of the "ordinary" by imposing a certain restraint upon the manifestation of his emotions; and by doing so he infuses into it the attitude of respect proper to a sacred action. That is why it is called "hieratic." Secondly, in a ritual action, he adds "convention" to nature; by a certain uniformity in their religious behavior the adherents of a faith both realize and show that they share the same faith; hence there results a certain fixity of ritual required by the social and permanent character of worship.[24]

[24] Individual stylization and social convention, as modifications of normal human behavior, are not specific to ritual gesture but are found in every "civilization." They are an ingredient, more or less marked, of every form of "education" and of "culture." They are to be found in human activities such as speech, eating, love-making, work, etc. If they are enfeebled or disappear, the corresponding actions become less human and more material. It is, however, specific to ritual to accentuate these factors (stylization and convention) so as better to signify (as we shall see later on) the order of the sacred, to which rite pertains, and not merely the spiritual or social order.

b) *Art and Nature*

If we now examine the behavior of an artist, we shall find that in the exercise of his art he, too, departs from what might seem natural. The dancer does not walk, as ordinary people do, by simply putting one foot before the other. Sometimes he leaps, as if freed from his own weight; at other times he glides like a being with wings who has no need, in his progress, for any contact with earth;[25] sometimes he stands still like a quivering aspen. Does he want to make us forget that we are glued to the earth and that we can only move about by the alternate use of those two levers which we call our legs? The poet, in his turn, seems to take pleasure in pulling to pieces the ordinary language which we call prose. He writes what he wants to say in the form of verses; he subjects words to numbers and durations; he uses the recurrence of accents, metric feet, calculation of syllables, rhymes and assonances. What is the purpose of all this "artifice"? And what painter cherishes the ideal of portraying nature exactly as it appears to the eye? And as for the musician, scorning the infinite variety of sounds that he can hear in the song of a bird, in the inflections of human speech or in the frequencies of a siren, he arbitrarily chooses just a few notes from which he constructs a scale.

So it is not by chance that the two words "natural" and "artificial" oppose each other as antinomic terms. When art intervenes it unmakes nature in order to make it otherwise. Yet nature is beautiful, so beautiful that the artist can never hope to surpass its beauty. If the artist is not content with nature as it is, that is because he has in mind some other order of beauty. He is trying to interpret the most profound yearning which is inscribed in the heart of man: to discover the world which lies beyond this visible world.[26] For this world will pass away, whereas man aspires to the eternal. He tends to fashion for himself that which nothing in the whole world displays to him. So the artist takes possession of nature in order to make it express something which it is not.[27] In this world he wants to make another world appear, a

---

[25] The first variant is more common in the West, the second in the Far East. "It is one of the rules of classical art in Japan that all natural elements are excluded. Nature in itself is pushed aside as being something raw. One must kill the natural elements and then attempt to reproduce the same action by means of art . . . for example, the smooth walk in the *Nô*" (Toshinobou Ashiara, *L'esprit de la danse japonaise*).

[26] Although they do not directly refer to the supernatural, these sentences of A. Malraux express well the attempt to pass beyond nature, which is an element of all art worthy of the name: "As against the representation of the world, artists want to create another world—not merely another representation—for their own use" (*Les voix du silence*, p. 599); "No matter where or when, sacred styles refuse to imitate life, and demand to transform it or transcend it . . . they require that the relationships between shapes in their work should be different from those which are to be seen in life" (*ibid.*, p. 593).

[27] Then what are we to say about the classical axiom: Art should imitate nature? Although careful attention to nature has been, and continues to be, a condition for any marked progress in all the arts, one can maintain without paradox that the deliberate adoption, since the Renaissance, of the principle of imitation of nature as the rational ideal of art has led to a

world fashioned according to his own supranatural desires. And so, by rhythm and cadence, the poet pretends that his words bring into existence the substance of what they express. The dancer portrays a new mode of existence, entirely free. The painter gives form and color to the invisible, and the musician, in the sonorous language of sound evolved by his own spirit, speaks of realities which transcend speech.

Art, like rite, wrests nature away from its worldly existence; it refuses to consider nature as something merely useful or pleasant. It modifies the perceptible form of things which already signify the invisible, in order to impress on them more deeply the lineaments of that reality of which it dreams. In conclusion, because art is a language whereby man expresses a spiritual message to others like himself, it enters, as does rite, into the "convention" presupposed by every civilization. Every culture has its own standards of esthetics through which its own social appreciation of what is beautiful and what is ugly is strongly refracted.[28]

c) *Sacred and Profane*

Rite and art behave in a similar manner toward nature—neither of them will adopt nature as it is. And the reason is the same in both cases—explicit in the first, often implicit in the second: both are looking beyond nature.

This common approach is proper to man in his religion, and is but the expression of his effort to make contact with the world of the divine or sacred. The presence and action of the transcendent Being cannot be manifested here below except by some kind of a breach, for God is the totally Other. His appearance in this world is not possible apart from a breach or rupture of the natural order. That is why sacred things or gestures necessarily show themselves as somehow wrested from the profane. A sacred place is railed off from cultivated land or walled off from the inhabited city, is removed from all ordinary natural use and dedicated exclusively to a religious

progressive secularization of art (i.e., to its confinement to the things of this world). The present crisis in art, which is turning towards the abstract and non-representative, is very significant. It is the resurgence of art's will to live, its refusal to allow itself to be immured in imitation, in reporting, in publicity, etc., all of these being just "worldly" forms of human relationships. It is easy to understand also that religious art is in special need of escaping from a simple "restoration of nature" which would empty it of all manifestations of the transcendent. It remains true, however, that Christian art, because it is the handmaid of revelation, will never be able to dispense with a representational content (music to accompany words; statues to be the objects of a spiritual cult, etc.). Representation and meaning, far from being alien, are of the very essence of all true symbolism.

[28] Perfection of form is the basis, in the object itself, of perceptible beauty. But the actual perception of beauty in the sensible sign depends on the subject. St. Thomas defines the beautiful as *id quod visum placet*. We can never insist too much on the extent to which the individual, in his act of appreciation, depends on his cultural milieu. Music provides many examples of this fact. One has only to listen to a melody conceived in a scale different from that to which one is accustomed, to derive the painful impression that it is "out of tune." Another example: to be properly appreciated, Coptic and Syrian ecclesiastical chant have to be sung in a nasal tone; to us this seems terribly disagreeable and ugly.

purpose. It is "consecrated." When God enters this world to sanctify it, there is a breach in the world's finitude. The sacred sign is an opening upon the "beyond." [29]

Therefore, to make Himself understood by men, the Word of God assumed a strange accent: "Do penance . . . Blessed are those who mourn . . . He who loses his soul shall save it." Just as His voice calmed the winds and the sea, just as it commanded the demons, so also it had to conquer the noise of this world and its sin. The voice of God resounded as a voice from on high: "Father, make thy name known. And at this, a voice came from heaven: 'I have made it known and will yet make it known.' Thereupon the multitude which stood listening declared that it had thundered; but some of them said, 'An angel has spoken to him'" (John 12:28-89).

On the level of signs, the sacred is contrasted with the profane as art is contrasted with nature.

d) *Cult and Art*

Thus one can understand how cult, which is made up of sacred signs, allies itself by preference with art; for the liturgy, like art, is not content with nature as a means for expressing its mystery.

The believer who approaches the mysteries of his faith can do so only through the medium of religious rites. But does not the artist, by means of shapes and sounds, most wonderfully evoke that new creation to which the man of religion aspires? And cult imparts the hidden reality which art only suggests in sensible signs. Nothing but a religious rite can fully grant what the artist wants. In fact, if faith be not vain, the rite of the believer "verifies" (makes true) the work of the artist. Only here can the sign truly effect what it signifies.

This efficacy is not by any means due to the rite itself, still less to art. It is an illusion for a man to think that he can acquire a spiritual reality by means of a human sign; it is magic to think that he can act upon God. Signs can mediate the divine only if God Himself has chosen to make use of them to mediate His grace, and this is true only if they are mysteries of revealed religion. Hence, in the Christian religion alone can a rite be truly a sacrament; only there can art be a living introduction to the new creation in the Holy Spirit.

[29] However, it would not be correct to identify the sacred with the breach or rupture we have mentioned. The one is only the manifestation of the other. We must ever remember that sacredness or profaneness are not *in* the things. There are only sacred things and profane things. For the real sign is not a thing but an act: a meeting of two liberties.

On the other hand, the manifestation of the holy God in this world is not limited to the breach by means of which He appears in it. It is directed to the sanctification of man and of the world; and this sanctification is an invisible act. It is here that "sacred" means something different for the Christian and for the pagan; the signs of the liturgy are not of the same order as those of art, because of their power to mediate supernatural grace.

e) *Practical Art and Fine Art in the Liturgy*

The Christian liturgy, worship of the true God revealed in Jesus Christ, shows clearly enough that it can less afford to dispense with art than can any other form of cult. The vestments of the sacred ministers, the literary forms of the Collects and Prefaces, the chant of common prayers, the movements of the ceremonial, the architecture of the place of worship, sacred actions and sacred objects are all more or less ritualized, thanks to the art of man.

Nevertheless, it is equally certain that Christian worship, which is worship in spirit and in truth, is in its celebration more free than any other from definite ties with this or that concrete form of art. Apart from the matter required for validity of the sacraments, which involves but simple and common elements such as water, oil, bread and wine, the liturgy is not by its nature bound up with any particular language, style of music, or architectural form.[30] The very diversity of the Christian rites, and the different ways in which they have developed during the course of history, is proof of this. Further, in case of necessity, it is possible to celebrate Mass not merely without any singing, or in some place other than a church, but even without vestments or any objects artistically made. It is sufficient to fulfill, in the name of the Church, with a little bread and wine, the command of our Lord: "Do this in memory of me."

We must examine this double statement more deeply because it will lead us to establish, within the very idea of liturgical art, a distinction of great importance. It is true, on the one hand, that the celebration always requires art. The sacrificial Supper of the Lord, even when celebrated in the most primitive circumstances, remains ever a ritual meal. The art of man enters into it necessarily, and that in several ways. First of all, in the material for sacrifice: the food for the ritual Sacrifice cannot be any fruit of the earth in its natural condition, such as wheat or grapes; it has to be a product of human work, bread kneaded and baked, wine pressed and fermented. Further, this meal does not retain any elements pertaining to an ordinary human meal except those needed for its symbolism: its ordering is completely governed by the "convention" of the New Alliance. It is not a matter of sustaining bodily life or even of enjoying a meal among good friends, but of doing again that which Jesus did—taking bread, breaking it and distributing it in an act of thanksgiving which calls to mind His death and resurrection. All these ceremonies, even when stripped to their bare essentials, are still "artificial" acts taken in the strict sense.

[30] See J. Wagner, "L'art liturgique et la pastorale," *La Maison Dieu*, 47–48 (1956), p. 108 ff. At the beginning of his remarkable article the author formulates the thesis that the liturgy "is not bound to make use of art, can do without its service or even renounce it." We would agree with the first part of the proposition, but think that the second must take into account the distinction between practical arts and fine arts which we are about to discuss.

On the other hand, it is possible to celebrate liturgy without necessarily making any demands on any of the fine arts. By works of fine art we mean whatever creative architects, sculptors, poets or musicians have produced at various times in history. Music, indeed, is more closely allied to the sacred rites than any of the other arts; yet, when liturgy is not celebrated in its solemn form, and in the administration of most of the sacraments, music is not employed at all.

The relationship between arts and liturgy can be studied from several viewpoints. One may concentrate on the creative act of the artist who is expressing himself, or else on the results of his artistic activity, namely, the work of art. Or again, the artist may be striving above all to achieve a work that is good and true (its beauty being the fruit of these qualities), or he may be concerned primarily with its formal quality as a sign (its moral effect being then secondary). Yet again, the person who sees or hears this work of art may seek primarily his own esthetic pleasure, or he may strive in the first place to make spiritual contact with the realities signified by the work of art. In these three pairs of alternatives the liturgy is not directly concerned with anything except the last one, namely, spiritual contact with the reality signified.

Worship is action. In rite and sacrament the individual or the community seeks to *sacrum facere*, to do this holy thing, to make it holy for God. If one of the arts is brought into this sacred action, the purpose of using this art is not to produce some work of art beautiful in its form, but to produce some spiritual reality of which this form is the effective sign. It is the religious action which is essential; the artistic action which conditions it is only relative and accessory.[31] The worthy and beautiful collective expression of community prayer normally calls for song; but it does not of itself require this or that particular melody.[32]

To this first distinction between the artistic activity of the subject and the objective work of art which he uses, there correspond two attitudes—or rather, two tendencies—on the part both of the creative artist and of the person who makes use of an already existing work of art.

One whose task it is to provide his fellow men with the works of art which they need for their spiritual worship can either put his fellow men first or he can put his work first. If he puts them first, he models himself on the artisan who, while intent on making something useful, strives above all to help those who use it to rise up to the highest spiritual dispositions. That is why he wants to make it as fine and as meaningful as possible. This chalice, a cup from which consecrated wine is to be drunk, must be rich and

---

[31] Not in the sense of being superfluous, but of being accidental. This is the way in which music, though not pertaining to the essence of liturgy, is nevertheless an integral part of it.

[32] Stated as a principle, this does not contradict the fact that, for reasons of discipline based on history and sociology, the liturgy does in certain instances prescribe particular forms of melodic recitative, and, in nearly all instances, particular literary forms.

beautiful because thereby it will teach men to respect and to adore the Sacrament of the New Testament. This melody, intended to express the people's
cry of supplication in a *Kyrie eleison*, or their thanksgiving in an *Alleluia*,
must be charged musically with emotion because thereby it will deepen the
sentiments of prayer or of praise expressed by the words. But it is also possible
for this artist to change his creative ideals [33] by striving primarily to produce
a work of art intended to be admired for its own sake, a precious thing to
win the esteem of connoisseurs, a refined piece which will stand as an
achievement of human skill, irrespective of whether it is actually used in
divine worship or not. The artistic *chef-d'oeuvre*, thus displayed as an
esthetic symbol of the religious thoughts or sentiments of a culture, will
more naturally find its true place in a museum or concert hall than in the
liturgy. In the celebration of the sacred mysteries no work of art should
set itself up as the aim and object of the soul's movements; a *chef-d'oeuvre*
which attracts too much attention to itself runs the risk of looking like a
hors d'oeuvre. The liturgy requires from its handmaids that they should
stimulate "prayer within beauty," not that they should "foster beauty within
prayer."

The point of view of the believer who is taking part in the rites corresponds to that of the creative artist; for in the liturgy none should be purely
spectators or purely auditors, but all should be agents. For them liturgical art
is always "practical" art, for every rite is concerned with faith in action. Worship, to adopt a distinction made by St. Augustine, finds place only for signs
that are *useful*—useful not merely to the ceremonies but to salvation; it
has no room for signs which are merely *pleasurable*. The former signs employ the attractions inherent in beautiful actions for the purpose of penetrating more deeply into the mystery; the latter draw both sensitive and
spiritual faculties to themselves as their goal. Now there is no denying that
some chants, such as simple psalmody, stimulate the singer to pray the inspired text, while certain performances of great works of art *"se font écouter,"*
i.e., demand for themselves the attention of the listeners.

There is, however, something common to all these aspects of liturgical art as

---

[33] By this we do not intend to cast aspersions on the qualities specific to the artist in favor
of those specific to the artisan, in order to define the functions of the man engaged in creating
liturgical art. But it is interesting to note that neither antiquity nor liturgy has ever needed
this distinction because, in both of them, the good artisan was an artist, and the artist never
ceased to be an artisan. The distinction became necessary only after the Renaissance. Although
the artist remained, as did the artisan, directly at the service of society, he became distinguished
as a man of genius, and society paid the tribute of admiration not only to his works but also
to his personality. The romantic idea of the artist and of his inspiration came to isolate him
from the common run of mortals and to endow with an aura of distinction the individual
work of art. The era of the museum—with its "Exhibition by X" or its "Concert of the works of
Z"—on the one hand, and the era of industrial utilitarianism with its technical levelling on the
other, do but accentuate this opposition. Observe, however, that the balance of this evolution
is not entirely negative; it has aided the progress of the arts. Moreover it is not by any means
irreversible.

viewed from three different standpoints—that of the sacred reality to be signified, that of him who is to provide the expression of it, and that of him who has to make it his own. All three of them show that worship presupposes, in the signs which constitute it, a personal action which is both on the plane of the senses and also spiritual (which we will designate as practical art), yet neither approves nor disapproves of the "beautiful things" which are its means of expression (which we will designate as "works of fine art"). The more any activity is truly that of its agent and the more fully it enters into the ritual action, the more suited it is for use in worship; whereas the more it becomes an esthetic entity tending to be a manifestation of human culture in its own right, the less suited it is for use in worship.

Hence, in the role which art fulfills in rite, we must distinguish between the greater or lesser part that it plays in constituting the rite. The consequences of this distinction will appear when we come to study the function of the items sung within the liturgy and the choice of their musical settings.[34]

B. LITURGY HAS NEED OF SONG

Among all the forms of art which liturgy draws into its service, music holds a privileged place, especially in the form of song. Sacred music, declared Pius XII, "is more closely associated with divine worship than most of the other fine arts, such as architecture, painting or sculpture. The function of these is to provide a worthy setting for the divine rites. But music, on the other hand, occupies the chief place in the actual performance of the ceremonies and sacred rites" (MSD 13).[34a] Let us examine the basis of this statement.

[34] Observe that even when the distinction between artistic action and the resulting work of art is clear, it still remains difficult to fix with any precision the line of demarcation between practical art and fine art, which also includes both action and the result of action, though with a different emphasis. The part of the "agent" is here very considerable. Even when he is singing the sober recitative of a Gospel chant, it is possible for a deacon to be "listening to himself" in a way which could divert the attention of the faithful from the message he proclaims to his melody or his voice, while the singer of a Mozart aria might succeed in causing himself to be utterly forgotten and yet draw his hearers into a pure act of prayer.

The education both of faith and of religious feeling plays a decisive part in these differencees. One man prefers a Mass celebrated without any decorative accessories according to the mere essentials of its rite, in a Romanesque crypt with bare walls; another prays with more fervor amid the splendors of a baroque church at a Mass adorned with the fullest ceremonies and accompanied by an orchestra.

No doubt there are many mansions in the house of the Father. Nevertheless, it is a defensible proposition that a refinement of esthetic taste and a deepening of faith both work in the same direction toward an appreciation of simplicity. Just as the superficial mind loves the gaudy and flamboyant, while the man of culture appreciates the purity of form patient neither of addition nor subtraction, so the less well instructed Christian seeks the reassuring assistance of signs which stimulate his religious feeling to help his too human piety, while a more mature faith prefers for its contemplation aids which are as transparent as possible. The more a sign is denuded of inessentials, the richer seems its evocative power in the spiritual order. (But this does not mean the sign should be disincarnate!)

[34a] Cf. CL 112.

The complete Christian rites, especially the sacraments, consist of actions conjoined with words.[35] Baptism, for example, consists essentially in a bath of water accompanied by a triple invocation of God's name. The action expresses by its symbolism the grace specific to the rite; the bath is a sign of death and resurrection. The words relate this action to the incarnate Word, who alone confers upon it its efficacy.

Now song enters into the sacred sign under the double aspect of action and of word. As an act of human supplication or praise it is action; as a flowering of the spoken language it is word in the fullest sense. We shall see this most clearly in the celebration of the Eucharist, the "center and summit of the liturgy" and the basis of song as a Christian rite. "The dignity and importance of sacred music," wrote Pius XII, "become all the greater in proportion as they are connected with the supreme act of Christian worship, the Eucharistic sacrifice of the altar" (MSD 15).

a) *Song as Ritual Action*

1) The celebration of the Eucharist includes four actions that were done by our Savior: He took bread and wine, He gave thanks, He broke the bread, and He distributed to those present. Of these, three are borrowed from the procedure of an ordinary meal—bringing food, distributing it, eating it. But one of them—the blessing, or giving thanks—belongs to a different order. That its religious and festive character may be apparent, the Lord's Supper is set within the praise of God. It is "eucharist," thanksgiving. We have already described how song is particularly suited to be an expression of praise and spiritual sacrifice. Hence we should not be surprised to find it at the very heart of the Mass, which is both sacrifice and praise.

We observe, first of all, that the anaphora, or great eucharistic prayer, is normally sung. Even though the Roman liturgy makes use of a different type of celebration (*missa lecta*) which substitutes spoken prayer for sung prayer; even though, as the result of historical vicissitudes, the important parts of our Canon, once in fact and still by nature public proclamation, have become secret and private;[36] even though the act of singing cannot be put on the same plane as the acts of consecration and communion which are required for the validity or integrity of the Mass: in spite of all legal distinctions and factual differences it remains true that the celebration of the Christian Eucharist is normally cast in the form of a sung thanksgiving. Thus we may well believe that Jesus, according to Jewish custom, sang the blessing which He pronounced in the Cenacle, just as He probably sang the ritual *Hallel* (Matt. 26:30). In principle, the Holy Liturgy of the Oriental rites is always celebrated thus.

[35] In classical terms, the "matter" and the "form."

[36] For historical details about the history of the audible Canon, see, for example, J. A. Jungmann, *The Mass of the Roman Rite.*

Besides this general statement, there are several detailed ritual indications that show us how the act of singing has its place in the Eucharist. In every rite the eucharistic prayer opens with a passage having a particularly lyrical character. [37] In the Roman rite it is the Preface. This begins with a chanted dialogue between the celebrant and the people: *Sursum corda—Habemus ad Dominum, Gratias agamus.* . . . In order that his thanks may ascend to God in the name of the Church visibly present, the celebrant makes sure that all are with him in a union of hearts, and he asks them to testify to this by song. Encouraged by the people's reply (*Dignum et iustum est*), and building up on the lyrical *élan* of the opening dialogue (*Vere dignum et justum est*), he launches into song and sends up to God the Church's thanksgiving for the benefits of creation and redemption.[38] Not content with recounting these marvels in speech, his voice clothes them in modulations on a text composed in artistic rhythm,[39] and adorns them with inflections which are both sober and solemn.[40] Finally the praise from the mouth of the president bursts forth also from the entire assembly in the seraphic hymn: *Sanctus, sanctus, sanctus.* After that the voice of the celebrant subsides, to recount with restraint and gravity the principal mysteries of our Savior (institution, passion, resurrection, ascension); and then it is raised again in the concluding doxology: *Per ipsum, et cum ipso, et in ipso, est tibi Deo Patri omnipotenti . . . omnis honor et gloria*, as a prelude to resuming the chant: *per omnia saecula saeculorum*, so that the people may ratify by their solemn *Amen* the Sacrifice of the New Testament. We should bear in mind that in the Oriental liturgies the account of the institution—the chief proclamation of the mystery of salvation within the Mass—is always chanted. In the Byzantine rite the people emphasize each of the two consecrations by a solemn *Amen*, while in the Coptic and Syriac rites they take part in the memorial of the Passover by troping the anamnesis: "We remember Thy death, Lord; we confess Thy resurrection; we await Thy return. Have mercy on us."

Singing, therefore, finds its place in the heart of the liturgy as an act of thanksgiving. Its principal manifestation is in the chanting of the Preface.[41]

---

[37] In the Oriental rites it is the dialogue followed by the prayer of praise: *Vere dignum*; in the Mozarabic rite it is the *contestatio*, then the *illatio*.

[38] Hence, it is a *todah*, a "confession" or public testimony. In the East they recall in the anaphora of every Mass all the great mysteries of Christ. In the West the Roman liturgy has chosen successive mysteries for which to give thanks according to the feast or season of the year; hence the "proper" Prefaces.

[39] This applies specially to the Prefaces of the fifth–sixth centuries, which have the oratorical *cursus* regulating the cadences according to certain rhythmic accent-patterns chosen for their euphony (see note 224).

[40] In the Coptic rite, for instance, the degree of ornamentation is regulated according to the dignity of the feast. Even in the Roman rite we have a ferial tone and a solemn tone.

[41] This lyrical aspect of the *confessio* is found, not only in the Mass, but also in solemn blessings or consecrations which have the form of a preface (those for the paschal candle, baptismal water, dedication of churches, ordination). The structure is: dialogue; modulated recitative; simple recitative; doxology and conclusion, as may easily be seen by examining one

The *Alleluia* before the Gospel can be likened to this as being an Easter acclamation to the Word of God. Thanskgiving, however, does not exhaust the mystery of song, for it may also be supplication and communion. We can verify the fact ritually without going beyond the Mass.

2. Even though the Christian sends up through Christ his thanks for the redemption which God has granted to him, he is still here below as a suppliant. Supplication, therefore, is just as essential to the Church's prayer as is thanksgiving.[42] We find it even in the midst of the great eucharistic prayer, for sacrifice is also propitiation. It is a prayer of intercession. But, in the Roman rite as it is now, it does not give rise to any chant.[43] In other places its most common ritual and choral form is the litany; to the intentions proposed by the deacon, the people reply with a brief invocation. According to the findings of comparative liturgy, the most important form of ritual supplication is the *Oratio fidelium*, or "prayer of the faithful," situated between the liturgy of the word and the eucharistic liturgy of the Mass. Although it has disappeared from the Roman Mass, it found a new form in the *Kyrie*, which, in turn suffering the loss of its petitions, has become a mere cry of appeal, a sung act of supplication.[44] The chant for the fraction, *Agnus Dei*, is also a litany of petition. Finally, the presidential prayers of the celebrant (Collect, Secret and Postcommunion) with the *Oremus* which precedes them and the *Amen* which concludes them, are the chief examples of liturgical supplication. In this way the deprecative role of music is given a ritual basis.

of them. (See, for example, the very clear case of the *Exsultet* for the dedication of the paschal candle.)

The structure constitutes a masterpiece of dramatic lyricism which may be paralleled in some of the best works for the theater. One might represent it diagrammatically thus:

Preface   Canon   Consecration   Conclusion

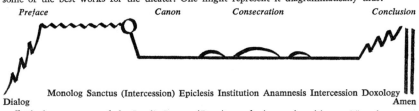

          Monolog Sanctus (Intercession) Epiclesis Institution Anamnesis Intercession Doxology
Dialog   Amen

[42] Cf. the two parts of the Lord's Prayer (*Pater*): confession and petition. 1 Timothy 2:1-3, which refers to the regulation of liturgical prayer, puts things in the inverse order: petition, thanksgiving. The fact that one implies the other is affirmed still more strongly in Philippians 4:6: "In every need make your requests known to God, praying and beseeching him, and giving him thanks as well."

[43] Intercession is in various places: the *Memento* for the living and *Memento* for the dead; in the *Supplices te rogamus*, and the *Nobis quoque peccatoribus* and, in a special form, in the epiclesis (*Quam oblationem*). In the Oriental liturgies intercessory prayer is highly developed, and finds its logical position towards the end of the anaphora.

[44] The prayer of intercession is one of the basic elements of Christian worship (cf. J. A. Jungmann, *Des lois de la célébration du culte liturgique* [Paris, 1956], pp. 146 ff.) It can be discerned in every type of celebration (e.g., on Good Friday, the Solemn Prayers; in the Paschal Vigil, the prayers after Canticles; and at the end of each monastic Hour of the Office, the *Kyrie eleison*; in the Roman Breviary, the *preces feriales*, etc.)

3. The social mystery of song is exemplified in all the rites which make use of music, especially in those which provide for the participation of the people in liturgical prayer. The unanimity of an *Amen* or of a *Sanctus* is an eloquent sign of the unity of the co-celebrants, provided that the rhythm ties the notes into one single cry and the melody brings all voices into union. The inclusion of music in a rite is strikingly evident here, since music is the very condition of the public nature of the rite. Because the liturgy is of its essence a communal acton, and because communal expression is naturally choral, it follows that liturgy evokes music.

There is no rite which can give a better illustration of this than Communion. The Communion at Mass is the final action in the Lord's Supper: the eating together of the consecrated Bread by the table-companions. But, taken alone, the visible and individual acts of the communicants do not appear to have sufficed to express the whole richness of the mystery of Communion. Its endowment with a solemn ritual involved not only a procession, a sacred action of a communal nature, but also song. The mere fact that our bodies are near to each other does not adequately express the interior relationship between members from whom Christ builds up His Mystical Body; hence it is the task of our voices to blend with one another and combine as a sign of that union in charity which is to nourish each and every one of us. We should let our song express our joy in eternal life; and we should, as it were, hear our own voice echoing in the hearts and on the lips of our brothers in tones of self-giving love.

b) *Song as Fulfillment of Sacred Word*

The great eucharistic prayer is made up of words expressing thanks in a song of praise. What is happening here in this liturgical rite which both typifies and gives a norm for Christian worship is paralleled in the entire liturgy. One never finds, in the course of Christian ceremonies, a rite (in the strict sense of that word) which is pure music: a song without any words, or the mere playing of an instrument.[45] Ritual music always occurs as a chant which presupposes words. "The primary function of sacred music," wrote St. Pius X, "is to clothe with appropriate melody the text which is proposed for the understanding of the faithful" (TLS 1). [45a]

This is so because of the very nature of Christian worship, which differs in this respect from that of other religions. Magical rites readily make use of instruments by themselves as incantations; another example is that of the long vocalizations on mystic vowels that were in use among the Gnostics of

[45] The exception is the ringing of bells, provided for by rubrics; but the nature of this is a signal rather than an exercise of musical art.

[45a] Cf. CL 112. Vatican II is especially explicit on this important point. The "main reason" for the pre-eminence of sacred music is its close relation to the words: (*excellens . . . eo praesertim quod ut cantus sacer verbis inhaeret*).

the third century.[46] As regards such practices, obscured as they are by the ambiguity inseparable from natural signs of the sacred, the Christian religion shows a contrast, for it is a revealed religion and a spiritual worship.

1. Revealed religion is based entirely on the word of God: mystery of the Word made flesh in Jesus, who speaks to us in the Spirit through the Holy Scripture read in church. In some well-known pages, Clement of Alexandria shows the contrast between the false allurements of the ancient myths of Amphion or Orpheus and the new song of the *Logos, Harmony and Symphony of the Father*:[47]

> The descendant of David, who yet existed before David as the *Logos* of God, despising the lyre and the harp, which are soulless instruments, through the Holy Spirit brought harmony into our world, and, in particular, into that microcosm which is man, body and soul. He uses this many-voiced instrument to sound God's praises, and He Himself sings in concord with this human instrument.[48]
>
> The prophets speak; the sound of music is heard everywhere.[49]

By reading Scripture in the liturgy, the Church is proclaiming the word of God; by recalling the series of His wonderful works, the Church is "confessing" her Savior and giving thanks to Him; by relying on His promises and remembering His acts of deliverance in the past, she is appealing to Him. She loves to do this especially by making use of the songs written by the Spirit Himself, the psalms. Our hymns to God are an echo of the Word which He communicates to us in the Spirit.

2. Christianity, as the religion of the Word, is also worship in spirit and in truth (John 4:24). As Clement says:

> He sings not in the manner of Terpander or Capion, still less in Phrygian, Lydian or Dorian modes, but in the mode which belongs to the new harmony, the mode which bears the name of God.[50]

Bound in no absolute way to a particular material circumstance, whether of place ("Neither on this mountain nor in Jerusalem . . . ," John 4:21), of culture or language ("We have each been hearing them tell of God's wonders in his own language . . . ," Acts 2:11) or music ("not . . . in Phrygian, Lydian or Dorian modes . . ."), the worship based on the "Truth" of the *Logos* and of Spirit of God is essentially *logikos* (Rom. 12:1), *rationabile*, that is, of a spiritual nature.[51] In the place of the bloody sacrifices of the Old

[46] See A. Gastoué, *Les origines du chant romain* (Paris, 1907), pp. 24 ff.
[47] *Protreptic*, XII, 120, trans. C. Mondésert, SC 2 (Paris, 1949), p. 147.
[48] *Ibid.*, I, 5, p. 47.
[49] *Ibid.*, XII, 119, p. 182.
[50] *Ibid.*, I, 2, p. 44.
[51] On the biblical and liturgical meaning of the word *rationable*, see B. Botte–C. Mohrmann, *L'ordinaire de la messe*, (Paris–Louvain, 1953), pp. 119 ff.

Testament, the New Testament has substituted the sacrifice of the heart, which finds due expression on the lips of men.

But the expression of the mystery in the assembly, whether strictly liturgical or not, requires a certain intelligibility of the word as spoken or sung. St. Paul makes this clear in what he wrote concerning the charisms manifested in the Corinthian community, where glossalaly was tending to supplant prophecy—something which St. Paul held to be an abuse:

> What good can I do you by coming and talking to you in strange languages, instead of addressing you with a revelation, or a manifestation of inner knowledge, or a prophecy or words of instruction? Senseless things may be vocal, a flute, for instance, or a harp; but even with these there must be distinction between the sounds they give, or how can we recognize what melody the harp or flute is playing? If a trumpet, for that matter, gives out an uncertain note, who will arm himself for the battle? So it is with you; how can it be known what your message is, if you speak in a language whose accents cannot be understood? Your words will fall on empty air. . . .
>
> The man who speaks in strange tongues should pray for the power to interpret them. If I use a strange tongue when I offer prayer, my spirit is praying, but my mind reaps no advantage from it. What, then, is my drift? Why, I mean to use mind as well as spirit when I offer prayer. If thou dost pronounce a blessing in this spiritual fashion, how can one who takes his place among the uninstructed say *Amen* to thy thanksgiving? He cannot tell what thou art saying. Thou, true enough, art duly giving thanks, but the other's faith is not strengthened. . . .
>
> And now, what will happen if the uninstructed or the unbelievers come in when the whole church has met together, and find everyone speaking with strange tongues at once? Will they not say you are mad? . . .
>
> What am I urging, then, brethren? Why, when you meet together, each of you with a psalm to sing, or some doctrine to impart, or a revelation to give, or ready to speak in strange tongues, or to interpret them, see that all is done to your spiritual advantage. If there is speaking with strange tongues, see that someone is there to interpret for him. If he can find nobody to interpret, let him be silent in the church, conversing with his own spirit and with God (1 Cor. 14:6-28).

That which may edify merely a single individual has no place in public worship; every sound heard in the assembly should convey some message to all, for every sung text is "proposed for the understanding of the faithful" (TLS 1).[51a]

3. If the word holds such a predominant position in Christian worship, does it not render music superfluous? And is it not best to strip words of special sacredness from all melodic ornament so that their message may come through with more certainty? If anyone were to draw that conclusion he would show that he is laboring under a serious misconception of the nature of human language. Also, he would have overlooked several important meanings which pertain to the mystery of song. For, continues Pius X, "the specific purpose of sacred music is to impart a more powerful efficacy to the text itself" (*ibid.*).

The word which is merely spoken is a somewhat incomplete form of human language. It suffices for ordinary utilitarian communications. But as soon as the word becomes charged with emotion, as soon as it is filled with power, as soon as it tends to identify itself with the content of its message—when, in fine, it has to signify the sacredness of actions being performed—then it calls imperatively for number and melos, that is, for a musical form, as we have already said.[52] The complete word, the fully developed word, the sacred word, has the nature of song.[52a]

This is proved very strikingly by the manner in which the liturgy is celebrated in its solemn form. The merely spoken word has almost no place at all in this, except in the sermon.[53] (There are, of course, some spoken prayers of a private nature.) If a sacred minister is to announce the word of God in Scripture readings, if a deacon is to proclaim intentions for prayer or give directions, if the choir is to psalmodize, if the celebrant is to pray as president of the community (Orations), or to thank God in the name of all (Preface), if the people are to reply to the priest, or acclaim what he proposes, or utter suppliant prayers—all these are done in song.

Whether because it must be presented as a word of power and holiness endowed with divine efficacy, or because it is a thanksgiving being offered up (anaphora) or an intense supplication (*ektenie*, litany), or because it is a thoughtful meditation on divine wisdom (psalmody) or, in fine, because

---

[51a] Cf. CL 33: "When the Church . . . sings . . . the faith of those taking part is nourished and their minds are raised to God, so that they may offer him their rational service (*rationabile obsequium*)." Cf. CL 11, 14, 24, 34–36, 83–84, 90, etc. One of the main preoccupations of the Constitution is to ensure that the message is transmitted.

[52] See above, p. 20.

[52a] Cf. CL 112. Music "confers greater solemnity upon the sacred rites." CL 113: "Liturgical worship is given a more noble form when the divine offices are celebrated solemnly in song."

[53] Even as regards the sermon we can call on an immense tradition of preaching in a lyrical style going back to the origins of Christianity, from the Homily on the Passion of Melitus of Sardes (cf. J. Quasten, *Initiation aux Pères de l'Église*, [Paris, 1955], I, p. 247), reaching its apogee in the *Mimrê* and the *Madrâshê of St. Ephraem*—these even include a response from the people—and continuing to live on in the manner of preaching still customary among the American Negroes (e.g., J. W. Johnson, *God's Trombone*).

it should be communal and choral, word used in rite never finds its fullest and most perfect form except when set to music.[54]

From all this we can conclude, with St. Pius X, that music is an "integral part of solemn liturgy." [55] It is not of the essence of liturgy since, in the Roman rite, it is possible to celebrate liturgy without it. But it enters into the rite as a constitutive element of the normal and perfect form of the word in the liturgy; "Its principal function is to clothe with an appropriate melody the liturgical text which is proposed for the understanding of the faithful; its specific purpose is to give an increased efficacy to the text itself" (TLS 1).[55a]

[54] In our modern Western civilization, which hardly concedes any place to spontaneous lyricism, it is the liturgy alone which has preserved the tradition of this most excellent form of human speech.

In fact, improvised recitative, still quite common among Africans and some of the Arab tribes, hardly exists among us. Melodic recitation, used as a mnemonic device in pedagogy (e.g., in multiplication tables, commandments of God or of the Church) is held to be something out of date. The recitative still preserved in classical operas sounds rather ridiculous to our modern ears. Words and music have become divorced. But this has not happened without a serious impoverishment of the possibilities open to human language. A form which was typical of the "practical arts" has thus ceased to give any help toward the individual or social humanization of language. And the "fine arts," precisely because they are the domain of specialists, can never replace the "practical arts."

[55] TLS 1. The Italian text is: *parte integrante della solenne liturgia*; the Latin text is: *utpote solemnis liturgiae pars necessaria*. Neither of these phrases taken by itself can be held to constitute that definition of liturgical music which some have desired to find in them. It should be noted that in fact: (1) the word "part" is equivocal, since music is not a rite distinct from the liturgy, but only a particular way of carrying out a given liturgical rite; (2) the adjectives "integral" or "necessary" share the ambiguity of the noun to which they refer. One might express things more accurately thus: Music is a constitutive element of the solemn form of liturgical celebration; (3) the phrase is applicable solely to the music of solemn liturgy. Nevertheless, the text following these citations, which we shall give later, can be judged as the best formulation to be found in Roman documents concerning the ritual function of music in Christian worship.

[55a] Cf. CL 112. The opening of the Constitution's chapter on sacred music will henceforth rank as a text of fundamental importance: "The musical tradition of the universal Church is a treasure of inestimable value, greater even than that of any other art. The main reason for this pre-eminence is that, as sacred song united to words, it forms a necessary or integral part of the solemn liturgy."

To explain fully the precise meaning of this complex passage, it would be necessary to work through a somewhat long discussion. We have already insisted that music enters into the liturgy through its alliance with words, and in the form of song. By adopting and confirming this view, the Council's text not only supplements the formula of Pius X, but removes its ambiguity. In its form of song, music becomes "a necessary or integral part of the solemn liturgy." Thus, although music is not of itself to be considered as a rite, song is in fact a "part" of the liturgy in the same way as reading or prayer; it is, moreover, a part necessary to the integrity of the rites. Even though the texts of the "sung rites" (acclamations, psalms, processionals, hymns) can be stripped of their musical element for use in a simple form of celebration, they do not cease by their very nature to call for their musical garb. They do not attain their fullness of meaning except in the solemn liturgy in which their music confers upon them their normal form.

3 MUSIC

HANDMAID OF THE LITURGY

As an integral, though not necessary, element in Christian worship, music, like all the other arts, is dependent on the sacred action whose meaning it is intended to enrich. And when music is vocal it is dependent, in particular, on the ritual words of which it is the vehicle. As *Tra le sollecitudini* reminds us, "music is merely a part of the liturgy, and its humble handmaid" (TLS 23).

Nevertheless the art of music, because of its rich power of signification, is more intimately attuned to the various aspects of the Christian mystery than is any other of the arts; none of these is closer to the truths which the liturgy proclaims, since song is like a glorious vestment for its words. That is why *Musicae sacrae*, following *Divini cultus*, can say that music performs a "noble service" for liturgy.[56]

Serving the rite [57] humbly and nobly entails several consequences for music. This service is governed by conditions both negative and positive. One single principle emerges: the music of worship is functional.[57a]

[56] *"Excelsum ministerium"* (MSD 15); cf. *"nobilissima haec ars"* (ibid., 41).

[57] *"Musica sacra liturgiae, non haec illae inservire debet,"* Urban VIII, *Decreta auth.*, SCR 823, 21 Feb., 1643. *"Artes . . . quasi ancillae nobilissimae divino cultui inserviant,"* Pius XI, *Divini cultus,* Introd.

[57a] Cf. CL 122. The "Roman pontiffs, in recent times . . . have explained more precisely the ministerial function supplied by sacred music in the service of the Lord." The title of the present chapter, "Music, Handmaid of the Liturgy," was inspired by a phrase from Pius X. An even better title would have been suggested by the remarkable words of the Council's Constitution, had it been extant when the chapter was written, viz., "The Ministerial Function of Music in the Liturgy."

A. THE CONDITIONS OF SERVICE

a) *What this service excludes*

If we study the Church's attitude toward music, and the ways in which she has intervened to regulate its use in her worship, we find that her warnings can be reduced to three great negative principles.[58] (1) The music of worship cannot serve two masters: the world and the devil on the one hand, the God of holiness on the other. This amounts to a moral principle which may be formulated: avoidance of the profane. (2) Music must not refuse to serve the true God in order that it may serve itself. This is a theological principle: rejection of art for art's sake. (3) Music must not do any disservice to worship by distracting the faithful. This is a pastoral principle: the refusal of what is extraneous.

1. History shows us that from her very earliest days the Church has had to fight in order to preserve the holiness of the music used in liturgy and to prevent it from serving masters other than the true God: idols, or mere worldly vanity.

In the Mediterranean world wherein Christian worship developed, music—apart from that of the synagogue—was almost entirely involved in idolatrous religions and pagan civilization. Hence we should not be astonished to find that most of the patristic texts which make any reference to music consist of severe warnings about its dangers.[59] The motives for this severity were the needs of holiness and Christian morality. "Those who sing psalms," said St. John Chrysostom, "are filled with the Holy Spirit, but those who sing diabolical songs are filled by the devil." [60] Most of the tunes in vogue in those days came from the stage, and usually carried with them implications of licentious words. The melody could all too easily evoke the impious words which belonged to it.

The numerous prohibitions of those times concerning the use of musical instruments are likewise to be explained on moral grounds: the organ was then an instrument used in low comedy and worldly festivities, the flute was the instrument of prostitutes, etc. But nothing can be consecrated unless it first be exorcised; and, in an established culture, such a change is a prolonged undertaking fraught with difficulties.

The danger of the profane is, moreover, something that exists in all ages. Even when paganism had been driven back by the spread of the gospel, the Church still had to react against the invasion of the sanctuary by worldly

---

[58] It is not surprising that the positions which the Church has taken at various times in history with regard to music have been primarily negative. Just as dogma has become clarified through the condemnations of heresies, so also law often begins by making clear what things the Church, led by the Holy Spirit, rejects. This negative approach, contrary to first appearances, is that which leaves untouched the maximum number of possible correct approaches.

[59] On this point, consult J. Quasten, *Musik und Gesang* . . . , (Münster, 1930), or Th. Gérold, *Les Pères de l'Église*. . . .

[60] *Hom. ad Eph.* 5, 20; *Hom.* 19, 2 (PG 62, 129).

music. The first decree in the West known to us regarding the discipline of sacred music comes from St. Gregory the Great. He restricted to deacons the singing of the psalmodic verses and the reading of Scripture passages other than the Gospel. This was because promotion to these functions had been used as a mere pretext for vanity, or as a way of conferring honors on people, irrespective of whether they were morally worthy to fulfill such functions or not. The Pope declared that "the singer who is the servant of the altar offends God by his morals while he charms the people by his singing."[61] Here the point at issue is still the personal morality of the singers and the modesty of their performance. But we are coming to the time when music itself will win a place, within Christian worship, of an importance hitherto unknown. It is from about the beginning of the seventh century that we must date the reaction of the traditional monastic circles to the new developments of hymnody within the Divine Office; such concern with mere singing appeared to them exaggerated. They saw in it a serious deviation from the primitive monastic vocation. A certain Pambo wrote to his disciple:

> Alas and alack, my child, the time is not far distant when monks will be abandoning their solid nourishment, the word of the Holy Spirit, to become addicted to hymns and songs. What compunction, what tears ought to be occasioned by these tropers who behave thus in the church or in their cells, lifting up their voices like oxen? . . . Monks did not retire into solitude to comport themselves before God in giving themselves airs, in singing tunes, in conducting melodies, in waving their hands about and leaping from one foot to the other. . . .[62]

We must return later to the risks of *bel canto* from which some parts of Gregorian chant had not escaped by the beginning of the eighth century. But the dangers of profanation became much greater with the birth of polyphony. With this there appeared, for instance, the motet or "little word," which was originally based on the principle of one voice singing a liturgical text while other voices sang different texts, often in the vernacular, and sometimes totally profane in spirit.[63] It is well known that even in the great era

[61] Gregory I, *Registrum*, ed. P. Ewald, I, p. 363 (Council of Rome, 595).

[62] Paul Evergetinos (11th century), *Synagogé*, II, 11 (Venice, 1783), p. 371. Compare with Pseudo-Sylvanus: "To say the psalms with melodies (literally with "tones," but this is a technical word referring to ecclesiastical modes) is, firstly, pride; for this suggests to you that you are singing whereas your brother is not singing. Secondly, this hardens the heart . . . Think of these illustrious men, the fathers; they were simple men who knew neither tones nor tropes but just a few psalms; yet they have shone throughout the world like great lights. . . . And as for singing, it has led many to the lowest things on earth, and that is true not only of worldly people but even of priests who, through it, have become effeminate and have fallen into love of pleasure and other shameful vices. For singing is the affair of worldlings" (*Ibid.*; cf. PO 8, 180).

[63] See ch. 10, p. 145, for the reactions of Pope John XXII.

of polyphony, otherwise so Christian, it was common to borrow musical themes from well-known songs, the opening word of which served as a title for the work. There were polyphonic Masses with names such as *L'homme armé*, or even *Bayse-moi, ma mie*. Finally, during the whole of the Middle Ages, the Church was overrun by the fashion for "farcing," that is, inserting into the liturgical texts glosses whose contents went from bad to worse.

Such practices were denounced among the abuses submitted to the Council of Trent. The Council took note of them in one of the canons of Session XXII by declaring: "That type of music in which there is an admixture of anything lascivious or impure, whether by the playing of the organ or by singing, is to be excluded from the churches . . . in order that the house of God may be said to be, and may actually be, a house of prayer." [64] In the succeeding centuries it became necessary to fight against the operatic style, which was ever more and more worldly. [65] It invaded sacred worship to such an extent that Pius X, first as Cardinal of Venice and later as Pope, had to use the full authority of the Church to rid the liturgy of it.

The only text in Canon Law which directly and explicitly treats of liturgical music is concerned precisely with the need to protect it from all contamination by the profane. To this end it uses almost the same terms as those of the Council of Trent. [66]

Because the quality of being sacred or profane is not inherent in things themselves but results from the use which men make of them, the assessment of one or the other is sometimes evident, but sometimes relative. If music is reserved exclusively for liturgical use (as in Gregorian chant nowadays), then it becomes objectively consecrated. And music allied to words that are impious or immoral, or used as accompaniment for impious or immoral deeds, is objectively profane. But between these two extremes there are a great many musical compositions which cannot be judged except within their own cultural and religious context. [67]

As regards worldliness, it is possible for this to slip into the liturgical repertoire in all sorts of ways: for instance, by the pretentious flamboyance or esoteric style of the compositions, by the vanity of musicians or by the curiosity

---

[64] Session XXII (Sept. 17, 1562): *Decretum de observandis et evitandis in celebratione Missae.*

[65] Cf. Benedict XIV, *Annus qui* (1749).

[66] "*Musicae in quibus sive organo aliisve instrumentis sive cantu lascivum aut impurum aliquid misceatur, ab Ecclesiis omnino arceantur; et leges liturgicae circa musicam sacram serventur.*" (*Codex Juris Canonici*, 1264, n.i.)

[67] In our modern Western civilization the art of music is sometimes religious, sometimes neutral, sometimes secular and sometimes depraved. It can hardly be said nowadays to be pagan or diabolical. On the other hand, in mission countries where the attempt is made to integrate native music into the liturgy, the question of the sacredness of the music is of prime importance: melodies and rhythms allied to rites, dances, or instruments of paganism cannot be used as they are in the Church's worship without engendering scandal or confusion. Local music has to undergo an adaptation which is all the more necessary because, in its original form, it always has a certain religious background.

of the listeners. The serious warning of St. Pius X still remains in force: "It must be considered as a very grave abuse when the liturgy in ecclesiastical functions is made to appear secondary to, and, in a manner, at the service of, the music" (TLS 23).

2. The risk of music used in worship becoming secularized or profane has always been present. But for the handmaid to become the absolute mistress is a phenomenon only of recent times. The temptation has certainly arisen more than once in the course of liturgical history, and its pressure has weighed heavily upon the evolution of some of the rites. Music, however, remained God's daughter and the Church's servant. The novelty consisted in ascribing to the fine arts an end in the purely esthetic order. It is remarkable that pagan music, whether ancient or modern, even when it succumbs to the seductions of licentiousness or to the power of magic, somehow does not seem to lose its religious character. It was only the rise of rationalist humanism allied to the independent progress of the several fine arts which gave birth to the worship of beauty as such, and the reflection of this in the theory of art for art's sake. This subtle form of atheism, mixed with a kind of natural religiosity, is very common nowadays among artistic and musical fanatics. And a good number of the faithful, without themselves realizing it, become infected by this outlook. Does not our contemporary civilization present it as the most sophisticated approach to art?

It should occasion no surprise, then, that the encyclical *Musicae sacrae* took a firm stand on this point. Having recalled that art must be judged "in the light of the fundamental principle of the final purpose of man's life—the sacred and inviolable rule which governs every man and all his actions," and that these are "to show forth and imitate God's boundless perfection, for the praise and glory of the Creator," Pius XII continues:

> The well-worn saying "art for art's sake" leaves out of account the purpose that is deep in a creature's nature. Its users make the false claim that art must be completely free from laws that have a source other than art. But such claim either means nothing at all, or it means what is a grievous affront to God, the beginning and end of man's life (MSD 10).

The objection to the cliché is thus twofold. Firstly, to define art as existing for art's sake involves a contradiction. For, in fact, art is a "sign" and not a "thing." Its end cannot be in itself; its purpose is to lead us, by means of what our senses can perceive, to something ulterior which our senses are incapable of perceiving. To make art take its own esthetic form as its end is but to destroy it, for then it does not "signify" anything. "Art for art's sake" is, in truth, a negation and a perversion of art. Secondly, to make esthetic form the goal and resting-place of the human spirit is to deny all other truth. Art for art's sake is atheism. Anyone who accepts a work of art as the ultimate object of his admiration and satisfaction is giving worship to something on the plane of nature. Art for art's sake is idolatry.

3. Several times in the course of her history the Church has had to reflect upon, and occasionally to make a decision about, the opportuneness of admitting into her worship this or that specific instance of musical art. The point at issue was not to give authoritative teaching about the theological purpose of art, nor even moral guidance about the sacredness of worship. It was, rather, a pastoral question. The Church had to decide prudently whether every intervention of art, even of sacred art, would foster the prayer of the celebrating community, as it should, or whether, in certain cases, such intervention would not involve the risk of disturbing community prayer. From the decisions which have been made in this sphere, we can deduce a third negative principle for ensuring that art shall not derogate from worship: the refusal of what is extraneous.

From the early Christian centuries one could adduce several examples of reaction against "innovations" which had been upsetting the traditional ways of worship.[68] But, to confine ourselves to official documents nearer to our own time, place and culture, let us recall how Pope John XXII condemned the excesses of the *Ars nova* for lack of restraint in the vocal techniques which it was introducing into worship.[69] The Council of Trent, in its turn, discussed the opportuneness of certain forms of polyphony in which the sacred text was rendered unintelligible by being used as a mere pretext for vocal display.[70] Finally, in our own times, there is difference of opinion about the use of "modern" music in worship; some say it is a distraction from prayer, while others maintain that it can help prayer more than any other form of music.

We shall have to deal later with the connection between musical style and liturgical action.[71] In principle, the Church does not take sides in purely technical matters and leaves the field open to composers. But the point which interests us now is this: the evolution of musical style and development of musical techniques normally cause a reaction of shocked surprise at first. The general public requires time to assimilate these new forms. Moreover, strivings of this nature generally give rise to the production of works designated as *avant-garde*; with the passage of time some of these become recognized as classics, while others ever remain esoteric. Now the liturgy cannot be used as a field for technical experiments, nor can it embrace disconcerting art forms which would appeal only to a select few. Worship must help the faithful to enter into the mysteries by means of sensible signs; hence there must first of all be some evidence that these signs are in fact intelligible, or,

[68] The monastic texts quoted above are among these examples; one could also quote certain pages from Agobard of Lyons.

[69] See pp. 145ff.

[70] See pp. 146ff.

[71] See ch. 9, p. 128.

at least, not totally unintelligible. If compositions are intended to be listened to by the faithful (sung by a choir or played on the organ), then, to be of any help to the people's prayer they must seem beautiful to the people.[72] And if the faithful themselves are to take an active part in the singing, the music used for this purpose must be a familiar and easy means of expression for their prayer. Hence it is inconsistent to introduce into worship forms of art which disconcert the body of the faithful or simply leave them indifferent. That is why the Church refuses to accept in her liturgy that type of novelty which arouses astonishment—the unfamiliar which produces a shock or the esoteric which repels.

This triple concern—moral, theological and pastoral—explains why the Church, in the course of historical developments, has intervened in the sphere of sacred music to ensure that it shall ever remain at the service of the rite:

> Progress in the art of music shows clearly how much the Church has always wanted to make divine worship more magnificent and more attractive to the Christian people. It also makes it plain why the Church must likewise constantly see that music does not go beyond its proper limits and that, at the same time as true progress is being made, nothing worldly or unsuited to religious worship creeps unobserved into sacred music, thereby corrupting its true character (MSD 6).

b) *What this service requires*

The purpose of the following chapters will be to analyze the particular conditions which have to be fulfilled if the art of music is to succeed in its role of serving the liturgy. But even before we examine these, it is possible to formulate some general principles governing sacred music. To do this we may take the three qualities proposed by St. Pius X in his *Motu proprio* as fundamental criteria in this matter: (1) sanctity; (2) goodness of form (or true artistry); (3) "from which its other character of universality spontaneously springs." [73] These three qualities, moreover, sum up in positive terms the three norms we have deduced from the Church's discipline.

1. Sacred music "must be holy, and must therefore exclude all worldliness, not only in itself, but in the manner in which it is presented by those who execute it" (TLS 2). Holiness is here defined as the rejection of worldliness. In this sense, the application of this principle leads us back to the negative principle we enunciated before.

Yet holiness can also be described positively as "consecration." Music acquires this objective sanctity by becoming integrated into the sacred action,

---

[72] According to *Musicae sacrae* (26), the justification for polyphony is that it can "be a notable help in giving splendor to divine worship and in arousing feelings of devotion in the faithful."

[73] TLS 2.

and in proportion to its integration.[73a] A "consecration" of this kind originates in the practice of the Church and from her life. The manner in which the music is performed should likewise participate in the respect and hieratic character of the ritual action. In fact, to speak of "sacred music" or "ritual music" (when the rites are Christian) or of "holy music" is but to speak of the same thing in three different ways; the three expressions imply but one single underlying reality: grace.

2. Sacred music "must be true art, for otherwise it will be impossible for it to exercise on the minds of those who listen to it that efficacy which the Church aims at obtaining in admitting into her liturgy the art of musical sound" (*ibid.*).[73b] Here we have the application of the theological principle concerning the intrinsic purpose of art in the liturgy. Music is integrated into the rite considered as a sign of the mystery. Now its power of signifying depends on this: that supernatural realities are evoked by means of a world of sounds which are not merely natural but the result of art. The truth or genuineness of art resides thus in its sacramentalism.

The "goodness of form" required here is not only the perfection of form apprehended by the senses, but also the aptitude of this form for signifying that reality which is itself good and perfect. For the benefit which the Church seeks to derive from music is not that of the esthetic pleasure which music may give, but the spiritual elevation of the mind which it can cause; through the instrumentality of the senses, music is to transport the soul, not just into the order of intelligible beauty, but into that of grace.[74]

As we have already said, principles applicable to works of fine art are insufficient by themselves to be criteria of that genuineness of art required here. The art becomes more "genuine" if it becomes more effective in causing sensible things to speak of divine things, and conversely. As a matter of fact, the liturgical value of a musical composition is not necessarily proportional to its artistic value; nor is it the beauty of the music which actually causes its efficacy in the liturgy. Expressed otherwise: the more beautiful is not *ipso facto* the more holy, because the efficacy of grace is not on the same plane as esthetic sentiment. But the splendor of the mystery which the music has the task of revealing to us cannot reach us except by way of a certain spiritual beauty in its sign. That is why rite cannot be other than true art.

3. Sacred music "must, at the same time, be universal in the sense that while every nation is permitted to admit into its ecclesiastical compositions

---

[73a] Cf. CL 112. "Sacred music is to be considered the more holy in proportion as it is more closely connected with the liturgical action."

[73b] Cf. CL 121.

[74] The precise and specific purpose of Christian worship whereby Pius X justifies the need for "art" seems to exclude, as incompatible with the liturgy, all works by which man attempts only to bring back to himself his own familiar universe, and which provide him with nothing beyond satisfaction and pleasure. Art cannot be "sacred" except at the price of being uprooted and transferred from its own soil.

those special forms which may be said to constitute its native music, still these forms must be subordinated in such a manner to the general characteristics of sacred music that nobody of any nation may receive an impression other than good on hearing them" (*ibid.*).

Like the faith which it is to serve, sacred music cannot be other than catholic. Catholicity does not imply uniformity, but the unity of one, same spirit in a diversity of human signs. In like manners, the universality of sacred music does not rule out, as Pius X says, the expression of genius proper to each culture. To a certain degree this is even an intrinsic necessity; for any celebration has to be suited to those who celebrate. But no matter what musical style may be employed, it must always give the impression of signifying the realities of our faith.

There are several ways in which this proposition can be reduced to more precise terms. The first is that of Pius X himself; no one, even a foreigner, should receive a bad impression when hearing music in a church. This approximates the third principle, pastoral in nature, which we discussed above: the rejection of the extraneous, of whatever shocks and distracts—in a word, whatever does not edify.[75]

The encyclical *Musicae sacrae* understands this universality in a slightly different way: it means that the unity of faith calls for a certain unity in forms of worship.[76] For the Roman liturgy it applies this principle to Gregorian chant insofar as this chant transcends the particularisms of the various musical cultures; it applies the principle also to the Latin language, to which Gregorian chant is allied. Here, then, universality is primarily of the material order, and is realized in uniformity of sign (MSD 21).

Nevertheless the *motu proprio Tra le sollecitudini* suggests to us a deeper interpretation by saying that the quality of universality "follows of itself" from "goodness of form." In truth, every authentic work of art, although particular in its material and appearance to the senses, is universal in its message. As a sign of the absolute, beauty itself participates in the absolute. Hence true art has no age, no confines or degrees of value because, by its meaning, it is in contact with the whole of reality. Finally, through rite, art comes in contact with the supernatural order. That is why, in all ritual

---

[75] We must not force this principle right through to its utmost conclusion when we are dealing with a musical culture that is totally foreign. It is inevitable that a Western Christian who has not been previously warned about it should be disconcerted by some of the liturgical music of the Oriental rites; for in such music the intervals are different from ours and are subject to quite different canons of esthetics. The catholicity of the Church requires us to admit that, in certain relative spheres, some way of doing things which is different from our own may be an equally good and proper way of expressing the true faith. It is those who belong to the Oriental communities who are to judge, not we.

[76] This principle had already been formulated by Cardinal Sarto in his pastoral letter of May 1, 1895: "The Church has never ceased to take note of the universality of the music which she prescribes, in virtue of the traditional principle that, just as the faith is one, so also the form of prayer should be one and, as far as possible, even the way of singing should be one."

FRAGMENT FROM A HYMN TO THE BLESSED TRINITY
(Egypt: third century)

This hymn, the only known example of Christian music dating from the patristic period, was discovered in a papyrus from Oxyrhynchos.

Over its text is an alphabetic musical notation which has rendered it possible to establish the melody. The rhythm, however (metric in the Greek manner or tonic in the Semitic manner?) remains a subject of discussion.

The document was published by B. P. Grenfell and A. S. Hunt in The Oxyrhynchos Papyri, *Vol. 15, 1912. B. Staeblein has made a classification of the reconstructions proposed by various musicologists and has tabulated the results of their analyses in his article* Frühchristliche Musik, *in MGG 4, 1054.*

... ΠΟΤΑΜΩΝ ΡΟΘΙΩΝ ΠΑΣΑΙ ΥΜΝΟΥΝΤΩΝ Δ‾ΗΜΩΝ

[Π]ΑΤΕΡΑ Χ´ΥΙΟΝ Χ´ΑΓΙΟΝ ΠΝΕΥΜΑ ΠΑΣΑΙ ΔΥΝΑΜΕΙΣ

ΕΠΙΦΩΝΟΥΝΤΩΝ ΑΜΗΝ ΑΜΗΝ ΚΡΑΤΟΣ ΑΙΝΟΣ ....

Δ(ΩΤ)Η(ΡΙ) ΜΟΝΩ ΠΑΝΤΩΝ ΑΓΑΘΩΝ ΑΜΗΝ ΑΜΗΝ

"... neither the stars, sources of light, nor the springs whence flow the raging torrents are silent!

While we sing the praises of Father, Son and Holy Spirit, let all the powers cry out: Amen, Amen!

Power and glory (. . . . . .) to the sole giver of all good things: Amen, Amen!"

music, the man of faith can listen to eternal Truth, and the Christian perceives by his faith both the image and the echo of celestial song; it is the universal and catholic praise of the whole Christ:

> *Chorus Christi iam totus mundus est;*
> *Chorus Christi ab Oriente ad Occidentem consonat.*[77]

B. A FUNCTIONAL ART

The conditions of service do but manifest a situation which is proper to Christian music: by means of singing, the Church is undertaking an action designed to save, to sanctify and to worship; and for this sacred action she makes use of music as of an instrument.

Now the sacred action takes place on two planes. In the order of grace it is invisible and general; in the order of rite it is visible and particular. The invisible action, which is the more important, is at work in the mystery: singing increases faith, hope and charity because it is a living sign, within Christian worship, of prayer, of thanksgiving, of meditation and of communion. But the visible action, also indispensable to the celebration of the mystery, corresponds with a more precise logic of rites which both differ from and succeed each other.

The reality of salvation, though it is but a single entity and is made present in a certain manner in each rite, is too rich to be clearly brought out on any single occasion by one rite or one word. It is made explicit by many actions located in time, performed by a plurality of persons and varied in their importance. So each rite, though it cannot be separated from the total action nor stripped of its unlimited meaning within the mystery as a whole, yet aims at expressing a particular element of worship by the features specific to itself. This is what we shall call its "function."

The function, for example, of singing the Gospel is to proclaim the word of God. This particular purpose implies, as regards its music, a certain number of conditions to be fulfilled. Just as a melody in duple rhythm, however charming, cannot be used for dancing a minuet, just as an aria will not do as a fanfare at a military parade, so not every melody, however beautiful, is suited for proclaiming the Gospel. In the first place, it has to be for a soloist, for the word of God does not come forth from the assembly, but is rather, imparted to its by a sacred minister, the deacon. Next, it has to be a free recitative whose melody can be adapted to fit a canonical and pre-existing text which may not be altered. Again, the melody should be inconspicuous in comparison with the text which it aims to raise up to its full efficacy as inspired word; it should not drown the text in melismata which would destroy its character as a reading. Finally, the chant has to be sung, not by a professional musician, but by a sacred minister making an ordinary use of

[77] St. Augustine, *Enar. in Ps.* 149, 7 (PL 37, 1953).

the human voice; hence it must be simple and within the capacities of all.

From the viewpoint of the performance of a rite, we should, then, define music in Christian worship as a *functional art*. Every art within the liturgy is an art taken into service. The creator of a ballet furnishes the composer with choreographic details and informs him of the scenes, actors, figures and movements which are to contribute to his production. In like manner the liturgy provides the musician with a "program" in which each item calls for a definite practical solution, and these cannot be interchanged with one another. It is in fulfillment of its ritual function that music's role as handmaid of the liturgy takes actual shape.

C. TWO OBJECTIONS TO THE FUNCTIONAL VIEW OF ART

a) Someone may object that to define liturgical music as a "functional art" is to degrade this noble servant to a role which is merely utilitarian. Think of "dance music" or "military marches" or even "music while you work." Think of opera and ballet music, which many composers view as rather inferior forms precisely because they are made subject to a functional purpose.

But a servant is not ennobled or degraded by the dignity or humility of the work he does; he is assessed by the high or low estate of the master whom he serves. Whereas pagan civilizations viewed the status of a slave as something infamous, biblical revelation teaches us that the service of God should be the ideal of human life. He who made himself the Servant par excellence has completely reversed the values of the world in this matter. For music, as for those who believe in God, *servire est regnare*, "to serve [God] is to reign." And, as we have already said, only the liturgy realizes the purpose of art, which is to provide men with efficacious signs of the divine world. No music except liturgical music can make us hear the Word and His silence.

The function assigned to art in worship is never merely utilitarian. It is true, indeed, that the altar, to fulfill the needs of the rite, must serve as a table and that the Eucharist makes use of gestures needed for any meal; but we know also that the altar is Christ, like Jacob's ladder extended between earth and heaven, and that the Eucharist is Christ's paschal sacrifice. In like manner, the reciting note and the cadential minor third of the Roman Gospel chant are indeed useful and convenient for proclaiming the Latin text solemnly and audibly; but also and above all, they carry and signify the very voice of God, which, through our ears, brings faith and light and life to our souls. The function of art in rite is not physical but mystical.

b) Another objection, referred to in the encyclical *Musicae sacrae*, is expressed in an axiom dear to philosophical estheticism: art is essentially free in the choice of its means and in the creation of its forms. Art can no more be amenable to rational or moral considerations than to physical or natural factors, for it belongs to the transcendental and autonomous order of beauty.

If the artist is obliged to submit to constraints imposed upon him from outside his art, then his inspiration is violated and he cannot possibly achieve any true creation which is personal and free.[78]

This principle is only an application to the creative (or even interpretative) artist of the theory of "art for art's sake," and should be refuted by similar criticism: the practice of art does not contain its own end.[79] It is but the sign of an invisible reality; and for the artist this, in Christian worship, is a *datum*. In profane art it may well be praiseworthy for the artist to seek to transmit *his* personal message by means of his work; but the liturgy calls for a very different attitude: the aim of the creative artist is to express, not *his* faith, but the faith of the Church. He is to do this, not just for himself, but for all the members of the assembly.[80] Ritual art is liturgical art in the most precise meaning of that word, namely, public service.

In olden times no true artist ever complained of the program imposed on him, nor of its limits. The *datum*, on the contrary, was that which stimulated his imagination, gave form to the work he was to create, and demonstrated his competence; this voice, that instrument, those words, such and such a mode were, for the true musician, the creative impulse, according to the old adage which ever remains true, that art flourishes by constraint and dies by liberty.

The artist is primarily an artisan. It is this "good and faithful servant," this "man of art," that ritual, insofar as it is a practical art, needs most of all. If he knows also how to clothe his practical work with all the splendor of a fine art, he renders a service for which the liturgy will thank him in proportion as the faithful are led by it into the mystery which is celebrated.[81] Though the liturgy gives guidance to art, it does not impose any limits to its beauty.

[78] "They say that an artist's soul is guided by an inspiration that is free; accordingly it is not right to subject the artist to laws and rules, whether religious or moral, that are foreign to art itself. Such restrictions would only do great injustice to art's rightful worth, and bind and fetter the artist in his inspired activity" (MSD 9).

[79] The encyclical admits that "arguments of this kind obviously raise a difficult and important question, affecting every art and every artist." But it adds that "this question cannot be solved by artistic and esthetic considerations, but . . . must be decided in the light of the final purpose of man's life" (MSD 10).

[80] The desire of artists to produce works that are "original" or "personal" (it would be better to say "individual"), unlike anything produced by others, is a comparatively recent phenomenon, at least to the degree in which it appears nowadays. The artists of former times, who viewed art as a form of social service, knew nothing of it. A work of art is the more authentic, the more an artist makes contact with the universal, and the more every man can recognize in that work some expression of his own life. But if an artist seeks only to deliver *his* message and is intent above all on producing *his* work, he runs the risk of impoverishing its meaning and limiting its influence. On the contrary, the real masterpiece is one which is simultaneously the most personal and the most universal. (See "the Task of the Composer" at the end of this book, p. 214.)

[81] See below, note 271.

4   SACRED MUSIC

LITURGICAL MUSIC

RELIGIOUS MUSIC

Of the very large number of musical compositions to which we attribute a religious value, the Church retains only a portion as suited for use in her official worship. The rest find their place in non-liturgical and private worship. This distinction is founded on liturgical law. It enables us to formulate a primary functional law: music is a part of Christian worship to a greater or less extent according as the texts which it accompanies do or do not belong to the official liturgical books, and according to the closeness of the relationship between the singing and the liturgical actions.

To clarify this general rule it is sufficient to abstract from recent official documents[82] the clear ideas elaborated there, and to retain the practical terminology which these documents employ.

A. SACRED MUSIC

The expression "sacred music" is a generic term.[82a] It applies to all music which, by its inspiration, purpose and destination, or manner of use has a connection with faith. Music is sacred whenever, by its aid, "the sons of the

[82] The encyclical *Musicae sacrae disciplina* (Dec. 25, 1955) and the Instruction *De musica sacra et sacra liturgia* (Sept. 3, 1958).

[82a] No other term is employed in chapter VI of the Constitution on the Sacred Liturgy of the Second Vatican Council.

Church are enabled to render to God the praises due to Him with feelings of stronger faith, more lively hope and more ardent love . . . even outside church, in Christian homes or gatherings of the faithful. . . ." [83] It includes Gregorian chant, compositions which are ancient, classical or modern, destined for use in church or at sacred concerts, and also popular hymnody.[84] This list of headings should not be considered as exhaustive since, by supposition, the concept of sacred music has the widest possible connotation.

There is one query which may arise in this connection: should one include in this concept music composed for use in non-Christian worship? Insofar as this music seems linked with some idolatrous cult or may evoke memories of paganism, the holiness of Christian worship excludes it. But if it is purified of all attachments to its original environment and appears solely under the guise of a fine work of art, there is no reason why it should not be used in a Christian context for praising the true God. History shows that, just as pagan temples have been converted into Christian churches in places where paganism has died out, so also a number of melodies originating in folklore have been adopted for use in hymns or anthems, and granted recognition within Christian worship.[85]

Sacred music falls into two main categories, according as it is used directly or only indirectly in worship: liturgical music and religious music.

B. LITURGICAL MUSIC

Not all sacred music is liturgical, but only that which the Church admits, both in law and in practice, to the celebration of her official and public worship which, strictly understood, is the liturgy. Because it accompanies the principal rites of Christian worship, especially the Mass and the Divine Office, this liturgical music [85a] is the most important and noblest part of sacred music.[86] The definition calls for several comments:

[83] MSD 61.

[84] IMS 4.

[85] Such an adaptation is quite easy when there is a complete change of culture; thus a Western Catholic of today might very well be able to pray with an ancient Chinese melody. But a transposition is almost impossible when there is a living tradition: African pagan dance-music could not be used by convert African Catholics. There is but little difficulty in using the sacred music of non-Catholic churches; for the religious and social context of such music (without words or with an altered text) would have to be extremely precise before the use of it could savor of *communicatio in sacris*. Some harmonized composition of Bortniansky or a choral prelude for organ written by Bach would be entirely admissible in Catholic liturgy. (With regard to certain reservations, see pp. 210-211.)

[85a] The expression "liturgical music" does not occur in CL. Moreover, it was not used in IMS. Its use here, however, is justified from the very nature of things and also by the meaning customarily given to it nowadays.

[86] "The nearer sacred music is to the eucharistic sacrifice, the summit of Christian worship, the greater is its worth and importance . . . Sacred music has another function that is close to its sublime one at Mass. This is when it accompanies and adds beauty to other liturgical ceremonies, especially the Divine Office in choir. The greatest honor and praise must therefore be given to this liturgical music" (MSD 15). Cf. CL 112.

a) To begin with, the distinction between liturgical and non-liturgical music is not based on technical or esthetic considerations in the musical order, nor on qualities which this or that work must have as prerequisites. It depends in the first instance on the nature of the liturgical action which does or does not employ these works. Music is liturgical only when the Church recognizes it as *her* prayer.

b) In order that an action may be liturgical (in the strict sense), it must conform to certain conditions; one of these is that it must be carried out "in conformity with the liturgical books approved by the Holy See." [87] But, in the ceremonies which these books specify, music does not appear except when it accompanies texts intended to be sung. [88] It follows that liturgical music consists directly in the singing of the words of a rite, and indirectly in the instrumental music which may accompany this singing. [89] "The principal function of music," wrote St. Pius X in a decisive phrase, "is to clothe with appropriate melody the liturgical text which is proposed for the understanding of the faithful" (TLS 1).

c) The performance of ceremonies in accordance with the authorized liturgical books obliges us to make a canonical distinction between two categories of liturgical singing, and to establish a hierarchy between them.

The most sacred texts are the publicly sung texts of the celebrant and of his ministers, together with the responses made to these by the choir or the people. [90] These texts may not be sung to any kind of music chosen at will. The melodies which the liturgical books assign to these words of the rite are obligatory. [91] Like the texts which they accompany, these melodies have a particular value in the rite; they remain solely vocal and all instrumental accompaniment of them is forbidden. [92]

There are other texts to be sung, consisting of psalms or hymns, executed by the choir, the assembly as a whole, or the *schola*. For these it is lawful to

[87] IMS 1. We must remember that, according to the definition given by this document, there are five conditions which an action must fulfil in order that it be a liturgical action. It must be (1) instituted by Christ or the Church, (2) performed in their name, (3) by persons deputed to do so, (4) according to the approved books, and (5) directed to God or the saints or the blessed. Cf. A. G. Martimort–F. Picard, *Liturgie et Musique*, coll. *Lex Orandi*, 28 (Paris, 1959), pp. 21 ff., also J. B. O'Connell, *Sacred Music and Liturgy* (London: Burns and Oates, 1959), p. 18.

[88] "The sublime purpose of sacred music consists in this: that by the beauty and magnificence of its melodies, it should enhance the voice of the sacrificing priest and also that of the Christian people as they praise Almighty God" (MSD 14).

[89] This is the reason why liturgical chant normally uses (apart from special indults) the language proper to the ritual actions, which is Latin (IMS 13). This point of law has been considerably mitigated by CL 36, 54, 63 and 101 in favor of the use of vernacular in liturgical singing.

[90] "Music can do nothing nobler, nothing more sublime, than to accompany the priest with its sweet sound as he offers the divine Victim, to give its joyful answer to the priest through the voices of those present at the sacrifice . . ." (MSD 15).

[91] Certain "traditional tones" authorized by custom in particular regions are also permitted.

[92] "Those parts of any liturgical service which, according to the rubrics, should be sung by the celebrating priest and his ministers are to be sung only to the Gregorian melodies as these

use other kinds of music adapted to the text, but taking into account the preferences which the Church has manifested for this or that category.

d) *Categories of liturgical music.* Apart from the pre-eminent category of chants having prescribed melodies, the canonical definition of liturgical music does not compel the choice of any particular type of music to be used. "The Church has always recognized and favored the progress of the arts, admitting to the service of the cult everything good and beautiful discovered by genius in the course of ages—always, however, with due regard to the liturgical laws" (TLS 5).[92a]

Nevertheless, the official documents do clearly indicate an order of preference. The first is held by Gregorian chant as published in the liturgical chant-books of the Roman rite; this is the principal and proper chant of the Roman Church. It can suffice by itself for the celebration of the liturgy, and, other things being equal, it should have preference over other music.[93] It possesses in the highest degree the qualities required of sacred music: holiness, artistic excellence, and universality.[94] Next in rank is classical polyphony *a cappella*, of which the Renaissance period furnishes the best examples.[95] Finally, all modern and contemporary music, provided that it corresponds with the ritual requirements of worship, is admitted into the liturgy.[96]

This analysis of the different categories of musical compositions, made on a roughly historical basis, supplies a first practical classification of strictly liturgical music. We shall have to insist, however, that it is inadequate, and we must supplement it by explaining other criteria flowing from the liturgical action which the music is intended to subserve.

C. RELIGIOUS MUSIC

All music which expresses religious sentiment but which is not designed for use in the liturgy is called "religious music." Under this heading would come, for example, sacred drama set to music, the oratorio, the cantata, the sacred song, and certain orchestral or instrumental compositions inspired by religious themes. Such works cannot be performed during the liturgy,

are printed in the typical editions; and accompaniment of these by any kind of musical instrument is forbidden.

And when the choir or the people reply, according to the rubrics, to these chants of the priest or his ministers, they also must use nothing but these same Gregorian melodies" (IMS 16b).

[92a] Cf. CL 112: "The Church approves of all forms of true art having the needed qualities, and admits them into divine worship."

[93] IMS 16; MSD 20; TLS 3; DC 4. Cf. CL 116, which specifies Gregorian as "the chant proper to the Roman *liturgy*."

[94] As we shall see later on when discussing the application of more detailed criteria, the corpus of Gregorian chant includes works of considerable diversity; some of them are far more suitable than others for use in liturgical celebrations.

[95] IMS 6, 17, 48-49; MSD 26-27; TLS 4.

[96] IMS 7, 18, 50; MSD 58; TLS 5. Cf. CL 116, second paragraph. Observe also that Vatican II acknowledges the special value in worship of the music and art traditional among peoples of the mission countries.

since they were designed for a different purpose. They may, indeed, find a place in a ceremony which is not strictly liturgical, but their normal place is the "sacred concert." [97] Since this kind of music has no direct connection with worship, it forms no part of the subject which we are studying here.

D. MUSIC "IN THE LITURGY"
MUSIC IN CEREMONIES NOT STRICTLY LITURGICAL

The classification of sacred music as *liturgical* or *religious* gives us a distinction which is both clear and fundamental. However, in consequence of the precision given to the definition of liturgical music, it does not cover all the music which, in fact, finds a place in Christian worship. There are two kinds of music used in worship which find no place under either heading; these are (a) music which accompanies a liturgical action, and (b) music performed during ceremonies which are not strictly liturgical.[97a]

a) The existence of music which, without being strictly liturgical, nevertheless accompanies liturgical actions can be exemplified in three ways. The first arises from the different degrees of celebration permitted by certain rites (especially the Mass). Thus for the *missa in cantu* (pontifical, solemn and sung Mass), its solemn celebration implies the use of liturgical chant, and vice versa. In the *missa lecta*, however, the celebrant does not sing at all; yet the people may take part in the liturgical actions by means of what the documents call "popular religious singing." [98] Such hymns do not use the words of the rite (Latin) but instead have texts written in the language of the people; that is why they cannot be called "liturgical." Nevertheless, they are intended to accompany the sacred action and to be suited to the various parts of the sacrifice.[99] Hence, although these chants are not "those of the liturgy," they are beyond all doubt "in the liturgy." [100]

[97] MSD 16. "There is also a kind of music which, though not directly devoted to liturgical use, must also be held in high esteem, since the things to which it gives expression and its purpose are a great help to religion. It is thus quite rightly known as 'religious music.' " In the *Instruction* religious music is given a more precise definition: "It is not intended for use in divine worship" (10); "Religious music must be completely excluded from all liturgical services; it may be admitted in exercises of piety" (20). Its proper place is at a sacred concert held in a concert hall, or, on certain conditions, in a church (55).

[97a] In consequence of the Constitution of Vatican II, these distinctions cannot be rigidly insisted upon, especially because now the people's own language has become admissible in some of the liturgical chants. Nevertheless, the distinctions remain both justifiable and useful.

[98] MSD 30; IMS 9, 19, 51. CL 118.

[99] "At Masses that are not solemn they (i.e., popular religious chants) can be a wonderful help in preventing those present from being like dumb and inert onlookers, since they enable the congregation to follow the ceremony in mind and voice and to join their devotion with the prayers of the priest. They must, however, be adapted to the different parts of the Mass" (MSD 30; cf. IMS 33).

[100] In *Musicae sacrae* the "popular religious singing" was ranked with "religious music." In the *Instruction* of 1958, since "religious music" was there defined as extra-liturgical, it became necessary to separate from it the "popular religious singing" which may accompany liturgical actions. It is the latter document which we are following here.

There exist also popular religious hymns even in the solemn liturgy, either in virtue of particular concessions (when they replace the liturgical chants),[101] or by reason of legitimate custom (when they are added to the liturgical chants).[102]

A third instance is provided by music played by the organ and other instruments. In the strict sense, purely instrumental music cannot be called "liturgical" music whenever it is not being used as an accompaniment to the words of the rite as sung. It is nonetheless admitted into the liturgy, whether solemn or not.[103]

b) The liturgy, though it is the most perfect form of Christian worship, is not by itself the entire worship of the Church.[104] There are also other forms for the Church's prayer which are both public and official (though to a lesser degree than the liturgy); they are forms authorized either by the Holy See or by the bishops and are called "exercises of piety," *pia exercitia* (IMS 1).[104a] In ceremonies which are not strictly liturgical—such as certain processions, pilgrimages, congresses, prayer-meetings for parishes or organizations—music, and especially singing, holds a very important place (MSD 31). Even though "religious music" may indeed be used at such gatherings (IMS 2), the normal preference is for popular religious singing of a kind which "originates in the liturgical chant itself" (MSD 30) in such a way that, though they are not *the* prayer of the Church, they appear as plainly as possible as *a* prayer of the Church.[105]

THE "GENRES" OF SACRED MUSIC

The Church's official documents have supplied us with a primary criterion which enables us to assess the worth of sacred music from the legal viewpoint according to the closeness or looseness of its connection with Christian worship. We established four degrees in this: (1) strictly liturgical chant (the chant *of* the liturgy); (2) chant and music which accompany the liturgy

---

[101] MSD 22; IMS 13b. An example is the *Deutches Hochamt* in Central Europe, and the similar form granted by special indults to certain missionary countries. Cf. A. G. Martimort, "Le problème des langues liturgiques de 1946 à 1957," *La Maison Dieu*, 53 (1958).

[102] MSD 23; IMS 13b. Such customs exist in some of the dioceses in France. Cf. *Directoire pour la pastorale de la Messe* (1956), 179.

[103] MSD 28-29; IMS 8, 60-68, 80-84. Organ music is an "ornament of the liturgy" (IMS 80). And even though its music is not strictly "liturgical music," the organ is itself a "liturgical instrument" (*instrumentum musicum liturgicum*: IMS 61) because it enters directly into the liturgy, especially by its accompaniment of the singing. For this reason it is a "sacred object" which has a ritual blessing (IMS 62). CL 120.

[104] "There are certain other pious practices which, though not belonging strictly to the liturgy, nevertheless enjoy a special importance and dignity, such that they are regarded as raised to liturgical rank, and have received repeated approval from this Apostolic See and the Episcopate" (MD 177).

[104a] CL distinguishes between *pia exercitia* and *sacra exercitia* (13) but recommends popular religious singing for both alike (118). To these should be added (but as ranking above them) the "Bible services" mentioned in art. 35, n. 4.

[105] See MD 179. Devotions are to be "influenced by the spirit and principles of the liturgy."

(singing *in* the liturgy); (3) song and music of ceremonies which are not strictly liturgical (singing *connected* with the liturgy); (4) religious music (music excluded from the liturgy, *extra*-liturgical).

But how are we to know to which of these categories any given piece of music belongs? The most recent document (IMS 4:48 ff.) gives a classification which divides musical works into six genres: (1) Gregorian chant; (2) sacred polyphony; (3) modern sacred music; (4) sacred music for the organ; (5) popular religious singing; (6) religious music. We shall have to refer back frequently to this interesting classification and its limitations, especially when discussing the various categories of sacred music (chapter 13). At the present stage of our study it suffices to point out that the classification gives only a partial answer to the question raised earlier: by what criteria are we to assess the liturgical value of a musical work?

The fact is that though Gregorian chant is always liturgical, and religious music always extra-liturgical, the other genres, such as classical polyphony or modern music, may find a place at any level. Organ music and popular religious singing may be found in any of the last three divisions.[106] Finally, among the great number of works which may be termed liturgical, no one would claim that all are equally well suited to the celebration of Christian worship. On what grounds would one justify a preference for Mass XVIII of the *Kyriale* rather than for Mass VIII, for Palestrina's *Missa brevis* rather than for Mozart's *Coronation Mass*, for a Mass written by William of Machaut rather than one by Stravinsky? We must, therefore, seek more detailed principles which will enable us to be more precise in our judgments.

[106] We may add that because the expression "popular religious singing" may not be applied to "liturgical chant" we are faced with the annoying inconvenience of thereby implying that singing by the Christian people is not itself liturgical chant, even though the documents explicitly state that it can be (e.g., MSD 14-15; IMS 25, etc.). This somewhat inconsistent terminology can unfortunately be traced in chapter VI of CL, art. 118, as compared with art. 30.

5 THE GREAT CLASSES

OF SUNG RITES

In Christian worship the art of music is distinguished by the function it fulfills; its primary task is to be the handmaid of the words of the rite. If we are to understand better the service which music thus renders to the words, we must naturally distinguish the various functions of the words which the music is to accompany. Viewing them from the standpoint of the nature of the spoken rites to be solemnized in music, we can divide the various items of singing into several great families which we will term "classes." This preliminary approach to the function of the singing will allow us at once to observe certain characteristics common to all pieces which fall within any one class.

The fundamental elements of Christian worship are normally reduced to three: the *reading* of sacred Scripture, the *singing* of psalms and hymns, and the *praying* of the celebrant and of the people.[107] All three of these ritual elements involve the use of words, but the second is not the only one to use music. In solemn liturgy, both readings and prayers are enhanced by rhythmic melodies.

The division of sung elements of the liturgy into readings, psalmody-hymnody, and prayer, because based on a correct analysis of the liturgical data, clearly brings to light the chief purposes of music in Christian worship.[108] At the same time it affords us the best classification of liturgical singing.

[107] See J. A. Jungmann, *Liturgical Worship* (New York: Pustet, 1941); and "La célébration du culte paroissial," *La Maison Dieu*, 20 (1949). Cf. CL 7: It is Christ who "speaks when the holy Scriptures are read in the Church. He is present when the Church prays and sings."

[108] This division agrees, for example, with the ancient and entirely functional division of the liturgical books into lectionary, antiphonary and sacramentary.

66

A. THE FIRST CLASS: READINGS

The singing of readings refers, in the first place, to the proclamation of the sacred Scriptures, whether in the first part of the Mass, or at vigils, or in the Divine Office: there are lessons, epistles, gospels, and *capitula*. One might add also the acts of martyrs and the lives of saints, the homilies of the Fathers and the martyrology. (In the past there were also the diptychs and, in Eastern rites, the *mimrê*.) In this first class the singing is always done by a soloist, whose function is to ensure the solemn proclamation of a sacred message by his melodic recitation of ritual words.

B. THE SECOND CLASS: PSALMODY-HYMNODY

This second category of ritual song is the one which employs music more than any other and which best exemplifies the various meanings and ways wherein music can serve the liturgy. That is why this element is specifically called "chant" or "singing," as opposed to "reading" or "prayer." In itself, singing, of course, can be prayer, and it can also be a vehicle for the reading of Holy Scripture; but the singing referred to in this second class of liturgical elements always has the nature of a *choral* expression of the assembly. This class of "song" properly so called has three subdivisions: (a) psalmody, (b) psalmodic hymnody, and (c) free hymnody.[109]

a) *Psalmody*

In Christian worship, psalmody holds the first place, both in law and in fact. Psalms and biblical canticles rank before all lyrical compositions of merely ecclesiastical origin, since they are the inspired word of God. This is why they have always been given a special preference, as is shown by the dominant place they hold in all the offices of the Church.[110]

Psalmody, as we shall see, assumes different forms according to the particular function it has to fulfill within worship, and to the part which the people are to take in it. When sung between the readings of the Foremass or of vigils, it takes the responsorial form. When it accompanies processions, it is more usually antiphonal. As employed in the singing of the Divine Office, it is, in the current practice of the Roman rite, in alternating form.

When making use of the psalms, the liturgy sometimes emphasizes that they are the inspired word of God by causing them to be "proclaimed" by a soloist, to whom the people make a "response"; at other times the emphasis is on lyrical self-expression by the assembly, which praises, thanks, or petitions God in a more developed refrain (antiphon); or the purpose may be

---

[109] In chapter 7, wherein we discuss lyrical forms, we shall explain in greater detail both the characteristics and historical foundation of this classification.

[110] At least in the Roman rite. In several of the Oriental rites psalmody has been sometimes rather submerged by later developments in hymnody.

meditation on the sacred text, which is then divided between two alternating bodies of singers. Psalmody, in the strict sense, never entirely loses its double character of word of God and prayer of the community.

b) *Psalmodic hymnody*

This is a development of two original forms of psalmody, the responsorial and antiphonal forms. Especially since the beginning of the seventh century, new forms appeared in almost every rite, as the result of the amplification of the recurring refrains and the reduction, or even suppression, of the psalm verses between which these refrains are interposed. Such forms are numerous in the East; examples are Byzantine tropes, *hypakoi* or canons; Syrian *onyâtâ* or *manyâtâ*. In the West they appear generally as antiphons (usually processional) and the longer responsories, and at times have texts which are not taken from the psalms.

In spite of the relative abundance of pieces to which psalmodic hymnody has given rise, this form does not fulfill any different or additional function in comparison with psalmody properly so called. It is but a derivative of psalmody, and its proliferation has not always exerted a favorable influence on the evolution of the rites. It enters into them as a musical enrichment of pre-existing sung items, either by modifying these or doing duty for them. Psalmodic hymnody has, for instance, replaced the ancient responsorial psalm in the prolix responsories of Matins (as also the biblical canticles in the Byzantine Canons of Odes); it evolves in some of the processions of the Mass (Introit and Offertory) and invades all other processions (on Palm Sunday, Candlemas, Rogation Days, etc.).

In psalmody itself the word of God retains its place; but in psalmodic hymnody it has either lost its importance or suffered total eclipse. It is the lyrical and musical element which has been brought into prominence. In consequence, psalmodic hymnody does not give rise to singing by the community, but only to that of a choir.

c) *Free hymnody*

This consists of chants composed for texts of ecclesiastical origin. It is a form of Christian singing which has flourished since the very beginning of the Church and has always had a place in worship alongside the inspired psalms. In every rite, in every culture and every language, it represents the immediate and spontaneous expression of the Church's faith by the assembly celebrating her worship.

Christian hymns have assumed very diverse literary and musical forms, ranging from the rhythmic prose of the *Gloria* or *Te Deum*, through the strophic poems of St. Ambrose, the Greek *kontakia*, the Syrian *qâlê*, all our Latin hymns from the Middle Ages, whether metric, tonic, syllabic, or simply isosyllabic, until the hymns of recent centuries, the chorales of the

Renaissance period, and the hymns of our own days. All these have one thing in common—they are to be sung by the people—hence the predominance of the system of strophes with equal numbers of syllables. They are, in fact, the most "popular" portion of the singing used in worship.

However, in contrast with the Oriental liturgies, the Roman rite admitted free hymnody only very late and to a restricted extent.[111] Apart from the *Gloria* and the *Te Deum*, hymns have not made their way into the liturgy except in the Divine Office, as an enrichment of psalmodic prayer. Outside this liturgical usage, hymns are in practice employed only as singing "in" the liturgy (*missa lecta*) and in ceremonies not strictly liturgical which call for a considerable amount of participation by the people.

C. THE THIRD CLASS: PRAYER

Although both psalmody and hymnody are prayer, understood in a broad sense, here we mean by that term a ritual action which is strictly euchological, expressing petition or praise, and performed (a) by the entire assembly, directly or under the direction of the deacon, or (b) by the celebrant in his capacity of president and mediator. All these prayers, when they are public by nature, are sung in the solemn forms of liturgy.

a) The climaxes of liturgical action are underlined by acclamations of the people, who thereby express their active faith in the mystery being celebrated. The people prolong the Preface by their unanimous *Sanctus*; they welcome the Gospel by the praise of Christ (*Alleluia! Gloria tibi, Domine*); they conclude the Canon and the prayers by their *Amen*.

When the people's prayer becomes more intense, it borrows the form of the litany: *Kyrie eleison! Agnus Dei . . . miserere nobis!* But normally this developed prayer of the people needs to be directed; and, especially in the East, the direction is given by the deacon.[112] His office is to announce the intentions for which common prayer is to be offered, and to these all reply *Kyrie eleison! Te rogamus, audi nos!* In these instances the chant consists of brief and sonorous melodic formulae.

b) It is, however, always the celebrant who is charged with the presidential function of praying in the name of the Church, and of formulating this prayer at essential points of the liturgy. Sometimes he sings the Church's expression of thanks (in consecratory prefaces and blessings); sometimes he collects up the petitions of the assembly (in collects and similar prayer). Unlike the people, he makes no use of poetry or of florid melody, but employs

---

[111] As late as the eleventh century hymns were still not allowed in St. Peter's in Rome. But they had been widespread in other churches of the West for a long time—in Milan, Gaul, Spain, Ireland. The Benedictine Office included hymns of the Ambrosian type from the very beginning.

[112] Unlike the celebrant or the assembly, the deacon does not himself pray, but he controls the prayer of the people. (There are exceptions to this, such as the blessing of the paschal candle found in the Roman rite.) The same rule holds today for the office of "commentator" (IMS 96).

instead a grave and cadenced prose set to melodic formulas which are sober and restrained.

We should observe that the prayer of the celebrant, offered in the name of the people (*Oremus*), is always preceded by a call to the congregation (*Dominus vobiscum*; dialogue before the Preface) so that they may unite themselves with it, and the prayer is terminated by a formal conclusion that they may ratify it: *Amen*.

This division of ritual song into three great classes, founded on the distinction between reading, communal singing, and prayer (communal or presidential), shows us the broad outlines of a liturgico-musical program. But, when seeking to determine the function of any particular piece of music, one cannot be satisfied merely to know the class to which it belongs. For example, if one asks: What is the Church's purpose in the Communion antiphon?, it is insufficient to reply: Psalmody. For there are many kinds of psalmody. The proper selection of music for liturgical singing requires that its function should be specified more exactly. For this has an influence, more or less direct, on the various factors at work in the sung composition, depending on exact meaning and the role which it fulfills in the celebration as a whole.

All singing presupposes someone to sing, a liturgical text to be sung, a form of song, and a melodic style. In the last analysis it is the rite itself which determines—and that in a more or less cogent way—the factors which go to make up a musical work.

1) It is the liturgical action which distributes the roles by fixing which persons within the assembly shall have the task of singing this or that item.

2) It is the text to be sung which, by its recitations, alternations and responses, dictates the form of song to be adopted.

3) It is the conjunction of singers and song forms which, in turn, requires or excludes the musical genre: recitative or air, monody or polyphony.

All three of these special functional laws have to be known and understood by anyone who undertakes to judge whether any particular musical composition is more or less well suited to its liturgical purpose.

6 THE AGENTS

IN LITURGICAL SINGING

AND THEIR ROLE

As in every Christian rite, singing is an activity both personal and communal. The essence of the liturgy does not lie in its external ceremonies.[113] It is celebrated by and on behalf of persons who by it participate in the salvific Passover of Christ. Liturgical singing must, therefore, be for each of the faithful a personal activity of which he is both the agent and the beneficiary: an act of supplication or of praise, of meditation or communion. Christian worship makes no provision for mere "hearers"[114] or "spectators"; each one is an agent and a participator. That is the reason why the Church forbids the use of "mechanical music" (produced by record-players or tape-recorders) in the liturgy.[115] Even though the chants of the liturgy are at stake, even if the recordings are far better than those which could be achieved by the local choir, mechanical reproductions cannot be the personal action of members

[113] "It is a total misunderstanding of the true meaning of the liturgy to regard it as the merely external and visible element in divine worship, or as the outward splendor of ceremonial; it is equally wrong to see in it a mere catalogue of rules and regulations issued by the hierarchy of the Church for the conduct of the sacred rites" (MD 25). Cf. CL 11, 14, 19, etc.

[114] Except for those who are, in the strict sense, "non-initiates," that is, neither catechumens nor baptized, but who attend the liturgy as interested sympathizers. In a material way they can join their voices to those of the faithful, but they are incapable of "singing in the Holy Spirit."

[115] IMS 71.

71

of the celebrating community. They would lack that element which is the essence of rite as "practical art," that which makes any human act both significant and efficacious.

Though liturgical singing must always be a personal act, it does not follow that each member of the faithful must take an external part with his own voice in every sung rite. If an orchestra is playing a symphony, not all the musicians are playing continually all the time. Although each one actually plays only at the times predetermined by the score, it is nevertheless the orchestra as a whole which, all the time, is playing one single symphony. It is similar in the liturgy. Each celebration of it is a complex activity done in a communal manner.[115a] It is rather like a lyrical drama which employs individual actors, dialogue and spoken chorus, all equally required for the integrity of the work. When a person listen to the deacon-soloist at the Gospel, he is taking part in the action just as much as when he is making some response. And one who is prevented by his function or by accident from joining his voice with that of the assembly is nevertheless participating in the sung prayer.

A. THE CORPORATE STRUCTURE OF THE SINGING ASSEMBLY

When Christians come together to form a liturgical assembly, they are a visible manifestation of the Mystical Body of Christ. The assembly is no haphazard crowd, but a living organism in which the parts and members are coordinated hierarchically like those of the Church of which they are the sacred sign.[115b] Now, in the celebration of the liturgy there is nothing which more clearly manifests the organic structure of the assembly than the singing. It is when the members raise their voices that they reveal their respective roles in the common action; it is from what they sing that one can recognize their function and their rank within the assembly.

Just as the first impression one receives of a living human being is that he has a head and a body, so also the liturgical assembly manifests itself primarily as celebrant and people—two personal entities with whom there corresponds, in every church, the spatial arrangement of sanctuary and nave. This appears with especial clarity at the sung Mass, wherein the music is "to enhance the voice of the sacrificing priest and also that of the Christian people as they praise Almighty God" (MSD 14). All liturgical singing is based on this choral structure, an image of the praise which Christ, the Head of the Body which is the Church (Col. 1.18), offers with the Church to the Father.

The higher the place occupied in the scale of living beings, the more differentiation there is in their organisms. And so the singing body which is the

[115a] Cf. CL 28.
[115b] Cf. CL 26.

Christian assembly has a structure more developed than that of mere head and members. Each of the two main constituents is diversified into agents with differing functions. Particular roles appear both in the sanctuary and in the nave. That of the celebrant is to preside and to offer. For other functions within the sanctuary there are sacred ministers, his assistants. Just as the head needs eyes and mouth, so the sanctuary needs the deacon to direct prayer and proclaim the Gospel, readers to chant from other books of Holy Scripture, and even a psalmist to chant psalms. The nave, in turn, though capable of responding to acclamations, litanies, and psalms, and of singing simple hymns, must have recourse to a choir when it desires that song should be embellished with the riches of the art of music in compositions too difficult for itself to perform.

Thus, by the voice of the celebrant and his ministers, and that of the people with their choir, the singing body of the assembly celebrates a festive liturgy which may be compared to a symphony. The voices indeed are diverse, but the work is one. The Fathers of the Church loved to underline this unity in diversity, so characteristic of Christian worship. "It is truly a great bond of union," wrote St. Ambrose, "that the multitude who form the assembly make up but one single chorus, just as the strings of the harp, though unequal in length, play harmoniously together. Even a skilled performer, playing on so few strings, may make a mistake; but in the liturgical singing of the community it is the Holy Spirit who is playing; from Him there is never any dissonance." [116] And St. John Chrysostom explains how the celebrating assembly can have but one voice: "Because we all form one body together, there must be in the Church but one voice. Is it the reader who speaks? He does it alone; even the bishop who is present listens in silence. Is it the psalmist who chants? He chants alone; but when all reply to his chant, then it is as though but one voice were coming forth from one mouth." [117]

B. THE VARIOUS ROLES WITHIN THE SINGING ASSEMBLY

Those who sing liturgical chant can be divided into four categories according to the roles which they fulfill: the celebrant, the sacred ministers, the people, and the choir.

a) *The Celebrant*

"The celebrating priest presides over the whole liturgical action" (IMS 93). There can be no body without a head, no orchestra without a conductor. The head of that Body which is the Church is the risen Christ; the conductor of the choir of the baptized is the *Logos* of God. In the body and visible choir of the assembly, the Lord is present and active through the celebrant,

---

[117] *Hom. 36 in 1 Cor.* (PG 61, 315).
[116] *In Ps.* 1 (PL 14, 925).

mediator between God and men. The celebrant lends his voice to Christ so that the prayer of the Church may be lifted up toward the Father.

The celebrant gives the note which starts up the unified song of the just, even as the Word of God, having resolved dissonance, inaugurated all justice. When the celebrant enters, the assembly arises to receive him with song. When he speaks, his voice is to be heard by all present.[118] No other voice, no sound from any instrument, is to be superimposed on his.[119] Because he speaks and acts *in persona Christi*, his singing may never be replaced by that of the community.[120]

The presiding celebrant is the principal channel of God's message to men; and he fulfills the same function for men's response to God.[120a] It is with the celebrant's voice that every prayer of petition begins and every prayer of praise concludes. It is he who invites the community to pray: *Oremus*; he invites them to glorify God: *Sursum corda*. For he is not praying just in his own name, but in that of the entire community. He is never to "give a solo" on his own behalf, like a concert singer who "renders an item." He is to make sure, first of all, that everyone is with him: *Dominus vobiscum*. He says, in the plural, "*We* pray . . . *we* offer." The petitions of the Church are unified in the representative of Him who alone is worthy to be heard by the Father; the praise of the Church becomes a single paean in Him who alone can give to God all honor and glory.

The pre-eminence of the celebrant's song finds expression in the music which is the vehicle of his prayer. Though the people's song readily employs the arts of poetry and the charms of rhythm, that of the celebrant employs a dignified prose, adorned very simply by the oratorical *cursus*. The choir may indulge in expressive and varied melodic inflections, but the celebrant refrains from the use of melismata. He makes no pretensions to be a virtuoso. Just a few notes, a few melodic formulas which are restrained in character and fixed by law serve him in his prayer or his thanksgiving. Here is no exercise of the fine arts, but only the perfection of practical art in the mouth of the "sacrificer," that is, the "artisan of the sacred." The splendor of the reality which is expressed bears no proportion to the artistry of the song

---

[118] "The celebrating priest, especially if the church is large and the faithful numerous, must be careful to say all those parts indicated by the rubrics as *clara voce* in a voice so loud that all the people can follow the sacred action fittingly and easily" (IMS 34).

[119] If the voice of the celebrant cannot be heard clearly by all without the aid of microphones and loudspeakers, then the church ought to be equipped with the needed apparatus. The *Directoire* of the French hierarchy orders this (n. 48), as do the corresponding documents issued by the hierarchies of several other countries. "The explanations and interventions to be given by the commentator . . . must not overlay any of the sacerdotal prayers" (IMS 96c); the organ is not to be played, even as an accompaniment, when the priest is singing (IMS 16b); and the use of the organ at a low Mass is strictly limited according to the same principle that the celebrant's voice is never to be obscured when he is functioning as president (IMS 29).

[120] MD 29, 38.

[120a] Cf. CL 33.

which expresses it. The hieratic style of the essential rite is held to be a better expression of it than sensuous or exotic ornamentations devised by man.

In that symphony which is the liturgy, the leading part is taken by the presiding celebrant. All other voices must attune themselves to his. Or, to use a simile dear to St. Ignatius of Antioch, others must be united with him as strings with a harp, "so that in the harmony of your concord, as you take your note from God in unity, you may be able to sing with one voice a hymn to the Father through Jesus Christ." [121]

b) *The Sacred Ministers*

The study of liturgical action, which draws upon both history and comparative liturgy for light, shows that within the sanctuary the celebrant is not the only one who is called upon to raise his voice in song.[121a] He delegates to other voices the proclamation of the word of God which he is to expound and the direction of the prayer which he is to conclude. And so we find that there are three other important functionaries: the deacon, the reader, and the psalmist.

1. The *deacon* does not normally preside at any liturgical action,[122] but controls it by addressing explanations and directions to the people. This function has been reduced to small proportions in the Roman liturgy as it now exists,[123] but it was much in evidence in early Roman liturgy, and is still so in the Oriental liturgies of today. He is always the leader of the community's prayer.

The intervenions which the deacon sings have a triple purpose. Firstly, they inform the faithful of the progress of the rite and of the part which they ought to play in it: *Procedamus in pace* (Let us go forward in peace) before a procession; *Flectamus genua* (Let us kneel down) before penitential prayers; let us recognize in the paschal candle the *Lumen Christi; Ite, missa est.* In the ancient or Oriental liturgies the deacon has a specially important part just before the anaphora; he is not only to dismiss the catechumens and

---

[121] *Ad Eph.* 4, 1-2. Ignatius is here addressing directly the *presbyterium* to exhort them to union in all things.

[121a] Cf. CL 113.

[122] He has, however, the right to do so at solemn baptism, at burials, and at Communion outside of Mass. Cf. CL 35, n. 4, for Bible services.

[123] This is partly explained by the fact that our ceremonies were given their present form and became fixed at a time when, in the West, the people had little or no active part in the rites. The chief function of the deacon had thus become to assist the celebrant. The restoration of active participation by the people has brought to light anew the fact that community prayer needs some official to direct and control it. Hence a new functionary has made his appearance— the "commentator" (IMS 96)—who is now doing much of what used to be the business of the the deacon. But the commentator is not truly a minister of the liturgy, since none of the liturgical texts are allotted to him, nor is he entrusted with any of the liturgical chants. Although he is now, in fact, performing a real liturgical function, he is nevertheless excluded from the sanctuary; this creates an anomaly quite at variance with the traditional principles of liturgical celebration.

the non-communicants, but also to call the faithful to attention and to silence.[124] Secondly, the deacon is to direct that which is technically called "the
prayer of the faithful"; he does it by proposing to them intentions, in the
form of a litany, to which they respond by phrases of petition. It is for him
to chant the community's prayers of intercession, an element no longer found
in the Roman Mass but an essential constituent of other liturgies.[125] Thirdly,
it is the office of the deacon to chant the most important of the Scripture
readings, the Gospel.

There is one word characteristic of his interventions—*kerussein, praedicare*,
that is, "to make proclamations" [126] It includes solemn announcements proclaimed in the manner of a "herald," and connotes that use of the singing
voice which gives power and dignity to the words proclaimed. But the functional nature of the deacon's interventions calls for the use of a syllabic recitative in which there is no place for melismata. We see this exemplified even
today in the instances cited above: *Flectamus genua! Lumen Christi!* [127] The
same simplicity of melody can be found in the announcements and litanies
of Oriental liturgies.

The liturgy resembles a lyrical drama in certain ways; in this is employed
an "announcer" whose functions are paralleled by the voice of the deacon
in the liturgy. The announcer introduces or concludes items; he explains

[124] The *Testamentum Domini* (a Syrian document of the fifth century) gives us the following
example of what happened before the *oratio fidelium* and the anaphora:
"The deacon shall proclaim thus:

> Let us arise.
> Let everyone take his place.
> Let the catechumens depart.
> Let there remain here no one who is impure or negligent.
> Lift up your eyes and your hearts; the angels are watching.
> Anyone lacking in trustfulness should go away.
> And now let us ask with one single heart . . ." (I, 35).

Even today, in the liturgy of St. John Chrysostom, the deacon says:

> "The doors! The doors! In wisdom let us be attentive.
> Let us behave, let us be filled with awe:
> Let us be attentive to offer the holy gifts in peace."

[125] Especially the *oratio fidelium*, or common prayer of the faithful, which concludes the
liturgy of the word and links it up with the eucharistic liturgy of the Mass; also the diaconal
liturgy at the beginning of the Mass of which the *Kyrie* is now the only vestige. The *oratio
fidelium* may well have been originally a sacerdotal prayer like the *orationes sollemnes* which
we still have on Good Friday. See the study of this form in ch. 7, pp. 94ff.

[126] *Kerussein* is a biblical word which means the proclamation of the Good Tidings. It is
the term regularly used in the ancient Greek documents when they refer to the role of the
deacon. The corresponding Latin word is *praedicare*; it has been retained in the Latin Pontifical
at the ordination of deacons: *Diaconum oportet . . . praedicare*. This does not mean "preaching," but "liturgical proclamation"—making announcements within the liturgy. The term
has become metamorphosed into the French word *prône*, which, since the Middle Ages, has
been a collection of prayers similar in style and form to the ancient diaconal prayers.

[127] The neumatic or melismatic settings for the *Ite missa est* are all of late composition. The
authentic type of *Ite* is found in Mass XV.

or connects events; he recalls or draws attention to features within the drama. As the name signifies, the deacon is to serve the community. It is not for him to be an artist achieving brilliant performances [128] but an agent whose voice is to encourage other voices to join in the symphony of petition and praise.

2. The *reader* fulfills the oldest and most general of all the functions instituted by the Church in the service of Christian worship: to impart God's word by the recitation of passages from Holy Scripture, the Lessons and Epistles, which find a place in the Mass or the Divine Office.[128a] Later on some of the readings were allotted to the subdeacon, as at present in the solemn Mass of the Roman rite. In ancient times every Christian community had its own reader (or readers), whose liturgical function gave rise to the order of lector (which nowadays has nothing to do with its corresponding function, although it continues to function in the Oriental rites). The reader, a young man or even a boy chosen for the clarity and power of his voice, was given an appropriate technical training, and normally remained in office as long as his voice sufficed for its duties.[129]

The words "reader" and "reading" should not mislead us. "To read" (*legere* in the liturgy) had a special meaning in ancient times. It was not just any kind of delivery of a text, still less a purely mental activity; it meant a public and rhetorical kind of declamation. Moreover, in both Christian and Jewish tradition, Holy Scripture was normally "chanted." "Chanting," in this restricted technical sense, is a rhythmo-melodic recitation of a text by means of simple stereotyped formulas readily adapted to intonations, to verbal accentuation, and especially to punctuations and cadences. Its object was in the first place practical: to make sure that the words of the text could easily be heard. Words which were chanted would carry better because they were spread out in time by reason of number and kept within range of audibility by means of melos. But the main object of chanting was religious: the chant, as it were, put a sacred vestment upon the words and thereby signified the sacred character of the message.[130]

But no more than the other ministers of the sanctuary is the reader intended to be a virtuoso singer charged with the duty of displaying his art. Thanks to the technique of recitation, which he is expected to master, he transmits a sacred text, endeavoring through music to give to it all its mysterious power. But the Holy Scripture is not *his* song. The liturgy provides him with dignified traditional chant-formulas; and what he chants is God's word.

[128] The *Exsultet* is a notable exception which raises practical problems for certain sacred ministers.

[128a] Cf. CL 29.

[129] Evidence for this appears in epigraphical and literary documents.

[130] See p. 24 and footnote 17.

3. The office of *psalmist* more clearly subserves a purpose explicitly musical; he is but a specialized type of reader skilled in the recitation of psalms, which are, by their own intrinsic nature, the lyrical part of the Bible.[131]

The psalmist became distinguished from the ordinary reader about the fourth century. From the many documents originating in the fourth, fifth and sixth centuries we learn both the exact details and the importance of his office.[132] He goes up into the ambo to sing the verses of the intervenient chants of the liturgy of the word. At vigils, and during the Offices of Matins and Vespers (whether parochial or monastic), it is he who gives out the inspired texts to which the community reply in responsorial or antiphonal form. For, in ancient times there was never a collective recitation of sacred texts; only readers and psalmists were charged with the transmission of the canonical word.[133] That is why the psalmist had the rank of a sacred minister in minor orders in many churches of the Orient; not a few have retained the practice till this day.[134] In the Roman liturgy, neither the order of psalmist nor the corresponding function has survived in its ancient form.[135] But the Roman-Frankish liturgy preserved for some time the role of a solo singer in some of the responsorial psalms, as is proved by the existence of a special book designed for his use and containing the music for verses of the Graduals—the *Cantatorium*.[136]

The somewhat rare verses of responsorial psalms still to be found in the Roman liturgy have come down to us in the Gregorian chant of the Graduals and of certain prolix responsories in the Divine Office;[137] they are set to melodies rich in melismata. All these are the final result of relatively late musical developments (seventh to ninth centuries) which radically altered the nature of responsorial psalmody by reducing the number of verses

---

[131] In Hebrew the book of Psalms bears the title: *sefer tehillim*, the "book of hymns." The word "psalm" (*mizmor*) refers to the playing of instruments to accompany song, and would correspond well enough with our own word "music."

[132] In the second book of the *Apostolic Constitutions* (II, 57) of the fourth century the direction for the intervenient chants of the liturgy of the word still refers to "another reader." But in the eighth book of the same work, the psalmist has become a minor order distinct from the reader. With reference to the office of psalmist in the early liturgy, many texts will be found in our study of the subject to be published later: *Antiphona*.

[133] Cf. Canon 15 of Laodicea, which reappears in many canonical collections: "Apart from the canonical psalmists who go up into the ambo and chant from the Codex [of the psalter], no one else is allowed to psalmodize in the church" (J. D. Mansi, *Sacrorum conciliorum nova et amplissima collectio* [Florence–Venice, 1757–1790], II, 567.

[134] With the Maronites it is a distinct order; the East Syrians confer it with the tonsure; traces of the order of psalmist are admixed with the order of lector among the Byzantines.

[135] It is important not to confuse the psalmist with the *cantor* (as we now understand this word). The cantor, whether he be the only singer or one among many, is but a chosen member of the congregation. The psalmist, on the other hand, is one of the ministers of the sanctuary.

[136] Evidence for this is the celebrated n. 359 of St. Gall, published in the second volume of *Paléographie grégorienne* (2nd series, 1924).

[137] For example, in the time after the Epiphany. In other seasons they have usually been replaced by non-psalmodic responsories, original compositions more correctly classified as **psalmodic hymnody.**

to be sung and turning the people's refrain into a choir part.[138] During the patristic era, the chanting of verses by the psalmist was, in fact, always considered as a recitation of the sacred text, and it was referred to as a "reading."[139] Even as late as St. Gregory's day, the Roman Council of 595 refers to it in similar terms when it reserves to subdeacons or others in minor orders *inter missarum sollemnia . . . psalmos vero et reliquas lectiones.*[140] The whole purpose, in the psalm no less than in the Epistle and Gospel, was the proclamation of the word of God. This word, proclaimed to the people from the ambo by the minister authorized to do so, was to be in fact an intelligible reading. Yet, in contrast with the other readings, the psalm is a text which is both poetic and lyrical. Thus it afforded an opportunity, not only for the insertion of a responsory by the people (*responsorium*), but also for a more rhythmic and melodic style of chanting.[141] Probably we have a surviving example of the kind of musical recitative used by the early psalmist in some of the short responsories of the Roman Office, even though these are now limited to a single verse and the *Gloria Patri*.[142]

Except in the light of the constitutive role of the psalmist in the structure of the symphonic edifice of Christian worship, it is impossible to understand the nature of choral and musical forms which some of the liturgical chants have retained. It is all the more necessary to refer to this role if there is to be any progress along the way opened by the *Instruction* of 1958 (27), which permits the restoration of an increased number of verses in the antiphonal and processional chants of the Mass. If these additional verses are to be used, the function of the psalmist will have to be restored, at least in part, after the manner exemplified in the one verse of the Introit wherein his function has been retained.[143]

[138] See later in this book for a discussion of responsories and the responsorial form of psalmody (ch. 7, pp. 96ff.), of the Gradual of the Mass (ch. 11), and successively developed strata of Gregorian chant (ch. 13).—P. Wagner (*Introduction to the Gregorian Melodies*, ch. 7), basing his arguments on a musical repertoire of late development, holds that the distinctive characteristics of responsorial chant are to be discerned in chants of an ornate and melismatic type. But in the light of the history of liturgical forms and of psalmody, such a position is untenable.

[139] For example, St. Augustine: "We have heard the Epistle, the psalm and the Gospel; all these three readings are in agreement" (*Serm.* 165; PL 38, 902).

[140] Gregory I, *Registrum*, ed. P. Ewald, I, p. 363.

[141] The Greek name of *psaltês* given to the psalmist is borrowed from the singer who accompanied himself on the lyre (*psallein* = to strike the chords of the instrument). On the occasional use of this instrument in liturgical chant, and on the use of tambourines, cymbals, hand-clapping in East and West, see ch. 11.

[142] There are two points to be noted: (1) in the ferial Office the texts of the short responsories are usually taken from the psalms; (2) the melodies for most of them are identical with the tones at present in use for the oldest popular antiphons of the Gregorian repertoire. Compare, for instance, the ordinary tune for short responses (such as *In manus tuas*, with the antiphons exemplified by *Notum fecit Dominus* or those for antiphons of irregular tone (see p. 196ff., and Plate II, p. 99).

[143] The restoration of the Gradual as a responsorial psalm and psalmic reading within the Mass makes the restoration of the psalmist's office still more indispensable. From the point of

It should be noted that everything sung from the sanctuary, the most important parts of the liturgy, is in the form of *solo* chants (by the celebrant, deacon, reader, and psalmist). This fact accords with the nature of Christian worship, based as it is on the proclamation of a revealed word, and celebrated by an assembly which has a hierarchic structure. God speaks to us through the channel of a human mouth; the Church's response is realized through the mediation of the priest.

In the nave of the church, as we shall see, the solo form has no essential place, because the singing from there is, by its nature, the expression of a plurality of persons, that is, choral. By contrast, the Church has reserved to the soloist of the sanctuary his sacred and imprescriptible role. But this soloist, considered as an artist, is very different from the one normally found in the world of profane music. In the latter, the stature of the soloist is measured by his technical ability, his personality, the artistry of his interpretation, and the musical worth of his repertoire. But in the sanctuary the sacred minister is not a professional singer; [144] his personality is hidden behind a sort of neutral and impersonal melody; in his singing there is no place for vocal display or virtuosity. The splendor of the mystery which is itself inaudible to human ears is most fittingly signified by a wholly evangelical poverty wedded to the most essential and permanent forms of the art of good speaking.

c) *The People*

In the liturgy it is the voice of the people which is to reply to the voice of the celebrant or of his ministers.

1. The celebrating assembly is the visible body of the Church at prayer, and in this the people have a position which is organic. After mentioning the sacred ministers (*nos servi tui*), the great eucharistic prayer of the Roman Mass makes mention of the people (*sed et plebs tua sancta*).[145] The people are not the entire assembly, but that part of the celebrating body which occupies the nave of the church. The voices from the sanctuary have, indeed, the greatest dignity, but only those from the nave can express, by their plurality combined in unity, the public and communal character of the Church's worship.

The singing of the people, therefore, is a constitutive element of the lit-

view of liturgical structure, such treatment of the Gradual is eminently desirable and important. The psalmist would be needed also if psalm-singing with participation by the people is to be reintroduced in the morning and evening offices. Already the attempts which have been made to restore the prayer of the psalms to the people (for example, at low Masses and vigil services) have demonstrated how valuable it is to employ a soloist to sing the verses of the psalms.

[144] Nevertheless, as we are reminded in IMS 95, it is proper to choose as celebrant and ministers those who are capable of doing full justice to the musical requirements of their office.

[145] The same pair of agents is indicated also in the *Hanc igitur*: "*oblationem servitutis nostrae* (clergy), *sed et cunctae familiae tuae* (laity)."

urgy.[145a] It is with the people and for the people that the sacrifice of praise is offered: "We, Thy servants, and with us all Thy holy people, offer to Thy divine majesty . . . the perfect Victim" (*Unde et memores*). For the liturgy is "the whole public worship of the Mystical Body of Jesus Christ, Head and members" (MD 20). That is why the expressed and public ratification of the people is provided for in the sacred rites themselves at all of the most important points of the liturgy. "The Mass, by its very nature, requires that all those who are present should take part in it in the manner which pertains to them," which means, as regards the people, "especially by answering, praying and singing" (IMS 22).

The celebrant calls for a sung response in his *Dominus vobiscum* and his *Gratias agamus Domino Deo nostro* (Let us give thanks to the Lord our God). The end of the Preface introduces the communal praise of the *Sanctus: nostras voces ut admitti iubeas, deprecamur* (we ask Thee to command that our voices be included). There is no public act which is not included by the unanimous *Amen* of the people.

If, after considering the rites objectively, we then view them from the standpoint of the people, their participation in liturgical singing appears no less necessary. The sacred signs constitute, for the faithful who take part in the liturgy, the channel of divine grace and the instrument of the Church's worship. The rites become means of sanctification and of worship for the baptized in proportion to the part which they play in them. Now "singing is the ideal form of participation in the sacred action second only to sacramental Communion."[146] From this we can understand the importance, in all restoration of the liturgy, of the people's song. St. Pius X recalled that, "for the renewal of the true Christian spirit, active participation in the sacred mysteries and in the public and solemn prayer of the Church is the primary and indispensable source" (TLS, Introd.). And Pius XI said very forcibly: "It is most necessary that the faithful should not assist at the sacred rites as detached and silent spectators, but . . . that their voices should alternate with those of the priest and choir, as the rubrics direct."[147] Within recent years both Pius XII and many episcopal directives have frequently inculcated these same principles.[148]

2. If this is the position held by the people's song in Christian worship, how is it that the Church's practice has varied so much from one period of

[145a] Cf. CL 33: "In the liturgy God speaks to his people. . . . And the people reply to God both by song and prayer."

[146] *Directoire* 149.

[147] DC 9.

[148] Cf. MD, especially nn. 23-26; MSD, especially nn. 14-15, 30-32, 41; IMS, especially nn. 22-23, 93, etc.; and the *Directoire* of the French hierarchy, especially nn. 127-138. Cf. CL 30: "To promote active participation, the people should be encouraged to take part by means of acclamations, responses, psalmody, antiphons and songs. . . ."

history to another, and why is it so necessary to insist on the matter in these our own days?

When we look at the patristic era (especially the fourth, fifth and sixth centuries), we find that the people's singing in the liturgy was taken for granted. Whether at Mass, at vigils, Lauds or Vespers, we hear the faithful throughout the Christian world answering the litanies of the deacon or the verses of the psalmist. This was so completely normal that St. Augustine avowed to Januarius:

> Apart from those moments when the Scriptures are being read or a sermon is preached, when the bishop is praying aloud or the deacon is specifying the intentions of the litany of community prayer, is there any time when the faithful assembled in the church are not singing? Truly I see nothing better, more useful or more holy that they could do.[149]

From so many eloquent testimonies, it should be enough to quote St. John Chrysostom's description of the singing at the Church of St. Irenaeus in Constantinople:

> The psalm which occurred just now in the office blended all voices together, and caused one single fully harmonious chant to arise; young and old, rich and poor, women and men, slaves and free, all sang one single melody . . . Here the prophet speaks and we all reply, all of us echo his words . . . Together we make up a single choir in perfect equality of rights and of expression whereby earth imitates heaven. Such is the noble character of the Church.[150]

The first blow suffered by active participation of the faithful in worship came at the end of the ancient culture when the barbarians invaded the West.[151] From that time those who entered the Church were strangers to the Mediterranean culture which had been the setting wherein the liturgical rites had evolved; they received neither the long instruction nor the biblical formation which, till then, had been given to the catechumens. The psalms, the very basis of liturgical chant, were hardly explained to them; Latin was only more or less well understood by the barbaric tribes converted to the Church. The liturgical chant was chiefly sustained in the sacred offices only by the local clergy or the monks.

In the eighth and ninth centuries, Charlemagne, following Pepin, labored

---

[149] *Ep.* 55, 18-19.

[150] *Hom.* 5 (PG 63, 486-7). The canons of St. Basil (Egyptian, 5th–6th centuries?) even imposed upon the entire community the obligation of taking part in the responsorial psalmody. "Bodily suffering" is the only excusing circumstance envisaged (Can. 97, *Die Kirchenrechtsquellen des Patriarchats Alexandrien*, ed. W. Riedel, Leipzig, 1900).

[151] The following short historical summary is an attempt to explain briefly how it came about that in the Roman rite the celebration of the rites became divorced from the singing of the people. For more detailed information recent historical works may be consulted.

to replace the Gallican liturgy with that of Rome; and the latter did not escape the disadvantages of an imported liturgy, admired by the educated but too remote from the ordinary people. The sacred action became more and more the affair of clerics. At the same time there came a wave of poetry and music from the East (the Mélodes of Jerusalem, in the seventh century). This profoundly modified the structure of the traditional chants. By the beginning of the eighth century there arose in many places the *scholae* of professional singers and virtuosos who developed the ancient melodies or created new repertoires. The execution of these highly artistic pieces was reserved to them. The people listened to them, at least in those places where they were performed—in cathedrals and monasteries. A few decrees expressed reminders that certain chants, such as the *Sanctus*, ought to be sung by all.[152] But the separation of sanctuary from nave, symbolized by the rood-screens of the Middle Ages, was almost complete. Developments in polyphony finally excluded the people altogether from strictly liturgical singing, not only in the psalmodic hymnody of the *scholae*, but even from their items in the Ordinary of the Mass.[153]

There can be no doubt that the people did do some singing during the Middle Ages, but it is difficult to establish when, how and what: hymns—sometimes farced with couplets in the vernacular language, proses or canticles, rather than the traditional chants of the liturgy. The legislation of the Council of Trent, reserving control of liturgical ceremonies to the Holy See, established a legal separation between the liturgical chants in Latin, generally executed by a choir of clerics or professional singers, and hymns in the people's own tongue. In virtue of this distinction, the singing which contemporary documents call "popular hymnody" cannot normally be ranked as "liturgical."

In spite of these historical vicissitudes of the practical or disciplinary type, it remains true that singing by the people is one of the constitutive elements of Christian worship.[154]

3. The people's part in liturgical song is classified according to the different ways in which it finds expression. The congregation is a partner of all the

---

[152] An example is the *Admonitio generalis* of Charlemagne, dated 789, according to which the two parts of the *Sanctus* should be sung together by celebrant and people (Aboretus, "Capitularia regum Francorum," 70: *Monumenta Germaniae historica*, Hanover–Hahn–Berlin, 1826 ff., I, 59).

[153] Pius Parsch used to say of this that the Church musician was guilty of two sins, one venial and one mortal! "The venial sin was committed very early during the classical period of the liturgy in the seventh century. The *schola* performed chants ever more and more artistic and complicated, with the result that the people could no longer take any part in them. The people became mere listeners because the *schola* was reserving to itself all the chants of the proper." The mortal sin was committed when choirs, deserting the vicinity of the altar, assumed a monopoly of the singing by means of polyphony, which excluded participation by the people even in the items of the Ordinary (*Le renouveau liturgique*, trans. M. Grandclaudon [Mulhouse, 1950], pp. 183–184).

[154] In this kind of singing, the literary language and the musical genre employed are only the means, to be assessed by the Church, directed toward the end, which is the active and intelligent participation of the faithful in worship. If a language or a genre proves to be such

chief ministers in the sanctuary, and its singing manifests the role it plays in the sacred actions.

It is, first of all, a partner of the chief readers to whom it listens. It greets the proclamation of the Gospel: *Gloria tibi, Domine!* It answers the psalmist by its refrains. Next it is the partner of the deacon who directs its prayer. It associates itself with his petitions, with the intentions of the litanic prayers which he proposes. It replies sometimes to his directions: *Procedamus in pace: In nomine Christi, Amen!—Lumen Christi: Deo gratias!—Ite, missa est: Deo gratias!* But above all it is the partner of the celebrant before and after all his prayers, as we have said, and in the anaphora (initial dialogue, *Sanctus*, the anamneses of the East, and the concluding *Amen*). Finally, it has its own prayers and hymns: the Lord's Prayer before Communion,[155] the *Gloria*, the Creed, and all hymns and canticles. Sometimes it sings these *una voce*, at other times it calls upon a choir to be its partner by alternation in singing.

When the congregation is a partner of one of the ministers of the sanctuary, that is, in its most essential interventions, its song ever retains a great melodic and rhythmic simplicity. It consists in acclamations or invocations in a syllabic or recitative style. But in the hymnody which falls to its share, the congregation has greater liberty. We should observe that while the prayer of the celebrant is almost always addressed to the Father through the Son as Mediator, that of the people is more ordinarily addressed to Christ[156] or to the saints. Moreover, its literary and musical form readily turns to poetry or melodious "tunes." Hence it more often bears the marks of the culture specific to each nation. As we shall see later, it is in the congregation's singing that the pastoral aspect of worship finds its most frequent applications.

d) *The Choir*

The solemn celebration of the liturgy normally requires the presence of a group of skilled singers to execute, in Gregorian chant, the items of psalmodic hymnody (Introit, Offertory, Communion, Alleluia),[157] and also to sing polyphonic items when these are used. We shall call this group of singers,

that it renders liturgical singing by the people impossible, then the means should be subordinated to the end, not conversely.

[155] In the solemn form of the Roman rite the *Pater* is still sung by the celebrant. But, from a study of comparative liturgy, it is really a communal prayer, and henceforth is to be treated as such in non-solemn forms of the Roman rite (IMS 32).

[156] The litanic invocations (and hence the *Kyrie*), the original form of the *Gloria*, the Eastern anamneses, and many of the psalm-refrains are addressed *ad Christum*.

The idea that "the" liturgical prayer is normally addressed *ad Patrem* is too widespread. It is true only of the prayer of the celebrant, who is a mediator. Nor can one say that prayer *ad Christum* is merely a reaction against Arianism, for many instances of it can be adduced from the first three centuries.

[157] The *Directoire pour la pastorale de la Messe* of the French hierarchy says clearly: "Liturgical singing requires the provision of a choir" (150). The *Instruction*, somewhat less categorically,

which has a special function in liturgical chant, by the modern and now generally used title of "choir," without seeking to determine precisely other more restricted meanings sometimes attached to this word.

1. Because the choir has a special technical competence, it is only by means of the choir that the art of singing can offer its greatest musical possibilities in the service of worship. Hence, when we speak of sacred music, we normally think first of the singing and of the repertoire of the choir. But it should be realized that, although the choir's music is ranked first from the standpoint of music, it actually comes last from the liturgical standpoint when ranked among the various agents of liturgical singing.

The choir, in fact, has no place among the sacred ministers of the sanctuary, who hold the primacy in dignity.[158] Every item which falls to the choir is one of the nave chants: [159] responsories of the psalms, psalmodic hymnody or free hymnody. The choir is a "section of the people." [160]

But within the singing body of the congregation, the people need a specialized agent so that their song may be enriched by all the resources which the art of music can contribute to the service of worship. The rites make clear what this agent should do. Sometimes the choir is to deputize for the people in the performance of musical items too difficult for them to sing (items of the Gregorian Proper or harmonized pieces), sometimes it is to alternate with the people (items from the Ordinary), sometimes to reinforce them (in the acclamations), sometimes to combine with them by adding its harmonies to their unison. In all these instances the choir is singing in the name of the people or with them.

2. In point of fact, the composition, function, and musical contribution of what we call the choir has varied greatly in the course of the history of the

says: "It is very desirable that all cathedral churches, and at least parish churches and other churches of some importance, should each have a regular choir or *schola cantorum*" (IMS 99). To accuse the liturgical movement of an intention to abolish choirs is quite false. On the contrary, it seeks to establish them in their proper role (P. Parsch, *Le renouveau liturgique*, p. 182; *La Maison Dieu*, 60, pp. 148 ff.; *La Maison Dieu*, 63, pp. 78 ff. *Église qui chante*, 15, pp. 3 ff.). It opposes nothing except that which, as regards the repertoire, intervention or location of the choir, is incompatible with the proper celebration of worship. Cf. CL 29 and 114.

[158] We have already pointed out that the liturgical function of the psalmist, a minister of the sanctuary, must be distinguished from that of choir-singer. Similarly, as regards the arrangement of "sacred space" within the church, one should not confuse the sanctuary with the "choir." This latter space, which obtains its name from the choir of singers or clerics who used to occupy it during the Middle Ages, is distinct from the sanctuary, even if, in the West, it is more or less coterminous with it. In the Eastern rites the chief separation of space has remained (for example, as the iconostasis) between the sanctuary and the rest of the church. Their choirs always occupy a position in front.

[159] Exceptions are the verses of the Gradual or prolix responsories which originally were performed by the psalmist at the ambo. Nowadays they are done by a subsection of the choir.

[160] "Between the celebrant and the people there are normally some intermediaries: some may be considered as assistants to the celebrant and his delegates to the people—the *ministers*; others are chosen from the people in order to stimulate the celebration—the *choir*" (*Directoire* 79).

liturgy. There is no evidence which would even suggest the presence of any specialized group of singers within the assembly during the first three centuries. Toward the end of the fourth century, in town churches of some importance and in places of pilgrimage, there began to appear a particular class of the faithful to fulfill, in liturgical singing, a role which stands out clearly. They were the local "monks,"[161] élite Christians of either sex who lived within the Christian community of that place, but had three distinguishing characteristics: celibacy, ascetic life, and diligence at liturgical prayer. The names given to such people emphasize sometimes the first of these characteristics: "monks," "ascetics," "renunciants"; sometimes the last: "zealots," "vigilants."[162]

In practice, the monks took the lead within the assembly—often grouped together in "choirs" — at all services held by the community: the daily offices of morning and evening, the vigils and the Masses. As regards the liturgy they were, then, by their very vocation, exemplary "observants." They could always be relied on to reply to the psalmist (at this time responsorial or antiphonal psalmody was the basis of liturgical singing), or to reinforce the acclamations, or, in addition, to sing hymns. These diligent singers were not a group of specialized musicians, but simply the élite of the congregation. If, here and there, they assumed the character of an institution, not merely ecclesiastical but even liturgical or choral, this was not due to any special musical competence but solely to their zeal. They were not yet a *schola cantorum*. But we can understand what a support these faithful singers were to a congregation made up of all-comers. The congregation as a whole looked after the acclamations, the answers to the litanies, and the commonly known psalm refrains, while the élite group could make themselves responsible for psalmody and hymnody of a more varied kind.

Toward the seventh century we find the beginnings of a profound evolution both in the style of composition and in the form of liturgical music. The change coincides with the appearance of a new type of chant which came to play a decisive role. In the East the cathedrals were losing prestige; monachism of the Palestinian community-type took over and gradually enriched liturgical life; it gave an ever more and more prominent place in worship to

[161] The name "monk" here bears the original meaning of the word *monachi*, that is, celibates. Pre-monachism, often the affair of individuals, is not to be confused with Pachomian cenobitism, still less with Benedictinism. Those we are referring to had no worship other than that of the local community. The latter, by contrast, gradually developed a worship of their own. In the fourth to the sixth centuries the worship of the cenobites retained a degree of privation which is in sharp contrast with the worship of the cathedrals. "The making of music is not fitting for monks, but only for priests and people in the world," is a maxim atttributed to St. Anthony.

[162] On all this little-known aspect of the history of ecclesiastical singing, we beg to refer readers to a work we are at present engaged on, *Antiphona*, in which numerous texts concerning the existence, nature and function of these singers of the fourth to the sixth century will be quoted and analyzed.

the chant. Inspired by the Mélodes of Jerusalem and the example of such men as Cosmas, John and Sophronios, a great flood of lyrical and hymnodic compositions swept into all the churches. The antiphonal psalmody of the Office and the Mass gave way, in the East, to intervenient chants on poetic texts, and in the West to the melodies of psalmodic responsories. Both the composition and performance of these works of choral art were made possible by the existence of the chant schools, centers of poetic and musical culture, traces of which can be found from Mesopotamia to Spain.[163] Under Pope Sergius I (687–701), who was of Syrian origin, there appeared in Rome what later came to be called the *schola cantorum*.[164] In the next century this had attained such prestige that the Franks used to go to Rome in order to learn this or that Roman chant; and *scholae cantorum* on the Roman model became widespread throughout the empire of Charlemagne. But the singers in these schools did not quite correspond to the ancient psalmists, nor to the choirs of ascetics. They were clerics,[165] professional chant-singers, trained from infancy to a very high technical standard. Their repertoire was totally different from that of the people. It was a development of all those items in the liturgy which were based on psalmody, and this development took place at the price of radical transformations. To these professionals, who perpetuate their role in the Roman liturgy as we have it now, we owe the composition of our present Gregorian propers.

A third stage in the history of the choir, a very complex and varied one, was governed by the development and liturgical use of polyphony. It has been exemplified in the "maîtrises" (professional church choirs of high reputation) of recent centuries and by the "musical" Mass. Although the repertoire has been extended to all the liturgical items not reserved to the ministers of the sanctuary, its chief development was in the items of the Ordinary of the Mass. It thus became common for all the liturgical singing which belonged to the nave of the church to be carried out exclusively by the choir. This, in fact, was the usual practice ever since the Renaissance in all important churches which had such a choir at their disposal.

With regard to the various roles, whose distribution is determined by the very nature of Christian worship, we cannot regard as a norm that historical evolution of the choir's role which, in order to give greater prominence to the achievements of art, has progressively invaded the rites to the detriment of the people's part in them. It would be incorrect, for example, to conclude that the singing in church is primarily entrusted to the choir, even if it is

[163] Historians have not yet determined the limits of this evolution or the channels of its influence.

[164] On the *schola cantorum* at Rome, see S. Corbin, *L'Église à la conquête de sa musique*, ch. 8.

[165] Consult A. G. Martimort–F. Picard, *Liturgie et musique*, p. 183, for further information on the pseudo-order of cantor in the Middle Ages, and on its Gallican origin. No doubt it was inspired by the ancient office of *psalmista*, still attested by Isidore of Seville (*De Eccles. off.* II, 12) as existing alongside the reader's office in the West.

composed of clerics.[166] The people should keep their fundamental role in the assembly, and the choir should be limited to its own subordinate function of embellishment or support. The restoration to the people of their active participation in the rites, desired by the Church in these days, absolutely requires the correction of imbalance when the proper equilibruim has been disturbed. Likewise, it is only right that the people should be left with two possibilities: they must be able to express themselves in those chants which, by nature, belong to them; and also, with the aid of the more competent of their own members, they must be able to enrich their sung prayer by the inclusion of musical refinement beyond their own capabilities to the extent to which they judge that these would make their prayer more beautiful and more sincere.

3. In the present state of the liturgy, we may view the choir in several ways, whether juridic or practical.

From the juridic point of view, the Instruction of September 3, 1958 (93), states that the participation of the choir in the liturgical action differs according to the status of those who are its members. *Clerics*, if they are constituted as a *schola* and sing according to the rubrics, render a direct and special ministerial service in virtue of their clerical status. *Laity* of the male sex, if they are deputed to sing by competent ecclesiastical authority, if they are constituted as a *schola* and sing according to the rubrics, render a direct ministerial service by delegation. In other cases (choirs which are mixed or all feminine, and when the *schola* sings items not strictly liturgical), the participation is of that kind which belongs to every member of the faithful in virtue of his baptism.[167]

From the practical point of view, the choir can be used to serve worship in three ways which differ considerably from each other. In an ordinary congregation the choir may consist of a group of the faithful selected and assembled together, not necessarily on account of their technical competence, but because their zeal and good will render it possible for a special role to be entrusted to them: to lead and sustain the community singing, to alternate with the rest of the assembly, to sing certain verses or responses which they have practiced or for which they have the printed text. Their repertoire would be that of the congregation in general, and nothing exclusive to themselves. But their presence is needed because of the diversity of a crowd whose mem-

---

[166] The phrase of St. Pius X: "With the exception of the melodies proper to the celebrant at the altar and to the ministers . . . all the rest of the liturgical chant belongs to the choir of levites" (TLS 12)was a statement of fact concerning what the Church has actually done since the Middle Ages. It is not a statement of a juridic principle which would exclude the people from liturgical singing; for, if taken thus, it would conflict with all the rest of the same document, and with the teachings of Pius XII. Nor can we deduce from the phrase any difference of degree between the role of the people and of the choir. On this point see A. G. Martimort–F. Picard, *Liturgie et musique*, p. 183.

[167] This theoretical classification raises more problems than it solves. See A. G. Martimort–F. Picard, *Liturgie et musique*, pp. 180 ff. Cf. CL 29.

bers lack confidence in taking their parts, and whose voices are uneven in kind and quality. The choir assures an adequate performance of the sung prayer and fulfills an organic role of sustaining the others.[168]

Whenever a parish celebrates the solemn liturgy or other important or complex ceremonies, the singing will need a choir composed of clerics or faithful selected on account of their vocal ability or musical competence. Their task will be to sing the unison pieces (Gregorian propers) or harmonized items that are beyond the capacity of the people, whenever these are required by the liturgy or are desirable as embellishments to the congregational singing because they can be aids to community prayer. The *scholae* of religious communities, the professional choirs of the big churches, and the skilled amateurs of parish churches are normally of this type. Their task within the assembly is to make up for the deficiencies of the people; but also they should sustain the people's singing or alternate with them.

Finally, it is possible that a community may be so homogeneous and musically cultured that it can, as a whole, function as a choir (or as two alternating choirs) capable of singing Gregorian propers (apart from psalmodic verses which fall to the lot of soloists) or even polyphonic compositions. Congregation and choir are, in this case, identical. Here we have the ultimate possible as regards participation by the nave of the church in liturgical singing.

The position of the choir within the assembly depends on the role which it is to fulfill. Whether it is to lead the singing of the nave (which, in its entirety, is directed toward the sanctuary), or to supply that which expresses the participation of all in the mysteries, the choir is always to be a bond between the sacred action and the people. It should never monopolize the attention of all, concentrating this attention upon its own musical performance; it should never seem to be, as it were, on a concert platform, nor should it withdraw itself from the ranks of the Christian assembly. The liturgy demands that the choir should be in front of the assembly, at the point where sanctuary and nave meet.[169] This position expresses its true function, which is to channel the prayer of all towards the altar.

[168] A group like this, the élite of the congregation comparable to the choirs of ascetics of ancient days, is needed in every church service at which a large congregation is called on to take part in the singing. For when the people are many, and differ much in their educational and liturgical standard, their singing can hardly be confident, worthy, and prayerful without such aid.

[169] IMS 67. The same conclusion can be deduced from the position of the organ, which "should be situated near the high altar in a convenient place, unless long-standing custom or some other peculiar reason, with the approval of the Ordinary, justifies an exception."

One cannot do other than deplore intensely the existence of choirlofts which isolate the singers and run the risk of cutting the choir off from the sacred action. This undesirable consequence is practically inevitable wherever the choirloft has been built at the back of the nave. The attempt at solution by putting the choir behind the high altar, though preferable to the other practice, is still not fully satisfactory. The choir should really form a constituent part of the assembly.

7   LYRICAL FORMS

Every musical composition, considered as a whole, possesses a structure known as its "form." This is so whether it develops by the continual evolution of new melodic material as in a full-scale Gregorian antiphon, or by the indefinite repetition of the same motif as in a litany, or by alternation of a fixed refrain with variable couplets as in a responsory. Just as an architect arranges the different parts of a building so that each element of the work, whether used but once or many times, shall be integrated into the whole, so also the musician "composes" and orders his thematic material according to some form more or less well defined: lied or rondo, fugue or sonata, etc.[170] By applying the concept of form to liturgical singing we enter the domain of music more immediately than by studying the rites to be sung, their classification, or their agents.

[170] In the English language the word "form" can have quite a number of meanings; here we are using it only in reference to a work considered as a whole. It would indeed be possible to speak of the "form" of a phrase, of a section or of a sentence; one might apply the word to rhythm or to melody, each considered separately. But in music it is customary to restrict its meaning to indicate the nature of some composition as a whole, as when one says that a piece is in "rondo" form or in "sonata" form. This, moreover, is the sense in which Pius X employed the word in his *motu proprio* when referring to "parts of the Mass and the Office which must retain, even musically, that particular character and form which ecclesiastical tradition has assigned to them" (TLS 10).

Meanwhile we must not lose sight of the fact that no music is, strictly speaking, liturgical music unless it is vocal. Even if the forms hitherto presented to us by the only extant tradition of Christian song are practically all to be found again in the classical and modern repertoires of instrumental music in the West, these forms are never admitted into Christian worship as pretexts for the inclusion of non-vocal music. We are concerned always with melodies intended to be sung. For this reason, which springs from the very nature of Christian worship, it will be our task in this chapter to treat only of "lyrical" forms.[171]

It is not possible, by mere abstraction from the text which is sung, to consider formally as pure music any genuine compositions of vocal art. For rhythm and melody are inseparably combined with the word. It is the literary phrase which inspires the musical phrase, word by word, syllable by syllable.[172] Hence the study of lyrical forms is necessarily related to that of literary forms.

Moreover, liturgical music is the handmaid of a canonical text which has to be pronounced in the performance of a rite being celebrated, a rite which is itself but a part of some single ceremonial whole. The melodico-literary form of a chant, therefore, does not depend solely on the inspiration of the musician who composes it. It has to be suited to the ritual function proper to the chant concerned (reading, psalmody, hymnody, prayer), just as the shape of a hand must suit it to be a prehensile organ, and that of an ear must accord with that of an organ intended to hear. Also, it must fit in with the roles of the various agents to whom the performance of the chant is entrusted (celebrant, ministers, people, choir), just as the shape of a tree comprises a trunk, branches and leaves. Therefore, even before it becomes clothed in melody, a given liturgical chant has already a form of some kind—that of a recitative solo, a responsory, an isolated acclamation, or a dialogue. As St. Pius X wrote: "Different, therefore, must be the method of composing an Introit, a Gradual, an antiphon, a psalm, a hymn, a *Gloria in excelsis*" (TLS 10). There is a particular lyrical form to fit each piece of liturgical singing.

The close correspondence which binds together sacred singing and ritual action explains why we do not find in the liturgy all the forms which the art of music can freely use, but only those which are suited to Christian worship. And if, within this, certain forms preponderate, that is because they express both the hierarchic structure of the assembly and also the mystagogic significance of the rites to be accomplished.

[171] The adjective "lyrical" is used here in that modern sense ordinarily attached to it when one speaks of "lyrical art" (that is, concerned with song) as opposed to "symphonic art" (that is, concerned only with instruments). We are thereby excluding the ancient (etymological) sense of the word, namely, song with instrumental accompaniment (song accompanied on the lyre), as also the vague meaning applied to expressive art.

[172] This symbiosis is especially evident in Gregorian chant; it gives the secret of this chant's composition and furnishes the most reliable principle for its analysis.

In spite of their apparent diversity, the various lyrical forms employed in Christian worship can quite easily be classified under three main headings which we shall call direct forms, hypophonic forms, and alternating forms.[173]

A. DIRECT FORMS

We classify as being in direct form those chants which are sung without interruption and have texts which involve neither repetition (responsories or refrains) nor alternation of any kind (dialogues between a soloist and one or more choirs). This form may pertain entirely to a soloist or to a choir. Musically it may consist of a freely composed theme (A, the unitary type or lied), or else of a formula to be repeated any number of times (AAA . . .) or with variations (A, A', A''), or of musical ideas in sequence (ABC . . .).

Among solo chants emanating from the sanctuary and employing the direct form, we must assign the first place to *readings* and *prefaces*.[174] Their melodies consist of a kind of formula. A single melodic formula is adapted to each phrase of the text, and is repeated indefinitely, usually without any melodic variations except those imposed by the need to fit the text exactly.[175] To readings and prefaces we should have to add also direct *psalmody* (continuous recitation of a psalm by a soloist) if this style of psalmody were still in use.

Among chants emanating from the nave of the church we find a much greater variety in the direct forms employed by the people or the choir. The model for the choral direct form is found in the isolated *troparion*. This is a composition consisting of a single verse of variable length, the text of which is complete in itself and is set to a melody of unitary type.[176] Our Roman *antiphons,* when not integrated into a psalm, have a direct affinity with them. Certain isolated acclamations, such as the *Sanctus* which follows the Preface, are also in the direct form, even if they do sometimes display an element of formulation or the beginnings of melodic development.[177]

[173] This classification, though here expressed in terms of musical categories, is well adapted to Christian worship. From the strictly musical point of view, it would be sufficient to speak of unitary, binary or cyclic forms, of imitations and of developments. But here these technical terms are subordinated to the more ample categories which originate from the nature of the rites and the characteristics of the roles.

[174] One might perhaps also include the collects; but on account of the people's *Amen* which concludes them organically, it is more accurate to classify them among the hypophonic forms.

[175] It is quite exceptional for the melodic formula to give rise to any notable variations (as happens in the *Exsultet*). This does not apply to the Oriental liturgies, in which the singer retains a certain amount of liberty in singing the traditional formulas and vocal ornaments are quite customary.

[176] Oriental liturgies have a great many troparia (cf. M. Concheril, "Tropaire," *Encyclopédie de la musique*, III, pp. 815 ff.). A good example of a Latin troparion is *Te decet laus* (see A. Gastoué, *Les principaux chants liturgiques*, Paris, 1903) prescribed by the Rule of St. Benedict (ch. 11) at the end of dominical vigils.

[177] The alternation between two choirs sometimes introduced into the *Sanctus* of the Mass is not one of its constitutive features. It is, rather, one of the points which distinguish the

In ancient monastic usage, certain psalms which were called *in directum* perhaps gave place to a choral form of direct psalmody in which all the verses were sung one after another by the choir.[178] The metrical psalters of the Renaissance period, which enabled the people to sing the psalms, come into this category.

To the direct form there belong also certain *hymns*. When they do not prompt alternation by two choirs,[179] these hymns may take on the direct form (*Te Deum, Gloria* XV and, by analogy, *Credo* I, II, etc.), or they may become of the direct strophic type (AAA . . ., etc.). We should instance also the *Tract*, nowadays sung by two choirs, but originally beyond all doubt in the direct form (psalmody of the type set to ornamented formulas).[180]

The direct form is primarily suited to the sacred minister who is addressing the people or praying in their name. It is the typical form of sanctuary chant. And it provides also for the assembly a simple manner of singing pieces which are short or expressed in formulas. But it is not typical of song from the nave, for which Christian worship more readily turns to the hypophonic form.

B. HYPOPHONIC FORMS

The content of the liturgical celebration is a continual and mysterious dialogue between God and His people. By His word the Lord reveals Himself to His Church, and by her song the Church confesses her faith in her Lord. On the other hand, though the celebration is an act of the entire community, not a few parts of it are carried out through the ministry of mediators: the ministry of the priest, who represents God to the people and the people to God; the ministry of the deacon, who serves both the celebrant and the assembly; the ministry of the readers and of the psalmist, bearers of the inspired word. The mystery of these spiritual communications between God and His people through the mediation of ministers is admirably signified by liturgical singing, in which repeated apostrophe and response constitute a remarkable trait.

For the most part, however, liturgical dialogue does not take place between

Sanctus from the *Trisagion*. This latter seems to have been associated very early with the symbolism of two alternating choirs, doubtless in reference to Isaias 6:3.

[178] Nevertheless it is doubtful whether this psalm was in fact sung collectively (cf. *Rule of St. Benedict*, cc. 9 and 12; Ps. 3, at the beginning of vigils and Ps. 66 at Lauds for Sunday. Compare these with Ps. 69 in our litanies of the saints).

[179] Pieces like the *Gloria, Te Deum* and *Credo* were originally in direct form. Later they were sung by two alternating choirs in imitation of alternating psalmody.

[180] The origins of the Tract remain somewhat obscure. We should recall that the ancient Tracts in the eighth mode (such as the Canticles of the Paschal Vigil) are only responsorial psalms bereft of their refrains. To these the new *Ordo Hebdomadae Sanctae* has restored the name (though not the form) of *responsorium*. As for the others (second mode Tracts such as *Domine non secundum* . . .), rather than being responsories without refrain, they are more probably substitutes, during the season of Septagesima and Lent, for the *Alleluia* as the second interpolated chant, and made up of several psalm verses.

pairs of equals. It originates as though from on high, for it is God alone who holds the initiative in that salvation which the liturgy brings into action, whether He convokes or instructs or gives grace to utter petitions or thanks. And so the Church's song is like a response to the call which assembles her (con-vocation, *Ecclesia*), like the echo awakened by a prophetic appeal, the chorus of thanks carried up to the God of salvation.[180a] The Church's voice has been solicited, educed; her song is "hypophonic." This is shown by the preferential employment in the liturgy of lyrical forms which are dialogues or responsories.[181]

Musically, hypophonic forms are characterized by their employment of binary structures (the type AB and its variants). But they always involve the interplay of agents who differ in rank, being organized basically after the pattern of the dialogue between soloist and people. There are five great classical forms of hypophonic song which must be mentioned: dialogue, litany, responsorial psalmody, antiphonal psalmody, and responsorial hymnody.

a) *Dialogue*

In the liturgy, any minister who addresses the people or who speaks to God on their behalf usually requests their assent. Before each priestly action the celebrant greets the assembly: *Pax vobis*, or *Dominus vobiscum*, and awaits the reply: *Et cum spiritu tuo*. When the action is of special importance, as at the Preface, the dialogue is more developed. At the end of the collects and of the great eucharistic prayer all reply *Amen*. The musical simplicity of these greetings and responses precludes any melodic development. The binary musical theme appears usually in the form of antecedent and consequent (for example, *Dominus vobiscum — Et cum spiritu tuo; Per omnia saecula saeculorum — Amen; Pax Domini*, etc.), or as a formula repeated with variations (for example, the opening dialogue of the Preface, of the type aa', bb', cc'). The same remarks apply also to the proclamations (beginning of the Gospel) or directions (*Ite missa est, Procedamus in pace*) of the deacon.

b) *The Litany*

"Litany" is a generic term of modern origin which we use to designate various kinds of intercessory prayers [182] which have in common not only a euchological function but also a characteristic form: by means of a short invocation the people associate themselves with the intention announced by

---

[180a] Cf. CL 33.

[181] We call "hypophonic" those forms which, in general, can be reduced to the type "address-response." We reserve the term "responsorial" for those instances wherein there is a repetition by all of a text intoned in the first place by a soloist (or the *schola*).

[182] In Syriac these prayers are called *k̠arozuta* (proclamations); the Greek equivalent is *k̠erygma*, and the Latin *praedicatio*. (See note 126.) In the Byzantine liturgy they are called, according to circumstances, *ek̠tenie* (intense or prolonged prayer), *synapti* (collect), *litie* (supplication). In the Latin rites these are *preces, orationes*, etc. The terms *letaniae, litaniae* are normally used when they accompany some penitential procession.

the soloist.[183] Here we have one of the most fundamental and universal forms of community prayer which is found in every age and in every cult. It is the form par excellence for sung prayer.

In Christian worship, common prayer of intercession holds an organic position. Together with the reading of Holy Scripture and psalmody, it is one of its fundamental constituent elements. Therefore, in principle, it should find a place in every Christian assembly, according to the precept of Paul to Timothy (1 Tim. 2:1-3), and following the example of every liturgical tradition.[184]

The litanic form calls, on the one hand, for a soloist who leads the prayer, and, on the other, for a congregation which replies. We may distinguish: (1) the sacerdotal litany when the cantor is the celebrant himself (as in the solemn prayers on Good Friday); (2) the diaconal litany when the deacon is fulfilling his role as director of prayer (the most common form, habitual in the East); (3) the choral litany when it is led by cantors (as in our litanies of the saints).

The melodic structure is obviously binary. We have a recitative by the soloist who proclaims the intentions, and a refrain in which the people make their reply (type AB, or antecedent-consequent). The people's response consists in a short invocation: *Amen, Kyrie eleison, Te rogamus, audi nos*, etc. Usually the melody for this is syllabic, but it may be ornamented by a few expressive melismata. The soloist's part is capable of assuming several literary structures which determine the shape of the recitative. These can be reduced to three.[185]

1. The simplest form expresses the intention (such as the grace which is asked for) in a single proposition, often followed by the invitation *deprecamur*, "let us pray," which links it up with the people's answer:

Solo: For the holy Catholic Church, (let us pray to the Lord);
All: Lord, have mercy.[186]

The melody here is simply an antecedent with a consequent.

2. In a more elaborate form the invitation of the soloist is expressed in two propositions which formulate respectively the intention (introduced by *hyper, pro*, for . . .) and the petition (introduced by *'ina, ut*, that . . .); and it

---

[183] But there are also prayers of priestly intercession which do not call for any response by the people (e.g., in the second part of the anaphora, the Roman Canon, the Syrian *sedro*, etc.).

[184] This fundamental element has been somewhat radically excised from the Roman liturgy, both at Mass and in the Hours of the Office. One of the more important liturgical reforms ordered by Vatican II is the restoration, after the homily of the Mass, of the *Oratio communis* or "Prayer of the Faithful" (CL 53).

[185] For another classification see: J. B. Molin, *Pour un renouveau des prières du prône* (Bruges, 1961), p. 21 ff.

[186] On the type: *Dicamus omnes* (Irish, Milanese, short Gelasian) see F. Cabrol, "Litanies," DACL 9, 1563 ff.; *Divinae pacis* (Milanese and Irish), cf. *ibid.*; Liturgy of St. James, etc. For litanies which directly formulate the grace asked for: the Litany of the Saints, third section (*Ut ad veram penitentiam* . . .).

usually ends with an invitation to prayer (*deithomen, deprecamur*, we ask):

Solo: For the holy Church of God (a),
          that the Lord may preserve her in peace and unity (b),
          let us pray to the Lord (c).

All: Lord, have mercy.[187]

More clearly than ever the melody here is binary. The first phrase has three members, and educes a truly psalmodic formula with a flex (a), a mediation (b), and a termination (c). The people's reply forms a second phrase more or less separable from the first.

3. Besides these two fundamental types there are also some more complex forms, of which a good example is found in the solemn Roman prayers of Good Friday:

A. Celebrant: *Oremus pro* . . . (Intention). *Oremus.*
B. Deacon: *Flectamus genua.* Silence. *Levate.* (Directions and silent
                prayer of people)
C. Celebrant: *Omnipotens sempiterne Deus* . . . (Petition).
D. All: *Amen.*

Musically A, B, and C each form a complete element; but these three elements are connected together by the very movement of the prayer.

The litany, simple as it is supple, is the ideal form of liturgical prayer since it is both directed and unanimous.

c) *Responsorial Psalmody and the Responsory*

Like the litany, responsorial singing is instinctive in human nature and is the foundation of community singing. A cantor intones a refrain which is repeated by all, and then, between each communal repetition of this refrain, he interpolates couplets which vary to a greater or lesser degree. This is the well-known musical form known as the rondo (aA, bA, cA, etc).

It is significant that since the very beginning of Christian worship this form has been closely connected with the psalms and canticles, the songs par excellence of the Church. No doubt the Church inherited the form from the synagogue.[188] The interpolation of an *Alleluia* or a short passage of the same psalm to be repeated by all after each half of the psalm verse sung by a cantor is a practice both universal and frequent in the Christian liturgy of the fourth–fifth centuries, among the faithful as well as with the monks.

In this manner of praying the inspired text, the Church found an exact image of the cultual mystery: by the voice of the psalmist, an ordained minis-

---

[187] On the type: *Deprecatio Gelasii* (cf. B. Capelle "Le Kyrie de la messe et le pape Gélase," *Revue Bénédictine*, 1934, p. 138); *Constitutions Apostoliques*, VIII, 10, etc.

[188] The Bible itself suggests this mode of performance, for example, for the Canticle of Moses in Exodus 15 or Psalm 135. The *Mishnah*, witness of Jewish traditions contemporaneous with the first generation of Christians, described this manner of psalmody in greater detail. See H. Avenary, "Formal Structure of the Psalms and Canticles in Early Jewish and Christian Chant," *Musica disciplina*, VII (Amsterdam, 1953), pp. 1–9.

ter whose place is in the ambo, the word of God is addressed to the assembly which receives it and listens; but the assembly manifests its vital acceptance of the announced message by replying to the psalmist in a cry of supplication or praise: "Have mercy, Lord! Glory to thee, O Lord!" Or else the people meditate upon and assimilate the bread of the word by repeating one of the key-verses of the psalm: "Happy the man who fears the Lord! Taste and see that the Lord is good!" Responsorial psalmody is the image of the unceasing dialogue which takes place in the liturgy between the Bridegroom and His Bride.

Hence it is not surprising that this form is to be discerned as the origin of all the most essential psalms found in liturgical ceremonies, such as the intervenient chants in the office of readings which form the first part of the Mass (our Gradual, formerly called "responsorial psalm" or "responsory" derives from it);[189] as a constitutive element of vigils in the series reading–psalm–prayer (the canticles of the Paschal Vigil were once in responsorial form); as an essential part of all the hours of the Divine Office (our long responsories at Matins and our short reponsories at the Little Hours take its place); as a prayer to accompany lustration processions or those in special rites (Canticle of Simeon during the procession of Candlemas Day; psalms which occur during the rite of the dedication of a church).[190]

The typical form of responsorial psalmody, after the initial intonation, consists of inserting periodically into the recitation of the soloist a short extract from the psalm as a refrain (aA, bA, cA, etc). Originally this was done after every half verse, then after every verse, and later after a group of verses.

Psalmist: *Ipse invocabit me, alleluia: Pater meus es tu, alleluia.*
All: *Ipse invocabit me, alleluia: Pater meus es tu, alleluia.*
Psalmist v.1. *Misericordias Domini in aeternum cantabo* (Ps. 88:2).
All: *Ipse invocabit me, alleluia: Pater meus es tu, alleluia.*
Psalmist v.2. *In generationem et generationem annuntiabo veritatem
               tuam in ore meo.*
All: *Ipse invocabit me, alleluia: etc.*

The psalm is sung in this manner throughout.

A widely used variant of the responsorial form consists in using, after the initial intonation, not the entire refrain (*responsio a capite*), but only the end of it (*responsio a latere*) for repetition. In this case the concluding phrase must in itself provide a satisfactory meaning. Sometimes the entire refrain is used for alternate repetitions, as in our Invitatory at Matins, and in all

---

[189] On the nature of this psalm as a "lesson," see above p. 79.

[190] It would be a great mistake to see in this form of psalmody only a sign of archaism or of inability to adopt some more elaborate form. In particular, the practice of entrusting the recitation of verses to a soloist—a rule of ancient psalmody—cannot be attributed, in the case of monks who all took turns to act as psalmist and did it by heart, to any incapacity for singing these same verses all together.

THE TONES OF PSALMODIC REFRAINS

A great many of the psalmodic antiphons of the Office have been preserved in the Roman, Benedictine, Dominican and Ambrosian antiphonaries, as also in the Antiphonary of St. Peter's (from the purely Roman tradition of the twelfth century). These repeat certain melodic patterns or typical formulas. In them one can discern vestiges of the ancient interpolated refrains of the responsorial psalmody in vogue during the fifth–sixth centuries (see pp. 97 and 212). We give here two examples.

The first concerns a whole group of antiphons of the sixth mode which occur, in particular, in the third nocturn of Matins for Christmas, Epiphany and Ascension Day (perhaps they are traces of the old cathedral vigils?). The group is especially suitable for singing by the people. An elementary rhythm, based on the accentual structure of the text to which the melody is set, can easily be discerned.

The second example, called "irregular" because it does not fall within the classification according to the eight modes—imported from the East (about ninth century?) and adapted to the repertoire of the West—is certainly very old, and beyond doubt of Oriental origin. It belongs to the mode of "te" (whose universality in ancient times is shown by Plate IV); in contrast with the Latin psalm tones, which have an accentual structure, its cadences are syllabic. The difficulty in classifying this melodic formula with any one of the eight psalm tones has often led to its modification, for example, by giving it a first-tone termination.

The similarity between these tones and the melodies still in use for the short responsories (vestiges of the ancient responsorial psalm after the lessons) confirms both their antiquity and their original function.

SIXTH-MODE FORMULA

Ps. 88.   Matins of Christmas

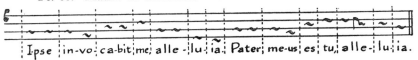

Ipse in-vo-ca-bit me, alle-lu-ia. Pater, me-us es tu, alle-lu-ia.

Ps. 97.   Matins of Christmas

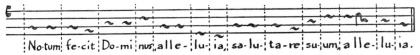

No-tum fe-cit Do-mi-nus, alle-lu-ia, sa-lu-ta-re su-um, alle-lu-ia.

Ps. 96.   Matins of the Ascension

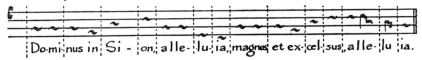

Do-mi-nus in Si - on, alle-lu-ia, magnus et ex-cel-sus, alle-lu-ia.

For comparison: Short Responsory (*Ant. Monast.*, ferial Vespers).

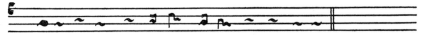

Bene-di-cam Do-mi-num in o-mni tempo-re.

FORMULA OF THE "IRREGULAR" MODE

Ps. 66.   Antiph. Romanum.

Il - lu - mi - na, Do-mi-ne, vul-tum tu - um su-per nos.

Ps. 103.   Antiph. of St. Peter's, Vat. B.79.

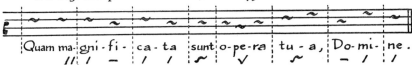

Quam ma-gni-fi - ca - ta sunt o-pe-ra tu - a, Do-mi-ne.

Ps. 97.   Antiph. Dominicanum. Toulouse 77.

Qui-a mi-ra-bi-li-a fe - cit Do-mi-nus.

For comparison: Short Responsory (*Ant. Monast.*, Lauds for Sunday)

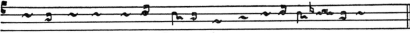

Incli-na cor me-um, De-us, in testimo-ni-a tu-a .

cases it concludes the chant. A remnant of this type is still extant in the short or long responsories of the Office [191] (aA, bA', cA' . . . . xA; or aA, bA', cA, dA', etc).

Psalmist: *Benedicam Dominum in omni tempore.*
All: *Benedicam Dominum in omni tempore.*
℣.   *Semper laus ejus in ore meo.*
℟.   *In omni tempore.*

    .   .   .   .

℣.   *Gloria Patri . . . .*
℟.   *Benedicam Dominum in omni tempore.*

Other variants of the purely responsorial type chiefly concern the text (use of refrains which are not from the psalms or not even from Holy Scripture) but do not directly concern the musical form.

Responsorial psalmody has practically disappeared from the Roman liturgy [192] to make room for a kind of responsory whose lyrical form is more or less changed and the text non-psalmodic. This transformation has come about by an amplification of the refrains (the texts being prolonged and the melody elaborated), and even more so by amplification of the verses (the primitive recitative being ornamented by melismatic developments). To compensate for this melodic extension, the number of the verses has been reduced and the repetition of the refrain omitted. In the Graduals as we have them now there is only one verse, and the initial refrain is not repeated. It is but a false responsory (Ab).[193] The long responsories of Matins still retain, together with one *responsio a latere*, at least one verse and the *Gloria Patri* (AbA' cA). But for the most part they are non-psalmodic chants composed on biblical texts subtly modified in view of the repetitions, an expedient at which the Frankish composers excelled. The processional responsories (Palm Sunday, Candlemas) belong to the same type.[194] Only the short responsories of the Little Hours (such as *In manus tuas* at Compline) have remained free from melodic ornamentation. But they also have suffered the same reduction to a single verse plus the *Gloria Patri*, though they have retained the initial repetition (aA bA' cA).

[191] The *responsio a latere* was used especially in the Gallican, Spanish and Milanese liturgies. It seems to have come from the East, where it is found in several of the rites. We should observe also that a number of *troparia* are often concluded by an acclamation which is both short and separable, and which may well have been an ancient *responsio a latere* (see also note 386). These *troparia* are but developments of old psalm-refrains which could not be repeated after each verse because they were too long for the purpose.

[192] This is not true of every rite. For example, the Chaldean (East Syrian) rite has retained responsorial psalms. Cf. J. Mateos, *Lelya-Sapra, Essai d'interprétation des matines chaldéennes* (Rome, 1959), pp. 315 ff.

[193] This deformation can be seen clearly in the Gradual of June 24 (St. John the Baptist), in which the verse concludes with the words *et dixit mihi* which used to connect up with the repetition of the initial phrase. This, however, is now missing. But this non-psalmodic Gradual is of relatively late origin. In the thirteenth century the repetition was still being sung.

[194] On these last two types of long responsory, see chapter 12, pp. 179ff.

The transformation of the responsorial form had another consequence which resulted from its melodic ornamentation, and that is a change of executants. Though the verses remain, in principle, entrusted to a soloist, the developed refrain is now the exclusive perquisite of the choir.

The melodic treatment of the responsorial form is obviously different according as it concerns true psalmody or a derived form. In the first case, the refrain, destined by its nature to be sung by the people, is straightforward and simple.[195] The psalmist's verses consist merely of a modulated recitation of the text.[196] By contrast, in the long responsory, the refrain, being reserved to the choir, is of a type which approaches the lied. As for the verses, although the original psalmodic formula is not completely forgotten (as indicated by the order and succession of the cadences in many of the Gregorian Graduals), they are developed into broad vocalizations more akin to *bel canto* than to a rendering of the sacred text.

In spite of all the vicissitudes it has undergone in the course of the centuries, the responsorial form remains in Christian worship as the most traditional and the best way of including the entire assembly in the singing of psalms.

d) *Antiphonal Psalmody and the Antiphon*

Antiphonal psalmody appears in the fourth century as a development of responsorial psalmody. The verses themselves, in accordance with the ancient rule, are always entrusted to a soloist. But the main attention and interest are now concentrated in the refrain, which gives rise to a more lively and dramatic style of performance. According to a procedure formerly employed in choral games, the assembly is divided into two choirs who confront each other voice-against-voice (*antiphônein*); in this way the psalmody of certain vigils and processions was enlivened.

The structure of the whole remains hypophonic, since the refrains continue to adhere to inspired verses which they prolong and which the assembly sings always "under" the psalmist. But it is the alternation and opposition of the two choirs, the characteristic feature of this lyrical form, which has given to it its name. Just as the name "responsory" was given to a psalm chanted in the responsorial manner (*hypakoi, hypopsalma, responsorium*), so also a psalm whose refrain was sung by two opposing choirs was called *antiphona*.[197]

[195] Some examples of this may be seen on Plate II (p. 99). See also notes 142 and 422.

[196] This corresponds with their character as "readings" still attributed to them. But the text from St. Gregory cited on p. 79 gives presentiment of a change.

[197] It becomes necessary to define certain technical terms. There are so many different kinds of liturgical singing covered by the word *antiphona* in Greek or in Latin that it is impossible to translate it indifferently into English by the corresponding word "antiphon" without engendering serious misunderstandings. We prefer therefore to speak of:

a) *antiphonal psalmody* or *antiphony* when referring to responsorial psalmody performed by two choirs and to other pieces of like structure. We shall avoid the adjective "antiphonated" which has usually been applied to the alternating psalmody actually used now for the Divine Office.

The success of the antiphonal form was so great that it spread widely in the psalmody used for processions and at the beginning of the canonical Hours. It was also applied later to a great many pieces of psalmodic origin and even to some that are non-psalmodic. No useful purpose would be served by entering here into all the details of the forms which have been derived from it. It should be enough to set forth the structure of the archetype, which will explain the pieces not actually found within the Roman liturgy.[198]

The fully developed form, which now exists only in theory,[199] can be set forth in the following scheme:

Psalmist 1	A (refrain)
First choir	A (refrain)
Second choir	A (refrain)
Psalmist 2	b (first verse of psalm)
First choir	A (refrain)
Second choir	A (refrain)

b) an *antiphonal psalm* when referring to a psalm sung throughout in this manner.

c) an *antiphon* when referring to abridged psalmody typified by the Byzantine little antiphons or the Roman Introit. We use the word *antiphon*, therefore, to translate the Greek substantival adjective *antiphonon*, which is neuter in gender. In Latin, *antiphona* was originally neuter plural, as in Greek (v.g., as used by Etheria); but Occidentals later took it as a feminine singular.

d) an *anthem*, in order to have a word different from "antiphon" to apply to a psalmodic refrain taken all by itself, or to a self-sufficient composition, in accordance with modern usage outside Catholic circles. For example, what we would call an "Antiphon of Our Lady" (*Salve Regina* and the like) would, in this terminology, be called an "anthem," since it differs so completely, in structure and purpose, from those items described in (c) above, for which we reserve the word "antiphon."

The true nature of antiphony as practiced in ancient days has escaped most of the authors who have written about it and who, in consequence, are much at variance in their opinions. The view most commonly espoused is to see the essence of antiphony as alternation of verses sung collectively by two choirs—something which cannot be proved. The view we are defending here has been expounded repeatedly by A. Baumstark (e.g., *Nocturna Laus*, [Münster, 1957], pp. 124–125). It is the only view which accords with historical documents.

[198] The Oriental rites are especially rich in pieces which originated from antiphony: Chaldean *onyâtâ*, Syrian *manyâtâ qâlê*, Byzantine antiphons, various *troparia* and *hypakoi*, etc.

[199] It is not possible to adduce even one example of it from the psalms. But it is most interesting to note that the Roman *Improperia* of Good Friday have preserved this form almost exactly, but with a bilingual refrain:

℣	Two cantors	*Popul6 meus . . . .*
℟ {	1st choir	*Agios o Theos . . . .*
	2nd choir	*Sanctus Deus . . . .*
℣	First cantors	*Quia eduxi te . . . .*
℟ {	1st choir	*Agios o Theos . . . .*
	2nd choir	*Sanctus Deus . . . .*
℣	Second cantors	*Quid ultra debui . . . .*
℟ {	1st choir	*Agios o Theos . . . .*
	2nd choir	*Sanctus Deus . . . .*

Later on the *Improperia* go into ordinary responsorial form with a single refrain in unison: *Populé meus . . . .*

Psalmist 1   c (second verse of psalm)
  etc.
  etc.
Psalmist or **All**   Doxology
First and second choirs   A (refrain)

A simplified form used in the psalmody of the Office[200] and closely related
to the pieces which the Greeks call *antiphons*[201] has the following scheme:

Psalmist 1   verse 1 of psalm
First choir   refrain
Psalmist 2   verse 2 of psalm
Second choir   refrain
Psalmist 1   verse 3 of psalm
First choir   refrain
  etc.
  etc.

Our antiphons for the Introit, Offertory and Communion are derived from
this form by reduction of the two choirs to one single choir[202] and by a more
or less radical suppression of psalm verses:[202a]

[200] For example, in the cathedral Office at Constantinople during the Middle Ages, as described
by Simeon of Thessalonica, *De sacra precatione* (PG 155, 637 ff).

[201] The three "little antiphons" sung at the beginning of the Liturgy of St. John Chrysostom
consist of three psalm verses and a doxology sung by soloists, each one followed by a single
troparion sung in alternation by the two choirs. Equally typical are the *onyâtâ* of the Chaldean
liturgy, also designed for use during processions; they comprised originally two psalm verses
and a short doxology, each followed by a single refrain sung alternately by first choir, second
choir and both choirs together.

[202] *Ordo Romanus* I seems to suggest that the Introit involved two choirs, for it makes mention of *duae acies* of singers: that of the *paraphonistae* and that of the *infantes*; also there are
two soloists designated as cantors for the psalms. One may also ask whether the textual and
melodic repetitions which occur at the beginning of several Offertories (*Iubilate Deo, Precatus
est Moyses, De profundis*, etc.) may not indicate performance by two choirs antiphonally. The
absence of any *versus ad repetendum* in the Offertories is perhaps not unconnected with this
fact; alternation between two choirs could be done on the *versus ad repetendum* in the Introits
and Communions, whereas in the Offertories this could not be done except on the long *versus*.
On the other hand, the *Antiphonary* of Compiègne gives some examples of the *responsio a
latere* in the Offertories (v.g., J. Hesbert, *Antiphonale missarum sextuplex* [Brussels, 1935],
n. 37b). P. Wagner is of the opinion that the Offertory chants changed to the responsorial
form because of the ornate character of the verses (*Introduction to the Gregorian Melodies*,
p. 95). But this opinion is based on a very debatable idea of the forms characteristic of the
responsory and of the antiphon.

[202a] In consequence of recent research in the field of comparative liturgy—especially the facts
brought to light by *Typicon de la Grande Église*, published a short while ago by J. Mateos
(*Orientalia Christiana Analecta*, 165–166, Rome, 1962–63)—we are no longer of the opinion
that these items of processional hymnody are the end-products of reduction of the psalmody.
We are now inclined to think that they are original compositions built upon a proper troparion
(a prose strophe sung by the choir), enclosing two, three or four psalm-verses and the doxology,
and separated by an acclamation sung by the people, this acclamation often being merely the
detachable conclusion of the troparion. When looked at in this way, the "antiphon" of our
Roman processionals does not appear to be a developed refrain, but is the proper troparion (with

Typical scheme	Introit antiphon	Offertory antiphon	Communion antiphon
Verse 1	....	....	....
Refrain, 1st choir	Refrain, schola	Refrain, schola	Refrain, schola
Verse 2	Verse 1	....	....
Refrain, 2nd choir	....	....	....
etc.	....	....	....
Doxology	Doxology	....	....
Refrain, both choirs	Refrain, schola	....	....

We should point out that such a simplification was due partly to the short-ening or suppression of the processions which these chants had the function of accompanying. We know from documents of the eighth–ninth centuries that the Introit used to have as many verses as were needed to last out during the entrance procession.[203] We possess also some verses for Offertories and Communions, exemplified in those still found in the Requiem Mass.[204]

Musically these antiphons display two very contrasted elements. The open-ing refrain, considerably developed, often assumes the neumatic form of a piece for the choir. The music is broadly extended, a feature which is ex-plained by the ornamental purpose of these processional chants. Thus the main interest is centered on the refrain, both by the choice of its text and by the art which envelops it. On the other hand, the verses, at least in the Introit, are left as simple psalmody by a soloist.

Given the relationship between the responsorial and antiphonal forms of psalmody, it is not surprising that sometimes there has been a fusion between them and that mixed forms have arisen. At one time the Offertory antiphon was given some verses richly ornamented, rather like those of the Gradual. More interesting still is the occurrence, in the Antiphonaries of the eighth century, of a *versus ad repetendum*[205] drawn from the psalm, which was suit-able for use as an interpolated responsory in the psalm—something which was not possible with the long neumatic antiphon reserved to the *schola*. Thus there would have been a processional psalmody which was antiphonal by origin yet responsorial in fact:

> Neumatic antiphon by the *schola*
> Verse 1 by the psalmist

a biblical text in the West, a point of difference from the Oriental rites) which opens and closes the piece. The only genuine refrain would have been the *versus ad repetendum* (see later). On this question see our communication "Art und Form der liturgischen Prozessionsgesänge" in *Musik und Altar*, 1, 1964, p. 16, and the same study worked out in greater detail with support-ing notes in *Musique sacrée et langues modernes*, "Kinnor" 4 (Fleures: Paris, 1964).

[203] *Ordo* I, M. Andrieu, Les "*Ordines Romani*" du haut moyen âge (Louvain, 1931 ff.), II, pp. 67 ff.

[204] The preservation of the verses in the Offertory of Requiem Masses is due to the custom of making offerings at these.

[205] See J. Hesbert, *Antiphonale missarum sextuplex*. The nature and historical role of this *versus ad repetendum* remains obscure (see ch. 11, pp. 168ff.).

Versus ad repetendum by all
Verse 2 by the psalmist
Versus ad repetendum
    etc.
Gloria Patri . . . .
Neumatic antiphon.

Antiphony likewise made use of the technique of the *responsio a latere* for its refrains. We have an example in the invitatory *Venite exsultemus* of Matins, expressly referred to as an antiphon in the Rule of St. Benedict (ch. 9),[206] though its mode of performance seems to us nowadays to be responsorial.

Like the responsory, the antiphon also became detached from the psalmody to give rise to autonomous compositions. Most of them, such as the *Adorna thalamum* of Candlemas, the anthems for the distribution of ashes and for the procession with palms, and also the Marian anthems which conclude the Divine Office, are compositions in their own right. Although really derived from the anicent antiphonal refrains, they are not in fact anything more than long *troparia*. A few of them still retain traces of the *responsio a latere*.[207] Others, such as the *Ubi caritas* of the *Mandatum*, which consists of alternating verses and a refrain, bear the name of antiphon only by chance.[208]

The antiphons which nowadays precede and follow each psalm of the Divine Office obviously have a direct connection with the ancient refrain of antiphonal psalmody. But now they are associated with a psalmody of a completely different form. As the verses are no longer sung by a soloist but are alternated by two choirs, the psalm has no further need of any refrain. The antiphon serves merely as an introduction and a conclusion. This kind of psalmody can no longer be classified as hypophonic in form.[209]

[206] In the *Regula Magistri*, more archaic on this point, the invitatory is a *responsorium* sung by the abbot. Moreover, there is nothing to prove that the Roman *responsio a latere* is original.

[207] See ch. 12, pp. 180ff.

[208] In the case of the *Ubi caritas*, the name "antiphon" is adventitious; this piece used to be called a "hymn," and the liturgy has preserved only a small part of it. Its form is worth noting: it is composed in strophes of four isosyllabic verses (8 + 4), with a supplementary verse of nearly the same rhythm (8 + 4) serving as a refrain. The four verses of the strophe are treated melodically in the form AABB.

[209] Abstracting from certain antiphons of the ferial Office which, in the light of their dimensions and style, may well be old and authentic psalmodic refrains, most of the antiphons of our diurnal could never have fulfilled this function. They are too long and too ornate. (Yet we know that during the Middle Ages they used to repeat these antiphons sometimes on feast days, not just before and after the psalm but also before the doxology. This was called "tripling" or "triumphing" the antiphon.) The alteration of antiphonal psalmody into its present form can be explained thus: when more important and artistic antiphons were composed, their repetition after each verse would have prolonged the psalmody unduly. But the recitation of one verse after another by one or two psalmists without any intervening refrains would seem a rather impoverished way of doing things. So, in the West, the two choirs which used to alternate the antiphon now began to alternate the psalm verses collectively (see note 383). In

e) *Responsorial Hymnody*

The form consisting of verses and a refrain which underlies the most fundamental chants in Christian worship, such as the litany and psalmody, likewise flourished in the freer type of singing, hymnody. As this category of songs is by nature intended for the people, it is not surprising that it draws on the lyrical practice of the responsory.

As model of this type of singing it is proper to mention the Syrian *madrâshâ*, whose form was determined in masterly fashion by St. Ephrem. It is a kind of poetic and lyrical preaching, divided into regular strophes between which the people, as audience, expressed their faith, their praise or their petition by the aid of a short refrain (*onitá*).[210] The hypophonic form is here clearly discernible: the refrain is the response of the assembly to the message proclaimed by the preacher. In the wake of this hypophonic hymnody there flourished in the Orient a varied and abundant growth of hymns (*soghita*, *kontakion*, etc.) often combined with the antiphonal form.

St. Ambrose, a contemporary of St. Ephrem, is recognized as the father of Western hymnody; we know of him that, in order to get his Milanese people to sing, he imitated Oriental models. Now although those hymns which we call "Ambrosian" are late-comers into the Roman liturgy and to-day are sung verse by verse with two choirs in alternation, it can be argued that, as St. Ambrose created them, they used to have a refrain to be interpolated by the people, and that this disappeared only later on.[211]

Hymns with refrains are somewhat rare in the Roman liturgy as we have it now. But we should cite at least two famous examples: the *Pange lingua* of Venantius Fortunatus with the *Crux fidelis* used as a refrain, and the *responsio a latere*, *Dulce lignum*; also the *Gloria laus* of Theodulph of Orleans used in the palm procession.

In point of fact, responsorial hymnody, from about the end of the Middle Ages, was superseded by religious singing in the language of the people;

the East the process was exactly the opposite; they used to vary the intervening troparia by composing new texts, and ended up by abandoning the psalm verses. Thus the Canon of Odes to the *Orthros* in the Byzantine liturgy, formerly made up of nine biblical canticles, now consists of a series of poetic strophes alternated by two choirs.

[210] Plate III, p. 127, reproduces an example of Ephremian *madrâshâ*. But the original responsorial form has been lost; the strophes of a *madrâshâ* are now usually sung by two choirs as in our Latin hymns.

[211] See J. Handschin, *Gesungene Apologetik*, "Mélanges Mohlberg," (Rome, 1949), II, p. 103. This refrain would have consisted of one or two strophes of the hymn, or perhaps its doxology, as Ambrose himself suggested when he justified his innovation: "What could be more impressive than a profession of faith in the Blessed Trinity celebrated every day through the mouth of the entire people? All vie with each other (*certatim*) in professing their faith, and they learn at least the verses which proclaim the Father, the Son and the Holy Spirit" (*Serm. contra Auxentium*, 34; PL 16, 1017). The *certatim* could even point to Oriental antiphony: a division of the people into two choirs who try to outdo each other when alternating in the refrain.

this fulfilled an analogous function, though outside the liturgy itself. Most continental popular hymns, whether traditional or modern, have borrowed the musical form of the rondo, as secular songs also have done; the verses are executed by a soloist or by cantors, and the refrain is sung by all.

C. ALTERNATING FORMS

The practice of dividing the singing between two choirs, first introduced into the Church as antiphonal singing, finished by spreading over the whole field of liturgical singing. In many Eastern churches, in which it is justified on allegorical grounds, it was even considered to be one of the laws of church music. The West never went so far as that. Nevertheless, division between two choirs conquered not only psalmody but also pieces as different in style and form as those of the Ordinary of the Mass and even the strophic hymns of the canonical Hours. It ended by inspiring new hymnodic compositions founded on binary repetition.

We should observe that alternation, as employed here, is not only original but also has engendered a new category of lyrical forms. Hypophonic forms indeed already contain alternations, but these always take place between executants of different rank, usually between sanctuary and nave or between psalmist and people (and, to be precise, also between a group of cantors and the choir). But in the new forms we find no minister of the solo. Everything takes place in the nave or in the "choir." It is the assembly itself (or only the choir of clerics, monks or singers) which is divided into two groups, homogeneous or not, which dialogue with each other as equals.[212] This alternation is used equally in psalmody and in hymnody.

a) *Alternating Psalmody*

When both responsorial and antiphonal forms of psalmody fell into desuetude, a new form appeared in the West. In the place of the ancient psalmist, who alone was responsible for singing the inspired verses, there was substituted the entire choir of psalm-singers; they were divided into two groups who sang consecutively, but in alternation, all the verses of the psalm. To do this, the two choirs normally employ the same musical formula indefinitely repeated and made to fit a smoothed-out verbal rhythm. On account of communal recitation this formula was incompatible with all those rhythmic and melodic variations which a good singer feels constrained to make in order to adapt it to the text of each verse. The price of this transformation was beyond doubt a notable impoverishment of the psalmody. What psal-

---

[212] One might call this form "antiphonic" in the strict sense, to distinguish it from the "hypophonic" form. But since the word "antiphonic" is historically linked with hypophonic psalmody sung by two choirs, we think it better to speak here of "alternating" forms, so as avoid all misunderstanding.

mody gained in volume it lost in lyrical quality and in respect for the inspired word.[213]

b) *Alternating Hymnody*

Hymns in free style, like the *Gloria in excelsis* or the *Te Deum*, poetic hymns in regular strophes such as those of the Divine Office, litanies like the *Kyrie* and *Agnus Dei*, even acclamations like the *Sanctus* or professions of faith like the *Credo*, have all undergone this treatment of division between two choirs. Certainly this practice is not illegitimate from the musical point of view, nor, in general, from the point of view of liturgy.[214] But here, contrary to the general law of Christian singing which we have studied up till now, the lyrical form finds no literary support and can be justified neither from the structure of the texts nor from any need to allot different portions of the rite to different agents. Moreover, the Gregorian melodies themselves do not here point to the employment of two choirs, except perhaps in rather late compositions such as *Kyrie* IX and *Credo* IV.

Things are quite different as regards an abundant repertoire which flourished from the time of the Middle Ages and was developed from a prolongation of the *Alleluia*. We refer to the "interpolated tropes," the proses or sequences. This literature, of very uneven value, has left only small traces in our present liturgy. But, in both its literary and musical aspects, it clearly shows the influence of the practice of choral alternation. The formal principle of the interpolated trope consists really of doubling each melodic phrase. One can see this by examining the *Victimae paschali laudes*[215] or the *Lauda Sion*. When some phrase has been given out in a first couplet, it is repeated in a second couplet which corresponds with the first in its caesurae, the number of its syllables, and (later) its accents. The rest of the composition follows in accordance with this single principle. The result is a very characteristic alternation, and a lyrical form well suited to popular use (type aa,

[213] And perhaps also in value as contemplative prayer. Collective recitation requires more "activity" on the part of the psalm-singers; but the constant and rapid changing of the words which have to be said imposes a constraint from which the mere listening to those same words is quite free. With a responsory, on the other hand, the repetition of a single formula combined with listening to the scriptural text accords well with the laws of true vocal prayer, which finds a spiritual savor in repeating a phrase of few words.

[214] This is so, but the practice gives rise to some peculiarities, such as that of imposing on the *Kyrie* (which has a ternary structure) a melodic alternation which is binary; or again, that of alternating the three *Agnus Dei's* between two choirs, even though each one of them obviously ends with an invocation: *Agnus Dei, qui tollis peccata mundi,* followed by a response: *miserere nobis* or *dona nobis pacem.*

[215] The *Victimae paschali laudes* is attributed to Wipo, a chaplain in the Burgundian court during the first half of the eleventh century. The following points should be noted as regards the analysis of this Sequence: (1) the first strophe, unmatched, serves as an introduction (a, bb, etc.); (2) there follows cd, ed, instead of cc, dd—or, if preferred, two strophes in one (the same phenomenon can be seen in the *Landa Sion* in strophes 5-6, 7-8); (3) the penultimate strophe, symmetrical with the last, has been suppressed in the Roman antiphonary).

bb, cc, etc.) which gives opportunity for amplifications, imitations and interpolations. It has survived in quite a number of popular songs.

The traditional lyrical forms we have been studying correspond, above all, with the approved melodies of the Roman liturgy which are known as Gregorian chant, and in type they are exclusively monodic. Nevertheless, they embrace all the forms which are fundamental to Christian worship.

They do not, however, by any means exhaust the resources which the art of music has been able to apply to the texts of the liturgy. With the development of polyphony other forms made their appearance: the medieval motet, the *conductus*, the Renaissance motet, the canon, and above all the "cyclic Mass," which unites, in one musical whole, all the five pieces of the Ordinary. Then, in the operatic era, there entered into the liturgy new lyrical forms such as the Italian aria, and also instrumental forms derived from the fugue, the suite, or the sonata. Finally there came large-scale elaborate compositions destined to divide the liturgical texts of the *Credo, Te Deum* or *Magnificat* into sections, each treated according to one of the musical forms in vogue but related between themselves in such a way as to raise them up as great monuments of religious music.

Have these modern achievements of music thrown into doubt the lyrical forms which are proper to the celebration of Christian worship? When discussing musical idiom we shall have to return to the connections between the life of art and the life of the liturgy in order to establish that their evolution is partly in common but partly autonomous. At present we limit ourselves to some observations suggested here and now by the study of forms.

We begin by pointing out that, as regards the forms inherited from tradition, almost every one of the new forms we have just enumerated is linked with the use of polyphonic or instrumental music. Now even though the liturgy may welcome one or the other, it must remain true that liturgical song, in every one of its parts, must be capable of monodic execution. This principle precludes any piece of liturgical singing from assuming a form which, by nature, requires polyphony or instrumentation. On the other hand, the employment of polyphonic or instrumental music is perfectly compatible with traditional liturgical forms. *De facto* these have been continually exploited, at least partially, throughout every period and in every style. Litanies, responsories, psalms, alternated hymns, lessons at Tenebrae, etc., have never ceased to flourish, even subsequently to the Gregorian era. Furthermore, secular and instrumental music have made their own such liturgical forms as responsory and antiphony.

But if there is to be any attempt to adapt to liturgical texts forms which are radically new and, in origin, totally foreign to worship, then the literary structure of canonical texts must be taken into consideration. Otherwise there will appear a hiatus between words and music. We have to recognize that such a hiatus has often appeared in the course of the last eight centuries.

There arose an irresistible temptation to subject the sacred text to the music which it was desired to hear and to force the text to enter, sometimes happily but often quite unfortunately, into the musical forms whose employment was insisted on. Neither classical polyphony nor the operatic style can be exempted from these reproaches. In the latter case this is all too evident. What, for instance, could be more artificial than to apply to sections of liturgical texts not calling for repetition the *da capo* characteristic of the Italian aria? [216] Even in classical polyphony, a certain custom of imitation by successive entry of the different voices (which makes it difficult for listeners to follow the text) is not, as we shall see, unexceptionable from the liturgical point of view.[217]

But something more than mere material respect for the text and literary forms is required. The singing, in its form, must also fulfill the ritual function for which it is composed. The great polyphonic or symphonic compositions have not always been satisfactory from this point of view. In particular the works classified as "Masses," which treat the five parts of the Ordinary as five movements of a single cyclic composition, raise a question to which we must return later.[218] In style and inspiration a Palestrinian "Mass" is instinct with the sacred character, and this music, as Pius XI said, is "moulded by Christian wisdom;" but its musical forms, inspired by the liturgical and musical fashions of the sixteenth century, correspond rather imperfectly with the authentic ritual functions of the Mass chants. As for the great symphonic compositions of later date, such as the *Missa solemnis* of Beethoven, they are rightly preserved today as achievements of religious music to be sung only apart from the liturgy, because their use at the actual celebration of Mass completely deforms the normal course of the ritual action.[219]

An historical survey enables us to establish that, up till now, none of the recent advances in the art of music have modified the fundamental lyrical forms of Christian worship. Each century has but exploited them, with a more or less accurate perception of their true nature, by applying to them the style and idiom in vogue at the time. Will it always be so? It would be

---

[216] St. Pius X recalls this apropos of hymns: "In the hymns of the Church the traditional form of the hymns must be preserved. It is not lawful, therefore, to compose, for instance, a *Tantum ergo* in such a way that the first strophe presents a romanza, a cavatina or an adagio, and the *Genitori* an allegro" (TLS 11). And it is for the purpose of maintaining the authentic form of psalmody that he excluded absolutely from the liturgy psalms *di concerto* (ibid).

[217] See ch. 10, pp. 145ff.

[218] See ch. 13, pp. 201ff.

[219] The oft-repeated prohibition of interrupting the ceremony or of making the celebrant wait on account of unduly prolonged singing or instrumental music is only an expression of this same anxiety. It is rather striking to observe that in the Oriental rites the singing is always an "action" which in itself furthers the ceremony. How different it is with so many of our "harmonized" *Credos*, which, instead of being a straightforward enunciation of the rule of faith between the liturgy of the word and the liturgy of the Eucharist, hold up the entire ceremony in order to dramatize each of the dogmas. The *Credos* of Dufay or Ciconia, even in the fourteenth century, still kept to the right form.

possible, for instance, for the Church to modify the literary structure of some of the texts which have to be sung. This would be particularly desirable if certain pieces which have suffered in a special way from successive phases of liturgical decadence are ever to be restored. But in any case, if there is to be a literary restoration in certain instances (such as the responsorial psalm of the Gradual or the common prayer of intercession), this will not be done under the influence of formal musical principles, but with reference to the ritual action in the mystery to be celebrated and to those who are to be deputed to carry it out. The road to be taken will be the sequence mystery–rite–words–music, and it will be this which will give rise to the forms we have analyzed. We may presume that in order to bring to light their value and richness, it will not be necessary to evolve completely new forms. Nothing will be needed beyond arrangement of the existing forms according to the principles of the living music of the time and place.

We may conclude that the fundamental lyrical forms of liturgical song are too closely related to the very nature of Christian worship for their traditional structures ever to be substantially modified. But, within these universal forms, several musical idioms will have possibilities. It is in this way that true novelty will be achieved.

8 MUSICAL GENRES

The lyrical form of a piece which is to be sung does not predetermine the strictly musical aspect which its melody and rhythm may take. For example, a solo in the direct form might be treated as a free recitation slightly modulated, or as a metric air, or as a richly modulated melopoiea. This mode of being proper to the song itself we shall call the "musical genre." [220] Understood thus, the genre pertains directly to musical technique, or, more precisely, to the lyrical art, since there is no such thing as strictly liturgical music except sung music.

Nevertheless, art is no more independent of ritual action here than it is in the case of forms. The nature of a musical genre proper to a given item of song depends on the function of this song, on those who are to sing it, and on its literary form. Let us suppose we are concerned with the music for a Gospel. We must take into account that it (a) is a reading from Holy Scripture; (b) is to be sung by a deacon; (c) has a text which is prose. The genre

[220] We pointed out above (ch. 4, pp. 59ff.) that the *Instruction* of 1958, the practical application of *Musicae sacrae*, enumerates six "genres" of sacred music which are in the nature of "repertoires" classified according to an empirical principle which is historico-canonical by nature. We venture to employ the term here in a stricter and more technical sense to specify an aspect of the sung items which differs from the "classes" of ritual songs and from "lyrical forms." The idea of "genres" discussed here must be distinguished also from notions of musical "style" and of "idiom," which we shall consider in chapter 10.

required will thus be (a) a recitative, (b) by a soloist, (c) in free rhythm with a melodic formula. Observe that the margin of liberty in the choice of musical genre will be greater in proportion as the song is less directly implicated in the ritual action. The musical genre of a Preface is absolutely imperative, that of a *Gloria* is directive, but that of a hymn in an exercise of piety is only indicative.

So it is quite natural that the principle according to which genres are to be classified is musical rather than ritual; for lyrical forms just the opposite holds good. Nevertheless, the connection between genre and words is still the best criterion for distinguishing the different musical genres which are employed in Christian worship. The whole of the liturgical repertoire may be divided into two main genres: the *recitative* and the *air*.[221]

A. THE RECITATIVE

a) In recitative the text is enunciated in a way which gives it rhythm and melody. Simple rhythmo-melody is the most elementary form of singing, a first attempt to turn words into music. To give the words power and beauty (which are signs of the sacred), recitative introduces ordered movement into their utterance, striving for "number" and cadence; it tends to stabilize the pitch of the voice, fixing syllables on definite degrees of the musical scale so that they become "melos" (melody). In an "air," music acquires its own rhythmic and melodic autonomy, so that the sequence of sounds could, for example, be played on an instrument without any words, and it would still make sense. Recitative, on the other hand, is so bound up with the words that playing the melody without them would be meaningless. It is the text which gives to the melody the completion of its form; the melody alone cannot subsist without the words which give it existence.[222]

In liturgical singing recitative occupies the first place both in rank and in quantity. All chants from the sanctuary and a large proportion of the chants from the nave belong to this genre. The prayers and Prefaces of the celebrant, the readings from Scripture, from the Fathers and lives of the saints, proclamations, directions or intentions of the deacon, all the words addressed to the people or to God in the name of the people, are in recitative.[223] When the people reply to the celebrant or deacon, and in many of their acclamations, tney make use of this same genre. If we add to all these that very considerable part of worship which consists in the verses of psalmody in the strict sense

[221] The possible addition of instruments—something extrinsic to liturgical singing as such, and without direct influence on its genre—will be studied separately in chapter 13.

[222] For example, if I sing *fah-soh-lah-soh-fah*, no one could guess from which recitative I am quoting. This appears only if I begin to sing *Pater noster, qui es in coelis* in the ferial tone.

[223] An important exception: the verse of the Gradual (formerly verses of a psalm recited by the psalmist from the ambo), which is of the melismatic genre of Gregorian chant; it is sung, moreover, in the choir. We have already pointed out the anomaly of an ornate *Ite missa est* (note 127).

of that word, we reach the conclusion that recitative is an element of major importance in Christian music.

There is nothing surprising in this. Christian song, after all, is founded on the revealed word—a word announced solemnly in worship and thence lifted up to God in supplication or thanksgiving. The word remains the essential element in all sung ritual action. This is what is manifested by the recitative genre, in which the word is paramount.

b) We must distinguish several species of recitative according to the different ways in which its rhythm and its melody are presented. The rhythm of recitative is free if its text is prose, but measured if its text is poetry; the structure of its melodies may be of the rhetorical or of the psalmodic type.

1. If a prose text is to be cited in a melodic-rhythmic manner, the rhythm of the resulting recitative will be simply that of the word-phrases spoken in a natural way according to the characteristics of the language employed. The recitative is rhythmically *free*, in the sense that it borrows the duration of its notes from the variable and natural values of the syllables, words, and groupings of words into clauses and sentences, without giving to these notes any predetermined durations.

Yet we have to distinguish between two families of prose texts. The first, which comprises chiefly translations of Sacred Scripture, has not been purposely written in view of being set to melody and rhythm, but only as an ordinary literary text. The second, which includes a great many public prayers of the Roman liturgy (Prefaces, Collects, etc.), were originally composed with certain eurhythmic considerations in mind (*Kunstprosa*); these are manifested by balance of clauses within the sentence and striving for harmonious cadences. We have examples in the various kinds of Latin *cursus*.[224] Without achieving rigorously proportional durations, this second family of recitatives displays "number" and "art" to a degree not paralleled in the first. It is far more predisposed or suited to rhythmo-melodic declamation.

2. When we pass from prose to poetry we observe that those qualities which make a text intrinsically suited for cadenced recitation become essential and systematized. In poetry the creative spirit takes possession of the durations of the sounds of which a language is composed, only to give them back arranged in some rational order by means of a "meter."[225] According to the genius of the language, meter may be founded on a definite number of syllables of equal length, or on the proportions of syllables differing in length, or on

[224] The *cursus* arranges the conclusions of phrases according to predetermined sequences of accented and non-accented syllables which have been judged to be particularly agreeable. (According to the theorists of the Middlle Ages, these patterns were four in number.) They are to be found most frequently in Roman collects of the fifth and sixth centuries. See H. Leclercq, "Cursus," DACL, 3, 3193–3205.

[225] Here we use the word "poetry," not in the vague sense of some irrational *aura* which floats around the words, but in the original sense of *poïësis*, "formation" and "the art of speaking."

the regular recurrence of accents or of equal groups of phones. ("Phone" is a convenient technical term meaning the simplest of sounds—a single vowel sound or consonant sound all by itself). Thanks to the use of such mensuralist procedures (or of several of them simultaneously), phrases become organized into feet, lines, or strophes according to proportions more or less fixed. The rhythm of the recitative thus becomes the rational measure of movement. Poetry corresponds with a perfected form of the rhythm of recitative. It has been established that in antiquity, and right up till Renaissance days, all recitation of poetry was both metric and melodic. The same has ever remained true of recitative, for its rhythmic form, although perfected by music, still comes from its text and not from any durational structure inherent in its melody.

Christian worship has never permitted the sacred ministers, priest or deacon, to have recourse to the allure of poetic meters. All that can be allowed to them is the nobility of artistic prose.[226] But from the earliest times poetry has been a privilege of singers.[227] Chiefly, however, it was the privilege of the people in the form of their hymns. Most of the poetic hymns of the liturgy (whether metric, tonic or syllabic) have, actually built into their text, a rhythm which fits them for recitation. The melody of hymns of this type is but a pattern of tones for reciting rather than an air. This can be discerned clearly enough in some hymns of the ferial Little Hours (for example, in paschal time). By origin, therefore, poetic hymnody is only melodico-rhythmic recitation for soloist or choir.[228]

3. From the standpoint of its melody, the recitative is usually some kind of formula. This formula, intended for adaptation to each phrase of the text, has two essential elements: the reciting note and the cadences. (There is also a third, but accessory, element: the intonation). The reciting note is pitched

[226] See above, ch. 6, pp. 74ff. Attempts at versified texts have always been aberrations. A much more interesting exception is the ancient practice of metric preaching (the paschal homily of Melitus, the Syrian *mimrê* of Ephrem, of James of Saroug, etc.).

[227] This is so of the old Greek or Syrian hymns in which the verses were entrusted to soloists. In these two languages syllabism appears to have prevailed. The psalmist was treated far more strictly, since he was never permitted to use anything except the canonical and biblical texts. The Hebrew poetry of the psalms was cast originally in a type of metric progression called "tonic rhythm" which the old translations of the Bible were unable to employ. We do not know what rhythmic principles were observed by the old Greek and Latin psalmists when they recited verses of the psalms.

[228] Some readers may be surprised that we classify the ancient poetic hymns with recitative. But it is important not to be misled by our modern customs and viewpoints. (1) Nowadays we perform hymns without paying attention to their metric structure: every syllable is individualized, and lines, as such, hardly appear. (2) We pay far more attention to the melody, considered in itself, than we do to the rhythmic recitation of the text; thus we turn ornamental notes of secondary importance into cardinal notes in such a way as to endow the melody with an autonomous form and make it seem like an "air." The variants of hymn tunes in the manuscripts show which notes are, in fact, secondary. (3) After a certain date hymns are no longer treated as recitatives, but as texts to be fitted to an air (this tendency can already be discerned in the *Pange lingua* of Good Friday).

on a particular degree of the modal scale and is used for the enunciation of the text considered as a whole. This reciting note may be ornamented if the accentuation of the words suggests this (cf. the *Pater*) and there may be a secondary reciting note (as in the Prefaces).[229]

Cadences are melodic variations used to punctuate the ends of sentences or of their constituent clauses (flex). Technically these variations can assume a number of forms: simple inflection (as in the tone of a lesson); concluding melisma affecting the final syllable of the last word (as in the versicles which follow the hymns of Lauds and Vespers or the nocturns of Matins); a pattern to be applied syllabically to the last phones of a phrase (the last four syllables in many Greek recitatives; compare with the Latin psalmody of Introits); a formula to be adapted to the accents of the last or last two words (ordinary Latin psalmody); a blend of these forms according to the possibilities and genius of each language.[230] Normally the melody gives a note to each syllable, sometimes a group of two or three notes; but always this is done in a way which retains for the text its character as a recitation.

Whether there is any intonation or not, the structure of a recitative taken as a whole may be unitary, binary or ternary. It is unitary if the reciting note has nothing but a final cadence; it is binary if this final cadence is preceded by one secondary cadence, and ternary if it is preceded by two.[231] Most Latin liturgical formulas are conceived in terms of the binary form (Collects, Epistle, solemn Gospel, Prefaces, etc.), for this can be easily adapted to practically every sequence of phrases found in ordinary or artistic prose. Rhetorical recitatives fall into this category.

In recitatives for rhythmic poetry the melodic structure, by definition, copies the division of the poem into strophes, lines, feet and syllables, as may be gathered from a study of those hymns with rhythmo-melodic settings. The variety of possible systems of poetry likewise gives rise to a great number of recitative formulas. But there is no need for us to analyze these in detail.

4. We should, however, give some special attention to that type of recitative which is used for the psalms. Its structure naturally arises from that of Hebrew poetry. As everyone knows, the psalms are written in verses normally

---

[229] In some cases the reciting note may be reduced to small proportions by continuous melodic ornamentation, as in the *Exsultet*. But this is exceptional in the liturgy.

[230] The technique of recitative is, by hypothesis, entirely governed by the nature of the language used. Latin admits of the final melisma, syllabic progression, and, above all, the accentual principle connatural to itself. Modern French will not admit of syllabic progression because of the unpredictable occurrence of mute syllables and of stresses in a melodic formula designed syllabically; it cannot accept a terminal melisma except on a feminine concluding syllable; it cannot flow along acceptably without adaptation to stresses which originate sometimes from the words and sometimes from the syntax of the sentence. There are some languages—such as the Bantu tongues which dissociate verbal rhythmic and melodic accents from one another—which can attain an astonishing subtlety and richness in the recitative genre. Nearly all their music is, in fact, nothing else but this.

[231] There is nothing, of course, to prevent a formula from having more than three elements. The melodic formulas for hymns normally have four.

composed of two parallel halves. Considered as a unity, a psalm verse or distich calls for a chant in binary form [232] involving (often after intonation) a passing cadence or mediation to mark the end of the first half of the verse, and a final cadence to conclude the second.[233] Because the role given to psalmody in all the liturgical rites is so important, this structure has become characteristic of liturgical recitative. We find it again as the basis of ornate melodies, such as those of the verses in Graduals, Tracts, and long responsories.

c) Recitative is given great prominence in the liturgy, for all the chants of the sacred ministers and of the people's responses are in this genre. This prominence indicates the importance which Christian worship attaches to the word. But there is another interesting thing about recitative in the liturgy: in our modern Western civilization it is about the only way in which a "practical art" has been preserved in a living form for the many, not merely for the few.[234] Those who compose or improvise music are, of course, engaging in "practical art"; but for all others, music-making means reproducing some musical work already perfected. The average musician is an executant rather than a creator; he is the more highly esteemed the more faithfully he reproduces the actual notes written by the composer; his task is, so to speak, to sink himself into the work which he is to bring to life.[235] He interprets and does not create. By contrast, a singer who "vocalizes" a literary text is truly creating something, and the melody he evolves is always unique.[236] Now there is a very intimate connection between this creative activity and the mys-

[232] We have already pointed out, however, that in the early days of responsorial psalmody, it was not the entire verse but the half-verse that was taken as the unit of psalmody. This type is still in use in some of the Oriental rites. It is exemplified also in our own short responsories (with the ancient short doxology). The formula for the recitative is thus unitary, or rather, it makes use of the refrain as a consequent, as in the case of the simplest litanies.

[233] Verses of a ternary structure are reduced to binary form by the use of a flex after the first member within the first half of the psalm verse.

[234] See above, note 54, and later, note 333.

[235] This seeming fidelity to the original can, in fact, become an act of treason when applied to ancient compositions in which it was the task of the interpreter to vary, adorn and embellish a score which provided him only with an outline. To reproduce such a score as it stands would be like drawing a skeleton.

[236] Apart from Byzantine music, the liturgical chants of the Eastern churches have to this day been handed on by oral tradition. As such they have, on the whole, retained their close connection with practical art, which is always re-creation. Those who have attempted to set down these melodies in notation know well that an Oriental singer, even if he is repeating the same traditional piece, will never sing it twice in exactly the same way. Creation and interpretation are not regarded as formally distinct in the sense that one who "creates" music is accustomed to make use of musical formulas in the current idiom, while one who "interprets" it is not tied to the written note. In the West, the practical art of singing began to lose ground in the face of the growing practice of writing music down, and the circulation, from the tenth century onward, of the Romano-Frankish repertoire of music, known as Gregorian, which enjoyed such immense prestige. The practice of writing music down and performing it from the written notes became ever more widespread with the progress of polyphony and instrumental music.

tery of worship. The proclamation of the word is a "happening," something that takes place. And yet it is always something new—this particular celebration has never taken place before. The "memory" which it celebrates is not (as in a concert) some past creative act of the human genius, some composition now to be produced again (re-produced); what the liturgy renders present and active through the mysterious sign of the lyrical word is none other than the salvific action of God, the "new creation" achieved by the passion, death, resurrection and ascension of Christ our Lord.

B. THE AIR

The air is a musical genre in which both melody and rhythm acquire a substance of their own. It is better known and more usual among us than is recitative. It is, in fact, what we normally mean when we speak of "music," [237] and is the genre chiefly discussed in books which deal with liturgical singing or religious music. We shall concern ourselves here only with those aspects of it which bear upon the nature of Christian worship.

It is traditional in the West to distinguish between plain chant and figured music. [238] Plain chant, usually referred to under the generic name of "Gregorian chant" since its restoration at the end of the nineteenth century, comprises that traditional liturgical chant of the Roman Church of which neither the notation nor the execution involves measures of determined length with proportional subdivisions. Figured music comprises monodic, but especially polyphonic, works composed and written since the Middle Ages which do employ measures of determinate length in proportional subdivisions or multiples of a basic "time-unit."

This classification is empirical and lacks precision. The principles on which it is based, especially as regards plain chant, remain somewhat vague. [239] But it does lead us to make an observation which is important for our purpose: an air, although formally shaped as a melody, can be so closely allied to its text as to seem its perfect expression; and yet, on the other hand, it can seem to be a melody which is musically so self-sufficient that it may be deprived of its text, or fitted with another text, without suffering any change in its quality as a musical composition. Now beyond all doubt the perfect wedding of text to music is one of the most remarkable characteristics of Gregorian

---

[237] The general acceptance of such a meaning often indicates a certain misunderstanding of the strictly musical worth of recitative and of practical art.

[238] At least since the *Ars nova* (e.g., Jean de Musi, 14th century). Formerly the expression *planus cantus* referred to a chant in the lower register of the plagal modes (e.g., Guido of Arezzo); John XXII speaks only of *cantus ecclesiasticus* to designate the traditional chant of the Roman Church. But later the theorists draw a distinction between measured chant (*figuratus*, monodic or polyphonic) and plain chant "which is made up of simple notes of indeterminate value" (Tinctoris, 15th century). The expression *planus cantus* subsequently found its way into official documents (e.g., Benedict XIV).

[239] See ch. 13, pp. 193ff.

chant; it is this quality which explains why Gregorian chant is liturgical chant par excellence and why it remains, in this respect, the model for all music pertaining to a rite. By contrast, melody which is autonomous has a less immediate connection with the ritual action. The more it subsists in its own right and the more it diverts interest to itself, so much the more is its role in the ritual action merely adventitious and transitory. The liturgy does not absolutely reject such singing, and yet it can accept it only to the extent that it remains subservient to the rite.

a) Within the chants which have a really close collaboration between text and melody (for the Latin rite this means especially Gregorian chant), it is traditional to distinguish three species of the genre "air," according to the degree of melodic ornamentation found in each.

1. The simplest is the *syllabic* genre,[240] in which there is normally but one or two notes per syllable. Examples of this type are certain pieces from the Ordinary of the Mass (*Kyrie* XVI, *Gloria* XV, etc.) and some antiphons of the ferial Office. In the Byzantine rite this genre is called *hirmologic*.[241] It is especially well suited to pieces intended to be sung by the people, generally short items.

2. In the *neumatic* genre the syllables of the text can be ornamented by receiving a group of notes (neum) variable in size. To this genre belong such pieces as Gregorian Introits and Communions, and not a few antiphons. In the East this genre is called *sticheraric*.[242] In principle its text remains both audible and intelligible. It demands a trained choir, and is thus suited for pieces allotted to the *schola*.

3. In the *melismatic* genre certain syllables carry long ornaments or melodic developments, as exemplified in the verses of Graduals. The Greeks call this genre *asmatic*.[243] It is reserved for performance by a soloist with advanced vocal technique and specialist knowledge of music. In melismatic chant it normally becomes impossible to understand the text; interest has passed to the melody.

In practice it is often difficult to apply these categories. Just as one cannot draw a hard and fast line between recitative and air (as in *Sanctus* XVIII, which continues the recitative of the Preface), so also one finds an almost

---

[240] We retain here the word "genre," currently used in this sense, although strictly we ought to speak of "sub-genres," species of the genus air. The three categories are sometimes called "styles"; but we are reserving that word to designate another aspect of the art of music (see ch. 9).

[241] This comes from the word *hirmos* meaning a model strophe, first of a series, exhibiting the pattern according to which subsequent strophes are constructed.

[242] From *stichos*, the name for the tropes attached to the "stich" or half-verse of psalmody, in which this genre is habitually employed.

[243] From *asma*, song. It is sometimes also called *psallic*, because reserved for the cantor of psalms. This genre developed rather late in the Orient (chiefly in the fourteenth and fifteenth centuries); it points to a displacement of the center of interest in the ritual action, and indicates a diminution of liturgical sense.

insensible gradation from syllabic chant to neumatic, and from this to melismatic.

Though the interest of this classification is small from the musical point of view, it becomes great as soon as one establishes that the choice of a genre for any given chant depends on its ritual function, its performers, and its lyrical form. Thus if it is for a reading, the neumatic genre, and even more so the melismatic is inadmissible.[244] A refrain or hymn to be sung by the people suggests the choice of the syllabic genre, usually cannot accept the neumatic genre, and absolutely excludes the melismatic.[245] If the responsorial or antiphonal forms of psalmody are ever to be restored, for example, this could not be done except with careful attention to the melodic genres of the refrains.[246] Melodic genres, therefore, are related to the whole ritual action which is to be sung.

b) We must now ask whether the rhythmic genre of an air exerts as much influence on a celebration as does its melodic genre. Should it also be classified in similar categories? The traditional distinction between plain chant and figured music, and also the more modern contrast between the free rhythm of Gregorian and the measured rhythm of modern music, appear to give reasons for thinking so.

It is possible for the rhythm of a song, like its melody, to flow along in closest union with the text which it embellishes; but it is also possible for the rhythm to force the words to fit a pre-existing pattern more or less foreign to the text. Whatever may be the truth concerning the authentic rhythm of the various pieces of the Gregorian repertoire,[247] even an elementary analysis of them shows the extreme care for the text wherewith the discipline of most of them proceeds; verbal structures have influenced the flow of the music, not only in the distribution of the phrases, members and caesurae, but even in the treatment of individual words and the relative values of syllables. This can be seen most clearly in the syllabic genre and in the best pieces of the neumatic genre. To pray the text and to sing it amount to the same thing. This is the ideal for every sung rite.

But if the music runs according to a pre-established set of values, there is al-

---

[244] This raises a serious problem in connection with the verse of the Gradual.

[245] As regards the people's songs in the Ordinary of the Mass this is of especial importance.

[246] Thus, apart from a few exceptions, it is impossible to adopt the neumatic antiphon for the Communion as a refrain for truly functional psalmody.

[247] This specially difficult question is still very far from being solved and may perhaps remain always partially insoluble. The greatest weakness of all the theories worked out so far is that they attempt to apply some single principle of interpretation to a repertoire which is extremely diverse (ch. 13, pp. 192ff.). W must bear in mind also that the question of "authentic rhythm" belongs to history and musicology; but which interpretation is best for celebrating the liturgy is quite a different question. We cannot answer that from history and musicology; we must first of all conform to the rules given in the official Vatican edition, and then we must consider the various methods in common use and also the customs obtaining in different places.

ways a risk that its rhythmic movement may become so autonomous that the text has to take second place. The danger is enhanced by the fact that the rhythm can exert a formidable power of arousing excitement. The effectiveness of music in incantations depends above all on its rhythm, which can influence man both biologically and spiritually. Christian worship is willing to accept and make use of this power only if it can help the worshipper to enter more completely and intensely into the mystery being celebrated. There is no place in Christian worship for this power of rhythm if it does nothing but excite men and distract them or hinder them from entering into the mystery.[248] Of course, much depends on the moral dispositions of the individual; it is always possible for a man to give himself up to the influence of a rhythm instead of remaining in command of it. But, abstracting from this, we have some objective guarantee that worship will be genuinely "of the spirit" if the rhythms used in it are dictated by the text, which is the essential element of the rite.[249] Whereas if rhythm takes charge, and everything else is subjected to its requirements, singing within the liturgy could just as easily have a bad influence on worship as a good one. The danger is especially great when the rhythm is powerful and insistent, as in music of the orchestic genre, such as the march.[250]

It is extremely difficult to distinguish in technical terms between the kind of rhythm which brings out the spiritual quality of a text and the kind which obscures it. In olden times there was a distinction between plain chant and figured music, just as there is now between free rhythm and measured rhythm. But this does not help us as a line of demarcation. There can be no doubt that Gregorian chant assiduously cultivated verbal rhythm, whereas

---

[248] Like all created things, rhythm can be used or misused. According to his interior dispositions a man may use rhythm in the worship of the true God or misuse it to worship false gods. By its aid he can free his spirit or deliver it into subjection. For there is a perverted use of rhythm which drags the spirit down to the level of matter, turns man into a brute beast, and enslaves his soul to his bodily passions; he can become as though bewitched or possessed by the devil. But there is another use of rhythm which lifts a man up, exalts him, ennobles and spiritualizes even his physical emotions; it is in this way that good music employs rhythm. For rhythm has a remarkable power of unifying the entire personality from its psychosomatic depths to its spiritual heights. It sets man's whole being into movement, the muscles of his body and the powers of his mind, so that he "feels" the rhythm interiorly and tends to express it exteriorly—to move with it—in gesture. And every human gesture is a product, not only of man's body, but also of his soul. When placed at the service of prayer, rhythm can become a wonderfully efficacious means of rendering all our faculties "docile" to the Holy Spirit. It soothes the nerves and relaxes the muscles; it concentrates the memory into the vivid present; it frees the intellect from discursive activity and directs it to contemplation; it stimulates to love. Within the very act of prayer it more surely elicits "consent," not only of the appetitive will, but of the entire man to the transforming action of grace. Cf. *La Maison Dieu*, 33 (1953), p. 196.

[249] Hence the ritual superiority of recitative, even if it be metric in nature, because it derives its number from the word.

[250] *Mutatis mutandis*, one might say much the same thing about the melodic element of music. Just as rhythm has the power, as it were, to intoxicate and hypnotize people, so melody can put them into a trance or ecstasy. Sacred vocalizations were a Gnostic phenomenon.

modern music tends rather to produce a plethora of autonomous rhythms; yet in both cases the rhythm does require the intervention of a certain amount of rational number if it is to be truly musical,[251] and in both cases rhythm has been able to demonstrate its due subservience to word.[252] Of itself, rational number is not hostile to liberty of rhythm, which belongs really to a higher order than number. The spiritual character of a lyrical piece of music, therefore, does not depend on the presence or absence of number, but on the relationship which it bears to the act of singing.

Even though there is no generally accepted classification in this complex and much discussed matter, we must nevertheless formulate a few simple criteria of appreciation. We propose to distinguish three rhythmic genres to be applied to song. They will be ordered according to the degree of their rhythmic elaboration and the relationship of this to the text.[253]

1. We give the name *spontaneous* to the rhythm of a song in which the melodico-verbal flow bears no reference to any predetermined unit of time. Movement such as we find in rhetorical speaking lacks neither form nor proportion; it possesses an orderliness which the mind can perceive, appreciate, and even regulate (for example, in the *cursus* or balancing of periods). Yet the construction (*poïesis*) characteristic of any genuine "art" of movement does not, in oratory, attain the standard of fully musical rhythm.

This genre occurs in recitative or in certain melopoiae to be sung with *rubato* emancipated from all rational number. It is of its nature the affair of a solo singer (since choral singing presupposes conformity to communal objective time-values). It is more rhetoric than music.

2. We propose to give the name *numerical* [254] to the rhythm of a song which is strictly musical in the sense that its melodico-verbal flow is in terms of predetermined units of time. The movement is ordered according to values rationally defined in such a way that the mind directs them and appreciates them by referring particular durations to the abstract measure. This measure of movement requires at least a unit of time commensurate with itself; it can even rest content with this elementary arrangement of audible movement.

This genre is the one normally found in poetic recitative and simple airs. It renders possible a lyrical art which is completely musical and perfectly verbal. It is suited also to choral singing because based on a time unit which is both objective and communicable.

[251] See note 253.

[252] Think how the music is perfectly wedded to the words by the great polyphonists of the Renaissance; modern examples can be found in the lyrical music of such composers as Duparc and Debussy.

[253] Because different authors have different ideas of what is meant by rhythm, meter, number, measure, etc., and because these give rise to interminable discussions, it is necessary to state precisely how we interpret them here. See the "Excursus on the elements of musical rhythm" at the end of this chapter, p. 124.

[254] One might perhaps say "mensurable," were it not for fear of confusion with "mensurated," a word usually understood as referring to modern "barred music" which is orchestic in type.

3. We give the name *orchestic* to the rhythm of a song in which the mind, not content to refer durations to a simple measure of time, subjects the melodico-verbal flow to a compound rhythmic framework, abstractly predetermined according to definite numbers and proportions: 2, 3, 4, 5, often recurring (our modern "bar") and sometimes symmetrical (phrases, strophes).

This genre is related especially to dance music and to the use of percussion instruments. It can be employed in lyrical art provided that its frameworks are compatible with the structures of the words. It is suitable for choral singing so long as its rhythmic figures are not so complex or subtle as to be possible only to a soloist.

We must add here, as we did when discussing melodic genres, that the lines of demarcation between one rhythmic genre and another are frequently indistinct, and that blendings are possible. Spontaneous rhythm may incorporate certain elements from rational number (syllabism, *cursus*). On the other hand, numerical rhythm can make room for irrational values (by augmentation or diminution of certain values themselves incommensurable). In particular, the transition from the numerical to the orchestic genre can be so gradual as to be almost imperceptible.[255]

In conclusion, the air appears capable of assuming many different genres, both melodic and rhythmic, within liturgical singing. To analyze them all would be an endless process. For our present purpose it should be enough that we have indicated the general conditions according to which melos and number can demonstrate their fitness to serve, with varying degrees of success, the words which constitute the liturgical rites.

There is one conclusion, however, which has to be accepted by anyone who is studying the repertoires of the different rites as a whole. Apart from recitatives in spontaneous rhythm, the overwhelming majority of airs are derived from the very simplest form of the numerical genre: they are based on a single "time-unit." Think of the indivisible unit of time (*brevis*) which is the basis of Gregorian chant, or of the *chronos* of the music used for Oriental liturgies.[256] The polyphony of later days, right up to and including the Renaissance period, knew no measure other than the *tactus*. Early developments in choral singing likewise took for granted a similar beat. It is not difficult to explain this preference in an art which sets for itself the goal of being fully vocal; for here the musical rhythm originates from a text to be sung, a text in which the simplest element is the syllable. But the succession of syllables does not correspond, except in prosody, to a pre-established pattern like that of the recurrent framework of orchestic rhythm. The melodico-verbal flow which is desired is not that of free recitative but that

[255] On the occurrence of spontaneous, numerical and orchestic rhythms in the various pieces of the Gregorian repertoire, see chapter 13 and note 431.

[256] Even if we admit that the monotonous way in which the Orientals nowadays employ the *chronos* is a corruption (under Turkish influence?) of the ancient rhythmic practice, this last would have been much closer to Hebrew cantillation or Gregorian chant.

of measured music; and this cannot perfectly suit the phrasing of the text unless it has recourse to the most simple and the most supple manner of organizing time-values. And unitary rhythm is the only one which is, *a priori*, compatible with every possible kind of text. We cannot doubt that the reason why the traditional forms of liturgical music have generally adopted it is that it serves the ritual words with the maximum of docility.[257]

The use of polyphony and of musical instruments has a connection with musical genres. But this use does not follow (as does that of recitative or air) from the nature of the ritual action, as may be deduced from the fact that, in the history of Christian worship, neither polyphony nor instruments have been universally employed. We shall treat of these, therefore, in connection with those elements of music which are related to the celebrating community. This is the task to which we must now address ourselves.

EXCURSUS ON THE ELEMENTS OF MUSICAL RHYTHM

There are three elements which combine to make up musical rhythm and which enable us to perceive, as it were, three levels in the agogic aspect (motion) of music:

1) There is first the natural datum of physical or biological production: the *movement* of things or of living beings. Translated into audible phenomena (sequence of percussions, syllables or notes), this is the material of musical flow. In itself, considered merely as a "thing," it possesses neither number nor rhythm.

2) The intelligence then intervenes. Confronted with the natural data, it refers movement or duration to the abstract category of *time*. It introduces an analytic element—number—which enables it to compare and assess durations, i.e., to measure them. Durations thus become rational "values," which thenceforth can be apprehended as equal or unequal, as simple or complex, as integrated or subdivided. In order to handle these abstract values, the intellect uses, according to need, concepts of meter, measure and time. By so doing it takes possession of movement and masters it by recognizing that it is intelligible and endowed with rational order. Nevertheless, this analytical operation of the intellect remains something dead. Here number is but science; it is by no means living art.

3) The spirit now takes over the natural data thus rendered intelligible by number, in order to impress itself upon them freely. By means of its "art," which is *poïésis*, i.e., a constructive power, the spirit pours audible movement into definite moulds and injects its own mode of development, an

---

[257] This basic unit of time can be indivisible, as accepted in the current interpretation of Gregorian chant (in spite of some liquescent notes); or it can be divisible (by melodic ornamentation or by subdivision among two or three syllables) as in other categories. It is the genius of the language which determines the choice between these alternatives (compare the Huguenot chorale, in which the beats are subdivided into two, with the German chorale, which uses only one syllable per beat).

image of the spirit's own mind, clearly foreseen and freely willed in its evolution. The result is musical *rhythm*.

Hence, musical rhythm is in a different category from that natural rhythm which the spirit can recognize in the harmonious movement of things. This does not become music except by the intervention of "number," the analytical element which is the condition of *poïēsis*.

Rhythm is likewise to be distinguished from *measure*, the mere intellectual analysis of number. But it always presupposes measure. And we must bear in mind that this "measure" is susceptible of varying degrees of elaboration, ranging from mere perception of values as being equal, to exact appreciation of the subtlety of complex proportions. It is by means of measure (elaboration of number) that musical rhythms can be made to differ from one another.

The three elements of musical rhythm are not merely superimposed upon one another like three stories in a single building—they enter dialectically into a living unity. This statement is contained implicitly in the famous definition of Plato: "Rhythm is the ordering of movement," which contains not two, but three, terms relative to each other: (1) *movement*, which corresponds with matter; (2) *order*, which corresponds to form; and (3) *rhythm*, which synthesizes the ensemble.

The dialectic relationship of this living synthesis can be found wherever art is at work; in music it can be applied to melos just as well as to number. Natural sounds—whether of impassioned speech or of calm utterance—are, as regards their pitch, a continuum; they merge imperceptibly into each other. To evolve from them an *art* of sound, music introduces a discontinuity of pitch in the form of a scale made up of fixed degrees. Thereby it fashions for itself a world of melody in which the human spirit can feel at home. In like manner, the existence of a living being, made up of emotional states, strong and weak, is, as regards duration, a continuum. To evolve from this an *art* of movement, music introduces discontinunity in the form of temporal patterns made up of standardized durations. Having thus brought the world of duration under the sway of reason, the human spirit can move freely therein. Expressed otherwise: a sound cannot be apprehended as a "note" unless it be detached from its background of undifferentiated sounds and given a position in an abstract scale. In the same way a duration cannot be apprehended as a "value" (long or short) unless it be marked off from the sequence of natural duration and situated in an abstract measure. This can be represented schematically as follows:

1. In the natural order → objective existence → audible movement.

$$\downarrow$$

2. In the conceptual order → category of time → rational number, measure.

$$\downarrow$$

3. In the artistic order → free fabrication, *poïēsis* → musical rhythm.

In these conditions, what meaning is to be given to the expression "free rhythm" often used to distinguish Gregorian chant (as interpreted at present) from "measured music"? We have to say that here the word "free" is equivocal and gives rise to numerous misunderstandings, while the word "measure," to which it is opposed, is taken univocally as meaning, not rational number, but a certain rigid and recurring pattern of metric figures.

Musical rhythm is not a simple datum of nature, like movement, but a way in which the mind can apprehend duration and confer order upon it; it participates always in man's spiritual nature. Art and liberty are connected in such a way that to speak of free rhythm is a kind of tautology.

Measure, on the other hand, brings in the abstract and rational category of time. It is a way in which the reason can take charge in a human manner both of duration and of movement. Hence, it is in no way opposed to rhythm because it is of a different order.

In reality, rhythm and measure call out for one another in every kind of musical "art" worthy of that name. This is verified in Gregorian chant, which, as is generally agreed, presupposes a unit of time: the indivisible *brevis*. In this sense the rhythm of Gregorian chant should be called, after its own fashion, measured. It is a type of measure which differs, however, from that used in the fixed patterns of orchestic music.

TWO WITNESSES TO TRADITIONAL HYMNODY

Neither the written tradition of the Latin Middle Ages nor the purely oral tradition of the Syrian churches can guarantee with any certainty the authenticity of the melodies to which, even now, the poetic compositions of Ephrem or Ambrose are still sung. It is, in fact, most improbable that either the Syrian deacon or the Milanese bishop personally composed the melodies to which his hymns were first sung. Their purpose was to create a popular hymnody. It is said that Ephrem simply took over the music that was in vogue among the heretics whose errors he was attempting to combat, and that when Ambrose, in 386, desired to occupy in a pious way the people who were besieged in his basilica by Justin's soldiers, he provided them with hymns to sing and so must have made use of tunes which they already knew.

Nevertheless there is an uninterrupted tradition which, in the Milanese and Romano-Frankish rites on the one hand, and in the Chaldean, Maronite and Syrian rites on the other hand, has kept alive from the fourth century to our own day the tunes attributed to the Eastern and Western fathers of hymnody. These ancient heirlooms of Christian song are deserving of very great respect.

The Ephremian *madrâshâ* which we quote is taken from the Syrian liturgy (according to J. Jeannin, *Mélodies syriennes et chaldéennes*, II, no. 545, pp. 363/4). It is made up of two pairs of lines of eight feet, followed by two pairs of five feet, arranged in parallel distichs and sung to the same melody. Then follows a refrain from the doxology, made up of a pair of lines with eight feet, sung to the same air as the other lines with eight feet.

Its text sings of the mystery of Christ's Passion and seems to refer to the washing of feet. A non-rhythmic translation would be: "Who would not be astonished, Lord, to see Thy humble deeds, contemplating Thee, the mighty Master, before whom the disciples bow down! O Hero of the ages, O devouring Fire! Thou who, like a slave, dost serve those who are truly slaves. ℞. Glory to Thee, First-born of the Most High! Praise to Thy name for ever"

Ephremian Madrâshâ

Ambrosian Hymn

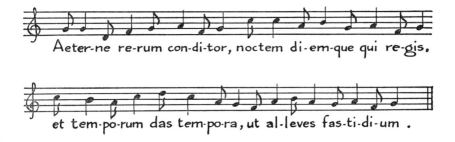

The hymn *Aeterne rerum Conditor*, whose Ambrosian authorship is attested by St. Augustine (*Retract.*, 1, 21), is found in Matins of the Milanese Office. The melody, though with variants, can be found in Ambrosian, Italian, German and Cistercian manuscripts (for the manuscript sources see Huglo-Agustoni-Cardine-Moneta-Caglio, *Fonti e paleografia del canto ambrosiano* [Milan, 1956], p. 100). The Roman antiphonary uses this hymn for Lauds on Sunday but with another melody.

9   IDIOM AND STYLE

In studying the principal laws governing music in Christian worship, we have, till now, regarded them from the standpoint of liturgical action by asking: "What does the Church desire and seek when singing her ceremonies?" But liturgy is not a salvific action independent of time. It is the celebration of the mystery by and in a Church situated in time. It is because of men and on their behalf that she expresses visibly realities which themselves are invisible, so that the faithful, enlightened and sanctified by these sacred signs, may give glory to God. The celebration of worship is thus necessarily bound up with those who celebrate it. Its signs must be their signs, its modes of expression must be theirs. The carrying-out of the liturgy is conditioned by the human cultures of this part and epiphany of the Church at prayer, this congregation *hic et nunc* assembled for the purpose of entering into the mystery of salvation. And so, after asking overselves, "What does the Church want?" we must add: "What will suit such and such a community of Christians that they may sing to their Lord?" In other words: "What music, particularized in time and space, is capable of appearing, to a given group of the faithful, as a living and sacred sign of the mystery?"

Even when we have acquired clear ideas about the nature of the rites to be sung as regards their functions, their agents, their forms and their genres, we have not thereby actually heard their music. I can know that a Gospel has the nature of a reading and is to be proclaimed by a deacon as a soloist, in direct form, by means of a melodic formula in recitative; nevertheless, the very same Gospel of Pentecost Sunday will sound quite different according as I may listen to it in Rome, Alexandria, Mosul, Antioch, Athens or Novgorod. From one place to another the intervals and melodic forms, the rhythm and diction, methods of voice production and singing differ according to the tastes, customs and genius of the peoples. A sung rite cannot be individualized except by taking a particular form in a certain musical idiom and liturgical style.

By "idiom" we mean here those audible resources or constituents of which an assembly may make use: musical scales, rhythmic figures, timbres and nuances. By "style" we mean the esthetic form given to these constituents in such a way that the work of art is considered to be beautiful or sacred.[258]

A. THE IDIOM OF SONG

a) Just as each nation speaks a language proper to itself, so each type of culture possesses a certain musical idiom. This is characterized by several elements. The most obvious is the adoption of certain melodic scales of varying richness in their number of degrees (defective scales, pentatonic, or heptatonic scales, etc.), more or less subject to modal forms (Greek *nomes,* Indian *ragas,* Jewish *taamim,* Gregorian *modes,* etc.). Rhythmic structures are no less characteristic. They depend mainly on the literary language and its arrangement in poetic meters (feet, lines) according to the influence of number and the quantity of syllables, intensive or rhythmic accents; then on the more or less mandatory employment of instruments (especially those of percussion); on dances whose movements require precise rhythms or symmetrical periods; finally, on conscious elaboration which invents abstract figures. No less distinctive of a musical idiom is the relationship between number and melos: certain peoples—for example, Africans—have developed and cultivated rhythm very intensely and yet have been but little concerned to establish differences between notes of a scale. Others have so refined their perception of pitch that they can distinguish minute intervals, and yet they seem quite uninterested in rhythmic developments. Finally, such things as vocal timbres and modification of the consonants proper to each spoken language enter into the determination of musical idioms.

b) The frontiers dividing musical idioms from one another are less definite

---

[258] Here we are giving to the word "style" its most common meaning: a mode of expression proper to a civilization, an epoch, or an individual. A comparison with architecture may help to understand the distinction we are making between constituents—idiom on the one hand and form-style on the other: a church can be built of stone, brick or cement, but the choice of any one of these constituent materials does not predetermine its style, which could be Romanesque, Gothic, or baroque. Later we shall have to distinguish between style (as such) and styles (in particular).

than those which separate written or spoken languages. There exist melodic patterns and quasi-spontaneous rhythmic figures which occur equally in cultures that are totally different.[259] It is well known how easily one civilization can adopt from another, wholly or in part, foreign music which has distinction or allure.[260] Because men of different races can more easily communicate with one another by music than by spoken languages, it has often been possible to graft the musical idiom of one culture onto the language of another. Many examples of this occur in the missionary expansion of Christianity: the apostles carried to the convert peoples, not only their gospel and their rites, but also the music of their Church.[261]

Nevertheless, the fact that some musical idioms can be spread to a certain extent into almost every culture does not disprove the diversity of musical idioms. The existence of such a diversity is even a condition for the evolution of music, which is ever seeking new ways of expression. Especially does it render possible the phenomenon of "culture," in which signs acquire precision of meaning and intensification of affective power only at the expense of the meaning which they acquired in a stable society. No idiom can become spiritually universal except by a process of semiological particularization. Now in music this process can embrace certain technical details which cannot be communicated from one people to another.[262] And it always implies at least a certain number of local habits or turns of mind which make some people judge that an air is "melodious" while others say it is "peculiar."

c) In practice, every liturgical celebration is carried out by an assembly in which the majority are at home with some particular musical idiom. Now singing is a ritual action which has to be performed by the co-celebrants. Hence liturgical singing has to make use of a musical idiom which is *within the powers of those who are engaged in worship*.[262a]

On the other hand, as regards its audible constituents, every musical idiom is *a priori* acceptable in liturgical singing provided that it will permit liturgical singing to exist as such.[263] Just as it is possible to build a church of stone, of wood, of brick or of cement, so also it is possible to sing in a mode, a key, or the twelve-tone scale. If there are any limitations, these come from the

[259] Think, for instance, of the pentatonic scale with no semitones which is common to ancient China, to most of the black races, and to the Celts, etc. It is the same with metric figures of the type anapest-dactyl.

[260] For example, the invasion, *via* America, of modern Western music by Negro rhythms, and the actual quasi-universality of Western music.

[261] Examples: the adoption of Byzantine chant when Russia was converted; European hymns spread throughout the whole world by missionaries of the past few generations; and, still more recently, the spread of Gregorian chant. The same may be said about non-Catholic churches and all the religious sects.

[262] It is very difficult for a European, whose ear is trained to tempered intervals, to assimilate, for example, Coptic or Arabic music. A man must practically abandon his own idiom before he can take to another. For most Europeans, an Oriental sings "out of tune," and conversely.

[262a] Cf. CL 121 and 119.

[263] As we shall see later, this is not so for all styles.

singers or from contingent ecclesiastical decisions,[264] not from any intrinsic incompatibility. The Church leaves the door open for progress in the art of music.[265] Just as every tongue may praise God, so every musical idiom can sing of Him.

The practical limitations imposed on singing in the liturgical assembly differ, within the musical idiom, according as they apply to chants from the sanctuary or from the nave, and, within the latter category, according as the music is intended to be listened to or sung by the people.

Chants from the sanctuary are allotted to soloists who are not virtuoso singers but *sacred ministers*. So that these chants may be sung with that sober gravity required by the rites and with the musical quality they ought never to lack, their idiom must be familiar to, and within the powers of, all who have the duty of singing them. Hence, normally they have to be extremely simple. But this simplicity is not poverty; it is a sign of controlled reverence and of a noble sense of proportion.

Chants from the nave comprise chiefly those items which the *people* are intended to sing and to make into their own prayer. It should be obvious that the musical idiom for this singing ought to be compatible with the common background of living musical culture of the community. The melody and rhythm, the relation of words to music, should be familiar enough to ensure that nobody feels himself excluded from the singing or distracted from the sacred action by being made to feel that he is an outsider.[266] For every baptized person, to sing at his worship is an inalienable right of which no celebration should deprive him. Here again the musical idiom will have to be simple and common, which does not mean that it has to be banal or vulgar.[267]

---

[264] Such as the rejection of the extraneous, of the profane, or of art for art's sake, of which we treated above (ch. 3, pp. 47ff.).

[265] "The Church has always recognized and favored the progress of the arts, admitting to the service of cult everything good and beautiful discovered by genius in the course of ages—always, however, with due regard to the liturgical laws" (TLS 5); "It is very important to give full scope to the arts of our times if, with due reverence and honor they put themselves at the service of our churches and sacred rites" (MD 190). Cf. CL 112 § 3.

[266] It is necessary to "take into account more the needs of the Christian community than the personal taste and judgment of the artist" (MD 190). This does not mean that one must take as the least common denominator the most unmusical and uncultured person in the community, nor acquiesce in the evident lack of practical musical culture displayed by some liturgical assemblies (a phenomenon, moreover, which is more striking in civilizations supposed to be advanced than in those recognized as primitive). We suppose here that children will have learned to sing, just as they have learned to speak, to read and to write; song ought to be for grown-ups a true means of personal expression and a sign of the beautiful. The teaching of singing and education in art are presupposed by liturgical pastoral work. One does not make laws out of exceptions, nor rules for conditions of poverty and misery.

[267] *Musicae sacrae* says, with regard to "popular religious hymns . . . mostly in the language of the people . . . ," that "their vocabulary must be simple, their tunes easy. They must be unpretentious, and not just a meaningless stream of words. They must be marked with a religious dignity and seriousness, however short and easy they may be" (MSD 30; cf. IMS 52). All these qualities should be required *a fortiori* for the liturgical chants of the people.

In practice, all rites contain a repertoire, more or less rich, of popular items which the faithful get to know by coming regularly to worship and which furnish the people with a common musical idiom. Sometimes this traditional musical idiom is specific to liturgical singing, like the "modes" of Gregorian chant. There is no disadvantage in this, provided that the idiom is really living; its exclusive use might even turn it into the objective constituent of a "sacred style." But such a sacred idiom ought to have some relation to ordinary, popular or artistic music. It should both inspire and be inspired by ordinary music, as has nearly always been the case throughout history. It is possible, however, for a complete breach to develop between liturgical singing on the one hand and the ordinary song of the people on the other; this could be the result of a lifeless performance of an unchanging repertoire, or of the purely material and exclusive use of an unintelligible language, or of the consequence of this—namely, that the people no longer sing in church. If such a breach occurs, there is a great risk that divine service may degenerate into an occasion for preserving musical works of the past or into a concert for the initiated. The idiom of liturgical music, whether it be traditional or new, must always be a living idiom because of the very nature of Christian worship.

Singing from the nave may include, in the second place, pieces sung by representatives of the assembly—the choir. The idiom of these pieces may exceed the bounds of what it would be possible for the people themselves to sing, for they are now listeners. It is, however, limited by the capabilities of the choir and ought not to exceed these.[268] On the other hand, the message which these works are intended to convey to those who listen to them ought to be intelligible. Any kind of music which is not a help to prayer in spirit and in truth has no place in Christian worship. Its idiom, therefore, should remain accessible and meaningful to the community as a whole.[269]

B. THE STYLE OF LITURGICAL MUSIC

The idiom of sacred music, considered simply as something which can be heard, is really nothing other than the idiom of music in general. Just as we use words of our own language when translating the Gospel into English,

---

[268] "It is scarcely necessary to add the warning that if the resources and skill available are unequal to works on such a scale, it is much better not to attempt them at all than to present something not worthy of divine worship and religious assemblies" (MSD 29; cf. IMS 60a).

[269] The remarks made in note 266 apply here also. This problem presents special difficulties in an epoch such as our own, when the art of music is trying to discover new idioms and certain composers are purposely evolving sound-systems never used before; such systems, to be accepted and appreciated, require to be heard either many times or by especially cultured ears. In this matter we must be neither too venturesome (what cannot be done today may be quite common tomorrow) nor too timid (listening to genuine music uplifts the spirit, and real masterpieces create their own public). Above all, we must avoid snobbery and "*avant-gardisme*" (all too common in this connection) and remind ourselves that the Church is the Kingdom of the poor and lowly whom we must never despise.

just as Jesus used words of the Aramaic language to reveal to us the Father's secrets, so also religious song uses the sounds of the melodies and instruments commonly employed.

a) But is there not a style specially fitted for liturgical use? Let us put the question more precisely: do we find that a given civilization, a particular epoch or an individual artist makes use of one means of expression in profane art and quite another in religious art? It seems generally accepted that they do, yet the idea may well be disputed. What purely objective difference of style can we discern in the Romanesque or Gothic used for churches and that used for building lordly palaces? What difference of style is to be found between Bossuet's *Histoire universelle* and his sermons? Between the religious motets and the secular chansons of Lassus? Between a Mass and an opera by Mozart? Any work of sacred art is destined to be used for a religious or liturgical purpose; admittedly this prohibits the employment of certain worldly effects and imposes on it subjects and forms appropriate to worship; but in other respects these limitations do not create a sacred style objectively distinct.

And yet public opinion does speak of "sacred style," of "liturgical expression," and of "hieratic forms"; does it thereby witness to some undeniable truth? Is there not really some specific quality which can enter into art as a sign of the sacred?

This proposition is certainly defensible. Yet, such a specific quality is not to be sought for in perceptible forms that can be particularized and assigned to material elements. It would be a gross mistake to think that one is producing something "sacred" or "Christian" just by building in Romanesque style, or by speaking in the style of Bossuet, or by composing in the style of Palestrina. If a style is sacred, this can only be because it signifies what is transcendent in the sphere of religion. Hence, sacred characteristics are not to be sought in the "thing" which does the signifying, but in its relation to the world of the divine. But this relation is something perceived by the observer; before he can interpret a sign as pointing to some reality, he must first have adopted, of his own free will, some definite attitude toward the reality signified. So there cannot be any such thing as a sacred style unless the sign be viewed through the eyes of faith. And the variety of sacred styles is thus only a projection of different kinds of religious faith, each endowed with its own social or individual character.

b) In this sense there can be no doubt that there does exist a sacred style which is specifically Christian, and within this there is such a thing as a "liturgical" style. The liturgy, in fact, endows art with a mode of being and a value of meaning which are proper to itself. What, then, are the main characteristics of the liturgical style? [270]

[270] Much has been written—and well written—about liturgical style. The reflections we put forth here only touch the fringe of this vast question. Moreover, they cannot avoid being, to a certain extent, somewhat subjective.

In the liturgy, art signifies primarily the making-present of some mystery of salvation. It has a bearing on the supernatural. It should lead the mind to the invisible. This means that it is incompatible with mere esthetic pleasure, which enslaves the senses to the delights of perceptible forms. It will not admit of human exuberance or of passionate excitement. Hence its modesty and transparence, hence its acknowledged sobriety and even austerity.

The mystery signified is, secondly, a historical revelation; for salvation is that brought by Christ and no other. Liturgical art is not a simple evocation of "the beyond" (no matter of what kind), nor is it a pretext for a vague mythical escape from reality. It is, in its own way, revelation—that is, the drawing-aside of the veil from the passage (passover) in Jesus from death to life. It contains a gnosis, a wisdom of the Spirit. It brings a knowledge by faith. It excludes, therefore, magical incantation or dionysiac ecstasy. This explains the spiritual and intelligible aspect of liturgical style. Statues and pictures are capable of having a liturgical style because they are material objects of the spiritual worship given to the historic persons whom they represent; music, too, can have liturgical style because it can always be the servant of words carrying revelation.

The mystery which is revealed is, moreover, transmitted by signs which are those of a Church, a visible society in which salvation is carried into effect. As in every visible society, the meaning of art depends on the convention [271] which governs social relationships. But liturgical art is meant to serve that society which is the Church; precisely because it is social, it excludes from its style whatever is merely individualistic. The purpose of the worship which liturgical art must serve is not to express the faith or sentiments of some individual member of the assembly; it is to express the faith and sentiments of the Church by means of signs which the believers can recognize as their own. The liturgical style is "ecclesial" because it reveals the human-divine personality of the Church expressing herself through her members in the charity of Christ.[272]

It is because of the splendor of the mystery which it should express that the liturgical style should also display the qualities of purity and spiritual

[271] This word is to be understood to mean, not something "arbitrary," but something "agreed." There is no "thing-sign" which can acquire its full power of signification without being inserted into some system of interpretation freely agreed to (even if it has some natural foundation for its symbolism). This is true of the sacraments and cult-mysteries, which draw their full meaning from the supreme convention agreed to between God and man—the Alliance in Jesus Christ, lived in the Church. Without this historico-social reference, the sign remains equivocal. As regards sacred art, the consequences of this principle are far-reaching. One, in particular, is the falsehood of the axiom: Every authentic work of art in which a true artist expresses his religious sentiments is, by this very fact, suited for use in worship. Nothing could be less certain; for this work of art must also be "recognized" by the Church and by the faithful as being a sign which expresses clearly their own objectively Christian faith.

[272] The well-known definition "*le style, c'est l'homme*" has to be understood, as regards liturgical art, as applying to the Church, and not to the Christian artist considered as an individual.

light and joy—reflections in the moral sphere of the theological depths presupposed by every sacred sign.[273]

c) The qualities of the liturgical style are first of all required in the work
of art considered in itself (literary text, musical composition, various forms
of church decoration). But they are even more necessary in the very act of
celebration. As we have said before, liturgical art, because it pertains to
ritual, is essentially a practical art.

This observation is of the highest importance for sacred music. Music,
unlike architecture, painting, or even the sacred text, is not a sign produced
once and for all. As an art of movement it does not exist except in time, and
even then only while it is actually being performed. Whatever has been
composed, even written down, is not yet music itself. Music has to be "made"
or "re-made" by being played or sung. Only in performance does it live and
speak; only in performance does it possess a style. Style, therefore, is not a
matter which concerns only the composer; it depends, even more, on the
interpreter. It is only when being actually played or sung that music is a sign.

This particular aspect of music's nature establishes between it and liturgy
an altogether special relationship—the two are "connatural." Liturgy is an
ever-renewed making-present of the mystery of salvation; music is an ever-
renewed making-present of audible signs. Liturgy repeats in time the events
of sacred history; music does not exist except by coming into existence; it is
forever being created and re-created. The one as a reality, and the other as
a sign are at the same time a memorial, a presence, and an anticipation. That
is why music is the liturgical art par excellence. More than any other art it
is free event and common history.

From this it follows that in the celebration of the liturgy the performance
and interpretation of the music is of prime importance. More attention ought
to be paid to the sacred action made up of the singing of ministers, choir,
and people than to the value of some work of art abstractly considered. No
doubt artistic excellence should be sought in the choice of repertoire, but
it is far more important in the performance of what has been chosen. For
the liturgical symbolism and spiritual effectiveness of singing depend, above
all, on the way in which the music is sung.[274] If it is well sung, even a simple
melody can bring to the liturgy all the living and sober beauty due to it. But

---

[273] Indeed, it would be possible to demonstrate from these three named characteristics that
the liturgical style should show forth the hope, the faith, and the charity of the Christians.

[274] In this matter of liturgical style, the prime importance of performance is not appreciated
as it should be. This is shown by certain discussions about the "quality" of works judged to
be admissible, or inadmissible, in worship. We limit ourselves here to a single contention:
abstracting from the functional requirements of liturgical art, and judging solely from the
musical point of view, we do not assess a piece of liturgical singing according to the principles
to be applied in the school or concert hall, because the situation is completely different. A short
acclamation, a preface, or the singing of a psalm may be of little interest at a concert or on a
phonograph record. But within a liturgical celebration such kinds of singing are irreplaceable
and even preponderant.

even a fine work of art, if sung laboriously or pretentiously, can sound insincere or out of place. Any ordinary Christian man can grasp this truth merely by his esthetic sense; he sees it even more clearly by his faith. For he knows that the very act of giving something to God has a far greater value than the poor gifts that are given; so also the act of singing to God, in which the voice signifies the spiritual sacrifice, is far more valuable than the work of art which is sung.

d) The quality of style in musical performance is also to be judged differently according to the liturgical agents concerned.

All that is reasonably demanded from a minister of the sanctuary, who sings by himself, is a correct and true rendering of a simple chant. Any apparent excessive preoccupation with the technique of singing would clash with the sacredness of his role. Even as bare, unfinished stone is just as suitable a material for the construction of an altar as is polished marble or resplendent gilt, so an entirely natural, untrained voice, though different from a flexible and cultured one, has the quality needed for its task.

Singing by the people also has a quality of its own. It should not be judged by the same norms as those properly employed when listening to a soloist or choir. A meadow full of flowers is beautiful even though many of them are only in bud while others are faded. Perhaps not one of them, if cut, would look well by itself in a vase; if a person wished to make up a bouquet he would have to pick and choose. It is like that with the singing from the nave. Its quality is due to its unanimity and fervor rather than to the excellence of its voices considered separately. In congregational singing, a certain amount of imprecision in both rhythm and pitch can pass muster, though it could not be tolerated in a choir. This slight lack of polish does not really impair the beauty of the singing any more than the assymmetry or inequality of the flowers mars the meadow's beauty. To a certain degree these imperfections even add charm to congregational singing. Finally, we must remember that in congregational singing everyone, by supposition, is an agent. To become instead a mere listener, a member of the assembly would have to isolate himself from the singing community. He would have to split himself into two parts, withdrawing from the common action in order to judge it as from the outside. A member of the congregation will appreciate the style of the community-singing only to the extent that he helps to create that style by joining in the singing himself.

On the other hand, the singing of the choir, for which the people are an audience, ought to contribute to the sung prayer all the qualities of style proper to a fine performance: precision, balance, and feeling. Here there is every justification for demanding excellence; it is, after all, for artistic reasons, not for ceremonial reasons, that certain items are reserved to the choir. Even so, the singing of a church choir should not be judged by the criteria that would be used to assess a concert performance. For at a concert a technical perfection of the highest professional standard is expected from every performer, and the audience has a legitimate interest in the personal interpretation of this artist or that conductor, but in worship the members of the choir are representatives of the people, and they should not cease to be "of the people." Even though chosen for their competence—and the more competent they are the better—they still remain amateurs who normally cannot be expected to rival professional singers in technical perfection and virtuosity. Fortunately no one expects them to concentrate on producing masterpieces. If they were consciously to strive after very studied or individualized interpretations, this would be a dangerous tendency; their chief concern should not be the music they perform but the worship which they help to celebrate. That is why their ideals should not be of this world but of the other world; they should aim beyond mere music toward a beautiful and living expression of prayer in faith and love.[275]

e) Even so, there still remains a very irritating question: what criteria should one invoke in order to decide whether a work and its performance really possess, as regards their style, those qualities of beauty and of sacredness which are required?

Beauty and sacredness of style arise respectively from esthetic judgment and religious sentiment. Now there is nothing absolute about either of these. They are essentially relative to culture, which is itself variable and unstable. In some of the Eastern Churches it is considered both beautiful and sacred to sing in a nasal tone; to us that is ugly and vulgar. Among us *portamento* is admitted in vocal technique; among them it is considered a lack of decency, even of modesty. In like manner, the religious sentiment of the baroque era took pleasure in signifying God's glory by means of flamboyant demonstrations of pomp and splendor; our own generation appears to seek its way toward God by means of simplicity and evangelical poverty. And within one and the same community this man prefers restraint and tranquillity while the other is not moved except by warm and colorful modes of expression.

Liturgy does not bring people together according to their level of culture, similarities, or tastes. Christian worship is open to all the baptized. And so the Church, in determining the style of her celebrations in any given epoch or region, is accustomed to take into account the religious sentiments and esthetic tastes prevalent among her children. This is relatively easy in communities which are homogeneous, exclusive, or stable, but it is a delicate affair in societies like our own which are diverse, open, and changeable. A "common" esthetic taste can only be the result of an equilibrium established between the better and the less well instructed faithful, between the more

---

[275] Who is there who has not had experiences such as the following: (a) a Church service leaves one with a memory of superb musical perfection; but when a tape-recording of it is played, it cannot survive a critical hearing; (b) someone possesses an extraordinarily well-trained voice; but when he sings at a liturgical function he seems to have no soul!

spiritual and more materially-minded characters, the more and the less intelligent minds, the more refined and the uncultured, the individualists and
the gregarious, the specialist and the man-in-the-street.

THE CHURCH AND THE EVOLUTION OF THE ARTS

Both in idiom and in style art is continually evolving. This necessarily has
repercussions on the liturgy, which requires a living art. What is the Church's
attitude toward evolution of the arts? She declares that in principle she is
willing to accept it,[276] but in practice shows prudence in doing so.[277]

At first sight the Church seems to maintain a kind of authoritarian indif-
ference when confronted with alterations in taste. Throughout the course of
many differing centuries she has preserved almost unchanged the most sacred
of her chants, such as the recitatives of the celebrant and certain acclamations
of the people. Even during those periods when, in the West, the kind of
art known as "gothic" was most despised, when plain chant was most de-
formed and least understood, the ancient melopoiae attached to the texts of
the liturgy did not perish.

But at the same time the liturgy, in the course of centuries, has strongly
felt the influence of successive changes of taste to such an extent that, under
social pressure, the very rites themselves have been partially modified and
changed. There has been mention of a "terrifying centrifugal force of art"
which, in the history of cultural forms, has sometimes seized some of the
ritual functions for its own purposes.[278] The facts cannot be denied. We have
examples in the appearance of antiphony as a new form of psalmody; the
wave of lyricism in the seventh–eighth centuries both in East and West,
coinciding with the rise of song-schools, and with the alienation of the people
from liturgical singing, which things in turn brought about a radical transformation of the responsorial and antiphonal forms of psalmody; the appearance, under the Carolingians, of the prestige attached to a melodic "repertoire"
ascribed to the authority of St. Gregory the Great, which later was to be
transcribed, even in its minutest details, into innumerable manuscripts; the
proliferation of tropes, proses and sequences, which carved out for themselves a considerable place among the chants of the Mass; the successive
conquests of polyphony, which gradually made its way into the liturgy;
the arrival of the organ, and then the classical orchestra, etc. One finishes
by wondering whether the dominant image of liturgical music throughout
the ages is not one of concurrence rather than of tradition.

No doubt it is essential to the life of liturgical forms that they be at the
same time stable yet mobile, traditional yet particular.[279] Even so, it can be
useful to examine critically the idea of progress in the arts and to see the
relationship between evolution of art and the evolution of worship.

---

[276] See note 265.   [277] See ch. 3.
[278] Josef A. Jungmann, *Des lois de la célébration du culte liturgique*, p. 132.

a) If we begin by discussing the idiom and resources of music, we can admit that, with the march of time and of civilization, a good deal of progress has been made: there has been the fixing of modes, the adoption of the key system and of equal temperament, the conquests of counterpoint and harmony, an increase in the number of instruments and improvements in the techniques of using them, etc. But this progress in resources, though it opens new technical possibilities to the art, does not automatically bring with it progress in the art itself. Art, the sign of the beautiful, borders on the absolute. Its greatness is not related causally to the material which it uses. It is possible to have more art in four notes from a shepherd's pipe than in a symphony from a full orchestra. So worship does not necessarily gain in beauty if it is enriched with melismata, polyphony or instruments. Everything depends on the way these resources are used—on the style.

b) A constant search, in celebration, for the spirit proper to liturgical expression has occasioned the appearance of successive styles which reflect, in a different way for each culture and epoch, something of the attitude of the Church at prayer: Gregorian style, Palestrinian style, harmonic style, etc. But are these changes any evidence of progress? The answer will vary according as one looks at the matter from the esthetic or the liturgical point of view.

As regards the history of art, the evolution of forms is an ineluctible fact depending on changes of idiom and of esthetic taste. There is a flow of artistic forms which come into existence and die for the very reason that their symbolic value in society increases or diminishes. The artist is always seeking more meaningful forms. Now the effectiveness of any sign depends above all on its power to arrest attention. The sign, by confronting people with something new, causes surprise. At this stage it attracts but remains partially uncomprehended. Then little by little it asserts itself, gains recognition and acceptance, and ends by becoming familiar. Society assimilates it into the contemporary idiom of symbolism. It becomes classical. Now a period of balance and tranquil possession has been reached. But in time and with use, the symbol becomes deadened; from being classic the style becomes academic and then banal. That which was once green has now faded. The form itself is not in question, but taste has changed and the search has begun for new ways of expression that will be more striking. Nevertheless, culture can restore life to old forms; it can, as it were, re-gild them and rescue them from neglect. One can begin again, for example, to appreciate Romanesque architecture or Gregorian chant.

[279] "In the liturgy there are human elements as well as divine. The latter, obviously, having been established by the divine Redeemer, cannot under any circumstances be changed by men; but the human elements may be modified in various ways approved by the hierarchy under the guidance of the Holy Spirit, according as time, circumstances and the needs of souls may demand . . . All these changes witness to the permanent life of the Church throughout the centuries" (MD 47).

In these continual fluctuations, where is progress? Authentic works of art themselves remain unchanged, and every age produces its own master-pieces which are ever young. But their value as signs can be perceived to a greater or lesser extent. The progress or decadence of art is ultimately re-ducible to the progress or decadence of culture.

The celebration of worship, for its part, is necessarily dependent on the prevailing culture, and its artistic forms undeniably reflect the fluctuations revealed by the history of art. Yet further, in a Christian civilization such as that of the Middle Ages, when religious art stood at the very center of culture, art and worship were in such close symbiosis that the history of music, for example, is, during this period, primarily and above all the his-tory of *sacred* music.

It would be a mistake, however, to conclude from this instance that the liturgy is, and should remain, the normal and privileged domain in which progress in the arts should take place. In cheap apologetics it has been said much too often that the progress of the arts is one of the glories of the Church, and that she would be failing in her mission if her worship would no longer accept or inspire the great masterpieces of human art. But history, as well as the intrinsic nature of worship, requires the admission of certain nuances into this view of things.

Throughout all the early centuries of her existence the Church showed herself more than reserved toward art, and the Fathers of the Church seem to have been particularly severe as regards the use of music. The Middle Ages give us a completely different picture; the Church was then the great mistress of culture. Nevertheless, even if the arts progressed within her bosom, they were not accorded immediate entry into her worship. The first pieces of music to be written down in the ninth century were extra-liturgi-cal pieces, and the first experiments in polyphony are likewise extra-liturgical. The religious drama, the *Ars nova*, the oratorio—all developed on the out-skirts of liturgy strictly understood. With the Renaissance the arts experienced a new efflorescence; at the same time they won their independence vis-à-vis Christian religious sentiment, and they never ceased to diverge ever more and more from worship. Insofar as they did enter it, one cannot say that the sacred rites were thereby always improved. Whether by causality or coinci-dence, the liturgy since those days seems to have been more often a sacred spectacle for the people than the primary source for their life of faith.

Will the liturgical renewal restore Christian worship to the center of artis-tic life? We cannot reply to that question without making some subdivisions.

1. To the extent that cult and culture are inseparable—because they are equally based on man's individual and social expression—we cannot doubt that the restoration to the faithful of active participation in the liturgy should bring about a kind of reconciliation between modern man and the signs of the Christian mystery. On the one hand, we may hope that contemporary

art may furnish worship with the living and partially new forms which it needs, especially in the sphere of congregational singing. On the other hand, the style proper to liturgical celebration, its characteristics of sobriety, transparence, and specifically Christian spirituality, should normally have some influence on the artistic expression of those who are nourished at this source. It is therefore to be expected that for the Church's faithful, and in the celebration of the Church's worship, art and liturgy should achieve a living interpenetration.

2. But can the Church make any claim to be the chief inspirer and patron of the arts in our modern civilization as she used to be in the past? Facts compel us to admit that there exists now a complete divorce between authentic liturgy, on the one hand, and public life and its arts on the other. Like our civilization, art has been secularized. It is more often a sign of man than a sign of God. Even when art does express a certain religious sentiment, this is very far from being that of the true Christian faith. Even works of the past, which were in fact inspired by the Christian spirit, are now accepted and appreciated as redounding to the credit of man and of his culture rather than as sources of the spirit of the gospel. The arts are playing their own game; they employ every available resource of modern technology; they celebrate their own achievements and those who brought them about; they constitute a human social phenomenon which is autonomous. Now the end proper to the liturgy is not the progress of human arts but the sanctification of the baptized for the glory of God. We must give up the idea that liturgical celebrations, in the performance of their music, ought to rival the standards of the concert hall, the radio, the theater, and the achievements of professional composers and performers. Their art is too equivocal in spirit, too different in plan, too heterogeneous in its productions to be directly allied to the requirements of a worship celebrated in spirit and in truth.

3. But, having taken note of these differences, even of these incompatibilities, we should not merely resign ourselves to them. The Church, the ark of eternal salvation, must even on this earth develop a new type of man by promoting a Christian culture, an evangelical civilization. A spirit of catharsis and wisdom must come forth from the Church, a spirit that should find expression in the liturgy to purify and turn to account every creation that is beautiful. The Christian must know how to welcome, outside his worship, everything that this age produces which is good, capable of intensifying his religious sentiments and those of all who feel drawn by the gospel. The task of "religious music" is important precisely because for the practicing Christian it extends the worship of God beyond the confines of the liturgy, and for the non-practicing it is an approach toward spiritual praise. In the second place, those of the faithful who collaborate in the artistic life of our civilization, whether as creators, interpreters or connoisseurs, must gradually infuse into it the supernatural light and warmth whose unique source is to be found in the Logos and in His Spirit.

10 POLYPHONY

AND MUSICAL INSTRUMENTS

From the standpoint of ritual action, liturgical music can only be monodic and vocal. Throughout nearly ten centuries of its history, Christian worship was in principle, and nearly always in fact, celebrated *una voce* and *a cappella*. The relatively late appearance of polyphony and the introduction of certain instruments are justified, therefore, not by the nature of Christian worship, which can always dispense with either, but by the interest which the celebrating community finds in them. They are admitted if they help the faithful in their common prayer, and in the measure to which they render it possible for the people better to approach the mystery celebrated by means of beauty expressed in music. Their reason is less ritual than pastoral.[280] Even if their introduction has sometimes partially reacted on the form of certain chants, this has not involved, in principle, any attack on the functional laws of liturgical singing; to these laws the use of polyphony and of musical instruments remains subject. In compensation, their importance can be considerable on

[280] "The Church has always held polyphonic vocal music in great honor. She has willingly given it a place at divine worship, not least in the Roman basilicas and for pontifical ceremonies, so that it may make the sacred rites still more magnificent. The power and brilliance of this kind of music were also increased by the fact that other musical instruments, besides the organ, were used to accompany the singers" (MD 5). N.B. The "always" (*semper*) at the beginning of the text above obviously means "since the appearance in history of the genre discussed."

the fringe of liturgy. In "religious music" they have prompted the emergence of new genres (sacred symphony, concert settings of psalms, oratorios, cantatas, etc.).

A. POLYPHONY

Polyphony, a word which means "many-voiced song," does not mean many voices singing the same melody together, but many voices singing different melodies at the same time. For a long time it was believed that plurality in melody was a creation of the Western Middle Ages; but the progress of ethnomusicology has shown today that this phenomenon is almost as widespread as music itself.

There is nothing surprising in this if one reflects on the natural diversity to be found among human voices. It is, in fact, a misuse of words to speak of "unison singing" if men, women and children are all singing the same melody; this is really an instance of elementary polyphony at the octave. Moreover, in each of the two registers there are high voices and low voices. If such voices are of narrow range and untrained, they naturally tend, as one may perceive with certain congregations, to sing a fourth below the melody if it is too high, or a fifth above the melody if it is too low, or they take other intervals which accord better with the modality in use among them. So true is this that we can recognize the classical division into four mixed voices of a choir made up of unselected personnel as being in accordance with the nature of things.[281]

In Christian worship, polyphony, which is choral by supposition, can be considered only for singing from the nave—for the people or choir. This being established, there is nothing in principle opposed to its use, provided that the functional laws of liturgical singing are observed. More than that, if those conditions are realized, polyphonic singing can be acknowledged as a beautiful sign or symbol of the liturgical community itself; for this is a unity in diversity, a single choir made up of diverse persons. Some of the Oriental rites which have adopted polyphony to a large extent testify to its very liturgical character.

Of itself, polyphony is compatible with all those songs from the nave which are not responses to some sacred minister (for these the canonical melody suffices). Technically it can be allied with all the choral lyrical forms, as also with the chief musical genres, recitative and air. However, it is more practical in the most popular melodic and rhythmic genres (syllabic and measured), and more difficult in the complex genres (melismatic air, spontaneous rhythm, or, by contrast, metric rhythm when this is complicated).

Polyphony, however, affords a new technical possibility which introduces an entirely novel element into the lyrical art; this is a vocal diversity due,

[281] On this subject see the reflections of M. Scriabine, "La musique d'enterrement," in *Le mystère de la mort et sa célébration*, LO 12 (Paris, 1951), p. 399.

not solely to the multiplicity of melodies, but to non-concomitant recitation
of the same text or to the superimposition of several different texts. Polyphony is thus divided into two great genres, according as the voices with different melodies sing the same words simultaneously (homophony), or sing the
same words successively at different times, or even sing different words
simultaneously (heterophony).

a) In simultaneous (*homophonic*) polyphony all the voices, though singing
different melodies, pronounce the same syllables of the text at the same time.
If one of the voices does sing a syllable "out of step," it is only for a moment
and occasionally in order to anticipate or retard some particular syllable
rhythmically, or to introduce a melodic ornament.

This is the most widespread form of polyphony, and it is found in many
musical cultures. In the West homophony saw the origins of polyphony in
the practice of the parallel organum (diophony) and then in descant involving contrary movement. Very soon the accompanying voices gained their
independence as regards the recitation of the text, and new forms arose.
Even so, homophony never disappeared from Western music and it continued to be cultivated especially in liturgical music. The most typical example
of it is found in the *faux-bourdon*, probably developed in Italy about the
fourteenth century; under various forms it has lived until our own day.[282]
On the fringes of the Roman liturgy are the collections of psalms and chorales
produced about the time of the Reformation; nearly all of them are entirely
homophonic. Finally, the abundant polyphony of the Oriental rites uses this
genre almost exclusively.

That homophonic polyphony is well suited to Christian worship is evident:
by its very nature it pays due regard to the communal recitation of the sacred
text without alteration. The word remains paramount; it imposes its rhythms
and its divisions on the music. We may add that it is also capable of use by
the congregation; though in practice we normally allot it to a choir, there
is nothing to prevent the whole congregation from taking part in it, provided that they have the taste and ability to do so and that the text is suited
to this treatment. Simultaneous melodic plurality establishes a correct equilibrium between words, song, and harmony; it has always been recognized
as expressing a sacred solemnity[283] and a religious fervor[284] all its own. It
provides the means to put at worship's service a part of the riches of musical

---

[282] See S. Clercx-Lejeune, "Aux origines du faux-bourdon," *Revue de Musicologie*, XI (1957),
pp. 151 ff.

[283] It is significant that the passage *Et incarnatus est*, traditionally emphasized in the *Credo*
since the eleventh century through devotion to the mystery of the Incarnation, is usually treated
homophonically in many of the Masses which, in all other parts, were written in imitative style.

[284] This is attested by the attraction constantly aroused, even among the Western peoples of
today, by the traditional classical music of the Slavic liturgy.—There are grounds for thinking
that homophony has not yet made its full contribution to the Roman liturgy because of the
heterophonic path taken by Western polyphony in the course of its development.

art, and to make the Church's prayer seem more noble, attractive and beautiful.

b) It was a logical development for polyphony to exploit musically the potentialities of its own nature by accentuating the individuality and independence of its voices. The resulting form of polyphony may be called *heterophonic*. Beginning with the ancient organum, the organal voices gained their autonomy. The thirteenth-century motet superimposed new melody and new text over the given liturgical chant and text. By means of complex counterpoints the *Ars nova* achieved polyrhythmic discoveries until finally there appeared the classical form of the Renaissance motet, in which every word or group of words, furnished with a definite melodic formula, is successively taken up in imitation by different voices. Until that time the entire composition was always governed by the *cantus firmus* which bound it directly to the given liturgical melody or text. Later on, each voice was treated as if it were an instrumental part. This involved the risk that the text would no longer be the material support of a composition now primarily musical, even if the work still tried to express its meaning.

Heterophonic polyphony, which superimposes different syllables, words or even texts in its different voices, has, from the time of its origin, confronted Christian worship with a difficult problem: the inversion of the text–music hierarchy. We have already examined the signs of it in the interventions which the Church has had to make on this point. She has never, in fact, ceased to recall and to maintain that the text must always remain audible.

The first famous intervention was that of Pope John XXII; confronted by the experiments of the *Ars nova*, he issued a decree from Avignon entitled *Docta sanctorum Patrum* in 1324-25. Its indictments are somewhat complex. It approves of consonances added to the traditional melodies, but takes exception to new airs, to the abandonment of the plainsong "modes", to the excess of disjunctive intervals, to mensuration, scansion, and division of time into semi-breves and ornamental minims, to the hockets and to the vernacular texts used in accompanying voices. In short, it warns against any too sudden break with tradition. But in a more definite way it requires that the "integrity of the chant as such should remain inviolate." Behind the irritated and not very well clarified reaction one can discern the intention of banning the musical spell, which "intoxicates the ears and benumbs the souls of the singers," in order to safeguard the primacy of the liturgical act of singing, which, according to tradition, ought to "keep the soul of each one awake without the words suffering." [285]

This decree did not succeed in halting the progress of heterophony, but that was never its intention. Still less did it succeed, as it should have done, in preventing the entry into the liturgy of the many excesses of an art which had become infatuated with its own learning. The decadence and liturgical an-

[285] A. L. Richter–A. Friedberg, *Corpus iuris canonici*, II, (Leipzig), 1256-1257.

archy which prevailed toward the end of the Middle Ages afforded plenty of opportunities for abuses. There were, indeed, a number of isolated protests made against them; [286] but the Church had to wait for the Council of Trent before they were clearly denounced, and for the reforms which followed the Council. Only by these reforms was a certain relative equilibrium restored.

The preparatory commission for the twenty-second session of the Council faced the question of figured music. Ought it not to be banned entirely from the Mass because of all the abuses to which it gave rise, and because it benefitted the ears rather than the spirit? [287] The general assembly on September 10, 1562, contented itself with requiring that all profane compromising should be avoided, and that the "words should be intelligible to all." [288] The definitive canon has not retained this last point. But it came into prominence again in the discussions of the commission nominated by Pius IV in 1563 to apply the decrees of the Council in the diocese of Rome. Under the presidency of Cardinals Vitellozi and Borromeo, there was an audition of chosen works on April 28, 1568, in order to decide whether the use of figured music did or did not permit of the hearing of the words.[289]

c) From the current of Tridentine reform was born a polyphonic style to which the name of Palestrina is attached, but in which Animuccia, Vittoria, Ingegneri and many others attained to eminence. This classical *polyphony* is a mixed genre between that of homophony and complete heterophony. The requirements of worship led those composers who were truly conscious of their role as Church musicians to a *via media* in which the word remained the soul of the music. Counterpoint stripped off its excesses, abandoned hockets and vocal flourishes. Imitations were limited to a group of syllables or words and became the principle of strict composition. Melody and harmony found their equilibrium. Taken as a whole, the result was admirable vocal music. These compositions, excellent from the musical point of view, are acceptable in the liturgy to the extent that they respect the function of the chants—something which the state of liturgy in those days rendered only partially possible.[290]

d) The rise of *symphonic music* and of the dramatic style was soon to compromise this beautiful equilibrium. Although the Palestrinian style remained

---

[286] See F. Romita, *Jus musicae liturgicae*, pp. 39 ff.

[287] *Concilium Tridentinum*, Acta, ed. Goerresiana, VIII, p. 918.

[288] *Ibid.*, p. 927.

[289] It was for this occasion that Palestrina is supposed to have written, among other things, his *Missa Papae Marcelli*. And in reply to the oral instruction given by Julius III to the Sistine choir: *quae proferebantur audiri atque percipi potest*, Palestrina is said to have answered that the fault was not that of music, but of the composers. About this session of April 28, 1565, see the texts of the diary of the Sistine choir in F. Romita, *Jus musicae liturgicae*, pp. 64 ff. On the question as a whole, see Cl. Rozier, "Éclairissements historiques sur trois points de musique sacrée," *Musique et liturgie*, 76–77 (1960), pp. 19–21.

[290] See chapter 13, pp. 202ff.

living before sinking into academism, pure heterophony recaptured its rights. The progress of instrumental music swept the choirs along in its wake, and there was an ever increasing tendency in the great religious musical compositions of the baroque age to treat the voices as self-sufficient parts, like the instruments themselves. Once again the text was drowned. In vain did Benedict XIV recall the golden rule of the primacy of the audible text.[291] Even though homophony, still occasionally used, could claim to observe the rule, the great fugal choruses rendered its observance quite impossible.

In his vigorous campaign for reform, St. Pius X clearly recalled in 1903: "The liturgical text must be sung as it is in the books, without alteration or inversion of the words, without undue repetition, without breaking syllables, and always in a manner intelligible to the faithful who listen." [292]

We cannot refrain from pointing out that, even in the use made of polyphony in our own days, the repertoire which is employed very often fails to comply with the clear norms imposed by the Church. It is true that the strictly musical problem is nowadays complicated by other problems which serve more or less as alibis. A text which is audible in itself does not thereby become intelligible to the faithful who listen to it if they do not know the language which is being sung. What is the use of requiring clear audibility for words which will not be understood? It can hardly be disputed that the use of a language unknown to the people renders us more easily unconscious or tolerant about this question of the intelligibility of the text, even though it be fundamental in liturgical singing. On the other hand, polyphony, by successive entries and independent voices, is, apart from rare exceptions, too difficult to be sung by the people. Of its very nature it can find a place only in the repertoire of the choir. But so long as the people cannot take any part in those items of singing which, by their nature, pertain to them, what object is there in limiting the art of the choir which has to perform them in default of the people? If, on the other hand, the various agents regain their proper role in the celebration, the result will be that heterophony can be employed only in a very restricted sphere of liturgical singing.

It would seem, then, that the heterophonic musical genre, except on certain very precise and limited conditions, is not capable of fulfilling the role of

[291] "If it is true, as we are informed, that figured music presents itself to the listening assembly as an object of pleasure because of the learned way in which the music is composed; if what the people relish in it is primarily the play of rhythm, the melody, the sweetness of the voices, and if most of the time *the words themselves cannot be clearly heard*; if all this is so, then in the future is must be the other way round. *The very opposite policy must henceforth prevail* in the Church's singing. The very first concern must be to ensure that the words can be clearly heard without any difficulty . . ." (*La liturgie . . .* , coll. "Les Enseignements pontificaux," [Paris, 1956], p. 56). Later, Benedict XIV develops this theme by the aid of many post-Tridentine conciliar texts.

[292] TLS 9. Pius XII says, more vaguely, that one must not "obscure the liturgical text by prolixity" (MSD 27). It is rather surprising that the *Instruction* of September 3, 1958, does formulate the principle of the primacy of the text.

humble servant to the texts and rites which the liturgy assigns to music. It can, however, find rightful employment in religious music and in sacred concerts.

B. MUSICAL INSTRUMENTS

a) The history of comparative religions proves that the use of musical instruments is almost universally allied with the phenomenon of religion.[293] By their power of charming, by their strange timbres—which are sought after as signs of the sacred by reason of their superhuman character—and even by the symbolism of their exterior forms, musical instruments have always filled an important ritual function of a mythical or magical kind.[294]

The attitude of the Church toward them is even more significant. In Christian worship the playing of an instrument all by itself has never constituted a religious rite properly so called.[295] A musical sound which accompanies no words is equivocal; even though capable of exalted spiritual meaning, it eludes the discursive intelligence if it be alone. Now, as St. Paul observes (1 Cor. 14), everything which is done in the assembly should be done for the "edification" of all (v. 26). What does this mean? The Apostle goes on to explain. Each one may have a psalm to sing (v. 26); but if this imparts no revelation, no knowledge, no prophecy, no instruction, "Thou, true enough, art duly giving thanks, but the other one's faith is not strengthened" (v. 17). In this case, as in glossalaly, the musician is "strengthening but his own faith" (v. 4). And the Apostle concludes: "What, then, is my drift? Why, I mean to use mind as well as spirit when I offer prayer, use mind as well as spirit when I sing psalms" (v. 15).[296] Already the irrational meaninglessness of his music is not overcome except with the aid of the *logos*.[297] But above all, its mythical ambiguity is not eliminated except by the revelation of the Christian mystery.[298] That is why Pius X, before discussing instrumental music, recalls that "the music proper to the Church is purely vocal music" (TLS 15).

---

[293] "Only one religion can give no place to music; it is the religion of 'No,' of nothing, of nirvana; the Buddhism of central India proscribes music in its worship" (G. Van der Leew, *La religion dans son essence et ses manifestations* [Paris, 1955], p. 369).

[294] See A. Schaeffner, *Origine des instruments de musique* (Paris, 1936).

[295] There is an exception in the case of bells; their sound, however, is a signal rather than music as such.

[296] Both the text and context of this passage have been given on p. 43. Calvin was but echoing St. Paul when he wrote in his preface to the psalter: "There is no edification where there is no doctrine." E. Kressmann, who quotes this, continues: "A composer can express his sentiments. Now these sentiments can be the fruit of faith, but must not be confused with faith because there can be no faith without doctrine; instrumental music is incapable of expressing dogma which only intelligible words can convey. It is a necessity in the Church: 'I will sing with understanding' " (*De la musique religieuse*, p. 84).

[297] "Music expresses the sentiments, but is not capable of defining them, and without the commentary of words, which are absent from instrumental music, the hearer always remains somewhat vague about the nature and object of the sentiment by which the musician is inspired" (P. Lasserre, *Philosophie du goût musical* [Paris, 1922], p. 43).

[298] See above, chapter 2, pp. 41ff.

b) As the Fathers of the Church observed, the use of musical instruments in Old Testament worship, abundantly attested to in the Scriptures, ought to be situated in the history of salvation; this shows the stages of a worship still carnal becoming more and more spiritual.

We should begin by noting that the various kinds of biblical instruments have very different relationships to worship.[299] One category is made up of the priestly instruments: horns (*shofar*) and trumpets. Their sound is a formidable and sacred symbol (the product of living breath), rather than a strictly musical performance. A second category is proper to the Levites and serves to accompany liturgical singing: harps (*nebel*) and lyres (*kinnor*). These stringed instruments, allied to the art of poetry, come much closer to music and to worship in spirit. As we see in the descriptions of the Chronicler, their playing strengthens and sustains the lyric word so effectively that those who play them are called "prophets" (1 Chr. 25:1-3). A third category comprises bells, reserved to priests and Levites of the highest rank, sistra, tambourines and cymbals, all of which have a place in the accompaniment of singing as being instruments of percussion. The flutes, pipes and oboes which make up the last category are lay instruments used in professional, family or social life, especially at marriages and funerals; they remain outside the sphere of liturgical worship.[300]

In spite of the more spiritual character of lyres and harps, instrumental music in the Old Testament never completely avoided the two dangers of ritualism and magic. Recalling the primacy of interior justice, Amos stigmatizes them as equivalent to bloody sacrifices:

> I hate and have rejected your festivities,
> and I will not receive the odor of your assemblies.
> And if you offer me holocausts and your gifts,
> I will not receive them;
> neither will I regard the vows of your fat beasts.
> Take away from me the tumult of your songs,
> and I will not hear the canticles of thy harp (Amos 5:21-23).

After the Exile, sacred instruments were confined to the liturgy of the Temple. Worship in the synagogues, genuine liturgy of the word, definitely excluded them.[301]

c) The New Testament fully confirms this evolution. Whereas singing

[299] See E. Gerson–Kiwi, "Musique" (in the Bible), *Supplément au Dictionnaire de la Bible*, V (Paris, 1957), c. 1415 ff.

[300] The mention of the *ugab* (flute or pipe) in Psalm 150:4 seems to be a poetic quotation as in Job 21:12 or 30:31. However, the *abub* (LXX: *aulos*; Vulg.: *tibia*) was probably used in the liturgy of the second Temple.

[301] There remained only the sounding of the *shofar*—an instrument for giving a signal rather than playing music, and more of a ritual than of an esthetic nature—on the great religious feasts of the year. The introduction of the organ into the synagogues of the West dates only from recent times.

always appears as a normal form of prayer and praise (Acts 16:25; James 5:13; Matt. 26:30) and even becomes the subject of positive legislation (Eph. 5:19; Col. 3:16), instruments receive only occasional mention, sometimes in connection with pagan customs (Matt. 9:23; 11:17; Luke 7:32; Apoc. 18:22), or explanatory comparisons (1 Cor. 14:7-8; Matt. 6:2; 1 Cor. 13:1; Apoc. 14:2), sometimes in an apocalyptic context where they have a symbolic value.[302] One never reads of Christ's disciples making use of them in their new form of worship. It seems, on the contrary, that St. Paul, strongly emphasizing the spiritual and interior nature of Christian music, desired to point out the comparative unimportance of its actual performance. The two characteristics which he retains: *to sing and praise God in one's heart* (Eph. 5:19; Col. 3:16) and *to sing psalms with understanding* (1 Cor. 14:15), concern vocal rather than instrumental music.

d) We cannot say definitely that during the patristic era Christians never made use of certain instruments, such as the lyre, to accompany their liturgical singing. Certain passing allusions or repeated prohibitions even lead to the conclusion that this was a well established practice.[303] Nevertheless the abundance and clearness of the texts in which the Fathers of the Church have

---

[302] This holds good for the trumpet, the signal of God's judgments, and especially of the Last Judgment (Matt. 24:31; 1 Thess. 4:16; 1 Cor. 15:52; Heb. 12:19, and eleven mentions in the Apocalypse). In our opinion it is true also of the harp which, according to the Apocalypse, the twenty-four heavenly ancients hold in their hands while singing the new song (5:8) and which the chosen victors of the beast used to accompany their singing of the Canticle of Moses (15:2).

Arguing from the principle that earthly liturgy is an image of the heavenly liturgy, and that the latter is necessarily symbolized and described in terms of the former, some authors have seen in the descriptions of the Apocalypse an echo of cultual practices usual among the first Christians (cf. F. J. Doelger, *Sol Salutis* [Munich, 1925], p. 128) especially in the case of the lyre, the most honored instrument of that era and one which was particularly suited to psalmody and hymnody. (J. Quasten, *Musik und Gesang*, p. 104). Certainly all apocalyptic imagery is based on something within human experience: attitudes at prayer, formulation of hymns, etc. But when the elect are described as "clothed in white robes, with palm-branches in their hands" (7:9), or "holding harps of God's fashioning" (15:2), and we are told of celestial hymns being sung by three or four choirs together (5:8-14), does that mean that in each of these details we have to see a description of the liturgical usages of the first generation of Christians? All this is but symbolic language of the apocalyptic genre; for our present purpose we cannot draw any certain conclusions from it.

[303] In this connection we must distinguish, on the one hand, between private playing of instruments and the customs at social-religious gatherings at which acceptable instruments were used, and, on the other hand, liturgical worship properly so-called in which there was nothing of the kind. Also Clement of Alexandria, after criticizing the use of diverse profane instruments at the "sober repast," that is, the *agape,* approves for this the use of the lyre: "If someone should discover you singing to the accompaniment of the harp or the lyre, you will incur no reproach; you are but imitating the just king of the Hebrews (David) giving thanks to God" (*Ped.* II, 4; PG 8, 444). St. Augustine makes mention of harp-playing during a funeral vigil in the chapel wherein lay the relics of St. Cyprian (*Enar.* II *in Ps.* 32, 5; PL 36, 279). On the other hand, canon 74 of St. Basil (Egypt, 4th–5th century) forbids the use of the lyre to every reader—even, it seems, outside worship—under the pain of censure: "Whenever a reader falls into playing a harp, he must confess it (?); if he falls repeatedly he will be excluded from the Church" (W. Riedel, *Die Kirchenrechtsquellen des Patriarchats Alexandrien*, p. 267).

discussed the question can leave us in no doubt about the content and firmness of their teaching: musical instruments are to be excluded from the worship of the New Alliance.

The motives adduced for this prohibition are of two kinds. The first motive for excluding musical instruments comes from the role they used to fulfill in ancient civilization and from their inseparable connection with idolatrous worship and depravity in morals. Even though the lyre could be accepted as respectable, the flute and the oboe were erotic instruments, the trumpet was bellicose and the organ, theatrical.[304] Thus, it was to reject the profane and to defend the sanctity of Christian worship that the Fathers excluded all the instruments in use in their day. In other times and circumstances this same principle was to have less severe requirements.

Another and more fundamental reason is developed by the Fathers: the use of material instruments was conceded by God to Israel, just as were sacrifices of animals, as a pedagogic measure to help their religious sense, which was still carnal.[305] With the coming of the Word and the imparting of the Spirit, the worship of the New Alliance consists in the sacrifice of the lips and the heart; it is expressed completely by word and song.[306] The playing of instruments, to which we are invited by the psalms we still sing, is verified to the full, not in the performance of music, but in the good actions of a Christian life: the true harp is Christ, our members are its strings, the orchestra is the Church.[307] Never can the vocal and spiritual praise of the Word

[304] For example, the entire Chapter IV of Book II of Clement of Alexandria's *Pedagogue* is very explicit. There he contrasts the Christian *agape* with the pagan banquets accompanied by their *aulos* and psalteries and cymbals and tambourines: "In truth these instruments should be excluded from the sober repast; they are more fitted to charm animals than men—or men deprived of their reason." He gives some examples; then he contrasts with them the songs of the Holy Spirit, interpreting in a purely allegorical way the instruments named in Psalm 150. He concludes: "The other (material) instruments are of no use . . . except for inciting to war, stimulating the passions, inflaming lust, arousing anger . . . We make use only of one single peaceful instrument, the *Logos*, by which we honor God; we do not use the ancient psaltery nor the trumpet nor the tambourine nor the *aulos*, accoutrement of the warlike . . . and of the dancers . . ." (PG 8, 440–444).

Many texts of a like nature can be found in M. Gerbert, *De cantu et musica sacra* (Saint-Blaise 1774), I, pp. 210 ff.; cf. H. Leclercq, "Instruments de musique," DACL, 7, 1161–1199; J. Quasten, *Musik und Gesang* . . . , pp. 1-6, 86-109; Th. Gérold, *Les Pères de l'Église* . . . , pp. 91-93.

[305] Thus Chrysostom: "Instruments were permitted to them out of regard for the weakness of their spirit, and because they had hardly emerged as yet from the cult of idols. Just as God allowed their sacrifices, so also He allowed their instruments, condescending to their weakness" (*In Ps.* 149; PG 55, 494).

[306] "The *Logos* of God, despising the lyre and the harp, soulless instruments, will rule by the Holy Spirit our world and especially this microcosm, man, his body and his soul: He uses this instrument of many tones to glorify God, and He Himself sings in harmony with the human instrument. 'For thou art for me a harp, a flute and a temple'; a harp by thy harmony, a flute by thy breath, a temple by thy reason, in such a way that one vibrates, the other breathes and the third shelters the Savior" (Clement of Alexandria, *Protreptic*, 1, 5).

[307] The allegorical interpretation of the Old Testament instruments is a *locus communis* among the Fathers. One might quote, among many others (see Th. Gérold, *Les Pères de*

of God be supplied or supplanted, in worship in spirit and in truth, by the sound of musical instruments alone.[308]

e) Nevertheless, once the singing is assured and the spirit is answering the voice, there is no reason why the choir of singers should not be supported or enriched by appropriate instruments. When the pagan culture of ancient times gave way to Christianity, the *aulos* of the courtesans and the organ of the comedians disappeared too. About halfway through the Middle Ages some musical instruments gained admittance into Christian worship.

Whereas the Byzantine rite has remained entirely faithful to the tradition of a purely vocal music, monodic or polyphonic, other rites have admitted certain instruments. But those admitted were not genuine musical instruments; they were but audible embellishments like little bells, carillons and cymbals used by the Armenians, Maronites and East Syrians. However, among the Copts of former times and the Ethiopians of today, instruments of percussion are used to mark the rhythm of the singing: sistra and rattles, drums and tambourines. At the time when these customs were introduced, it is probable that they were known in the West also. There are some manuscripts which lead us to think that the singers of the ninth century used to accompany themselves with castanets held in the hand.[309] But in all these cases the melody itself is executed by the voice alone.[310]

It was the Latin West which introduced genuine instruments into the liturgy either to accompany the singing or to play together. During the second half of the Middle Ages there appeared organs, vielles, rebecs, rotes, harps, guitars, lutes, psalteries, flutes, bagpipes, sackbuts and cornets; sometimes they supplied for or doubled the voices in polyphony, sometimes they accom-

l'Église . . . , pp. 125 ff.), the way in which St. Augustine interprets the playing of the instruments enumerated in Psalm 150: "It is you who are the trumpet, the psaltery, the harp, the tympanum, the chorus of dancers, the strings, organ and cymbals of jubilation, well sounding because concordant. It is you who are all these; there is no allusion here to anything despicable or ephemeral, or which would be mere amusement" (*Enar. in Ps.* 150; PL 37, 1965–1966).

[308] Pseudo-Justin (Syria, *ca.* 400) discusses the question: How is it that the faithful of the time of grace still make use of singing if it be true that this was granted to those of the time of the Law only because of their infantilism? And he answers: "It is not the act of singing which characterizes infantilism, but doing so to the accompaniment of inanimate instruments, dancing and shaking rattles. In the churches, therefore, the use of instruments and other childish things have been excluded from the singing, though singing itself has been retained." In truth, he remarks, "it is the word of God which, being understood, sung and heard, has power to banish the demons" in endowing the soul, by means of the Church's song, with the grace proper to faith (*Quest. ad Orthod.*, 107; PG 6, 1353–1355).

[309] See Th. Gérold, *Les Pères de l'Église . . .* , pp. 187-188. The interpretation of the text from Amalar about the *tabulae* (*De Eccles. Off.*, 16) has given rise to a controversy between J. Smits van Waasberghe and J. Jeannin in the *Revue du chant grégorien*, 36 (1932), nos. 2–6.

[310] According to Bar Hebraeus (a Syrian Jacobite of the thirteenth century) "All (?) the churches of the East and of the West" had adopted the organ in his day. But we do not know what sort of instrument this was, nor the use that was made of it. At any rate, it disappeared in the East with the Turkish invasion. In the West, on the contrary, it came into general use during the fifteenth century, though it was rare from the ninth to the fourteenth century.

panied processions which were enlivened by clerical or popular dances.[311] But the little information we have hardly permits us to specify exactly their relationship to the rites. Was their use habitual or exceptional? Was it really concerned with what we would now call liturgy, or only with other ceremonies of a more or less religious or folklore type?[312] Whatever may be the truth of matter, ecclesiastical customs in this sphere during this period of liturgical decadence should not now be regarded as having any normative value for us. Other sources imply that, in spite of the spread of these things in practice, the laws concerning them were not changed.[313]

f) A double phenomenon appears in the period subsequent to the Renaissance. On the one hand, there came a separation between vocal music (polyphony *a cappella*) and instrumental music, the development of which now permitted the appearance of the symphonic style and shaped the achievements of pure music. On the other hand, the Church, initiating and pursuing her reforms, was led gradually to clarify her attitude with regard to the use of musical instruments in her worship.[314]

At the Council of Trent there were denunciations especially of the many abuses which existed in church singing. Is this an indirect proof that instruments had no role as yet in worship? The only instrument mentioned in the decrees is the organ: its playing must be free from any element which would be *lascivum aut impurum*.[315] St. Charles Borromeo, at the Council held in Milan in 1565, does not admit of any instrument other than the organ,[316] and the same may be said of the *Ceremoniale Episcoporum* of 1600.

In spite of the firmness of ecclesiastical legislation, nothing stopped the

[311] We know that dances had invaded the rites from the number of conciliar texts which forbid them (see F. Romita, *Jus musicae liturgicae*, pp. 33 ff.) Dances and instrumental music have always been allied with each other.

[312] At this time there were no hard and fast lines of division between the sacred and the profane, between the liturgical, the devotional and the socio-religious; this may well have led to many dubious practices.—Note also that the examples normally given of the use of instruments, for instance on the feast days held by confraternities of minstrels like those of the Abbey of Fécamp in Normandy (see A. Gastoué, *L'Église et la musique* [Paris, 1936], pp. 114 ff.), or in processions, do not refer to genuinely liturgical celebrations. On the other hand, the exact role of instruments in polyphony, and their nature, are still matters of discussion among musicologists. Up till now, even the use of polyphony itself within the liturgy has not yet been sufficiently studied.

[313] Thus St. Thomas Aquinas (II^a II^ae, q. 91 a.2., ad 4) holds on purely and simply to the patristic position when he says the Church has excluded the instruments of the Old Testament, and that these "impress on the soul feelings of agreeable emotions rather than forming therein good interior dispositions"! At the same time Juan Egidio de Zamora, a Spanish Franciscan, historian and musician, notes that the organ "is the only instrument customary in the Church . . . all the others are normally excluded because of theatrical abuses" (quoted by H. Anglès, in Roland–Manuel, *Histoire de la musique*, [Paris, 1960], I, p. 1396).

[314] For the modern period, see the series of articles by G. Villior, "La musique instrumentale à l'Église," *Revue de Saint Chrodegand*, 1947 and 1948.

[315] *Sess.* XXII, September 17, 1562 (*Conc. Trid. Acta*, V, p. 963).

[316] "Organo tantum in ecclesia locus sit; tibiae, cornua et reliqua musica instrumenta excludantur" (J. D. Mansi, 34, 57).

symphonic wave of the baroque era nor the invasion of the church by sacred symphonies and orchestras. At the height of this period, about the middle of the eighteenth century, that great document, Benedict XIV's encyclical *Annus qui* (1749), reveals not only the general state of affairs then prevailing, but also a great liturgist's reflections on the facts. His position reveals careful thought. He adopts no extreme attitude. He begins by recalling the traditional exclusion of musical instruments, but then, with obvious sympathy, he gives the view of recent "authorities" and the arguments which had been adduced during the preceding few decades in favor of musical instruments. His conclusion is that "only the abuses should be reproved" (7). These consist, firstly, of the theatrical and profane musical genres, which are condemned outright (6). Then he tries to choose between the instruments which may be admitted and those which may not.[317] Next he defines their proper role in view of "a single principle": "These instruments must only be used to add, in some manner, a certain power to the words which themselves are the object of singing, so that the hearers may be more and more penetrated by the meaning of the words and that the faithful be thus led to give their attention to spiritual things."[318] But if instruments are played almost incessantly, drowning out the voices and the words, the right order has been inverted and this practice is to be condemned. Purely instrumental interludes are acceptable only when they are grave in style, and then only during the brief intervals which the office renders possible. In conclusion, he remits the application of these norms to the bishops.

This legislation, remarkable though perhaps too full of gradations, remained somewhat ineffectual. Not until the days of Pius X was the question taken up again in a clearly restrictive sense. The organ, which had been mainly a solo instrument in earlier times, became the usual instrument of accompaniment during the nineteenth century. Pius X "permits" it, provided it does not drown out the voices or interrupt the singing or the ceremonies. Other instruments are "tolerated," especially "a limited, judicious and proportionate selection of wind instruments," to the exclusion, however, of those which are "noisy or frivolous"; always the special permission of the Ordinary is required (TLS 15-21).

As these laws were applied in a somewhat haphazard manner, Pius XI returned to them forcefully: "We hereby declare that singing with orchestral accompaniment is not regarded by the Church as a more perfect form of music or as more suitable for sacred purposes. Voices, rather than instruments, ought to be heard in the church."[319]

---

[317] After consulting specialists, he accepts, besides the organ, the stringed instruments and the flute, because they "serve to reinforce and sustain the voice." But he excludes other instruments on account of their theatrical nature (11).

[318] (12). Translated in *The Liturgy* (Boston: St. Paul Editions, 1962), pp. 71-72.

[319] DC 7.

Pius XII was a little more mild. Having praised the organ,[320] he adds that "other instruments besides the organ can be called on to give useful help in the attainment of the high purpose of sacred music," and he names in the first place the stringed instruments.[321] He insists, however, on the technical proficiency required for their use.[322] Their employment is to be regulated by the local Ordinary.

g) The foregoing historical summary makes clear how complex and relative is the role of instruments in Christian worship. Taking actual legislation into account, let us attempt to disengage a few simple rules of judgment and conduct in this matter, which necessarily varies according to places, customs and musical cultures.[322a]

The fundamental principle: *vocal praise alone is essential to Christian worship*. Instruments are only accessory. The sacred ministers, who alone are envisaged by the liturgy as obliged to sing as soloists, are normally not to be accompanied. Instrumental accompaniment, then, comes into question only for choral singing, whether it be that of the assembly as a whole or that of the choir. In these cases the use of instruments is justified chiefly by the fact that they can render the singing more easy technically or more effective spiritually; hence their admission is to be assessed according to these two criteria. Secondly, instruments can reinforce the meaning of the rites, considered as a whole, by surrounding them with musical beauty; they should be admitted in the measure to which they clarify the mystery being celebrated. In practice, we must make sure that in applying this double principle we safeguard also the following three things: the primacy of the text, the sacred character of the instrumental playing, and its value as art.

1. In the liturgical act of singing, the text must retain the primacy which is its due. It must be easy to pronounce the words; the words must be the factors which determine the rhythmic and melodic development; the words must always be clearly audible.[323] Any kind of instrumentation which is

---

[320] To avoid repetitions, we are remitting everything that concerns the particular instance of the organ to the end of chapter 12, pp. 206ff.

[321] MSD 28-29. Pius XII was himself an amateur violinist.

[322] IMS 60-69. For the rest, nothing beyond the "sacred character" is required. This is a rather vague criterion, and it is surprising that it is not made explicit by any dicussion of the nature intrinsic to Christian worship, or by any reference to the ritual action or the text of the chants—such as Benedict XIV had rightly included—unless we count as such "the degree of rejoicing that marks the various days and liturgical seasons" (80). It is only the role of the organ which gives rise to some more precise observations (29 and 66).

[322a] Compare with the three points developed below, the conditions specified by CL 120 for the admission of instruments into divine worship: "Instruments other than the pipe organ may be admitted for use in divine worship . . . on condition that they are suitable, or can be made suitable, for such use, accord with the dignity of the sacred building, and truly contribute to the edification of the faithful."

[323] "It is to raise man's heart towards God that music has been adopted in the churches. As St. Isidore recalls: a musical instrument is used with the singing of sweet melody so that men's hearts may be swayed to compunction (*De Eccl. Off.*, I, 5). If such be the purpose, i'

sensuous or redolent of the dance, which relegates the words to the status of mere sounds, every profusion of timbres which drowns out the voices, is incompatible with spiritual worship.

It follows that instruments or groups of instruments can be, according to their nature, more or less suited to accompany choral singing. As the whole of ancient tradition shows, light percussion instruments constitute the family nearest to the fundamental lyrical art: they help the rhythm of the singers while leaving them absolute freedom as regards melos and word.[324] Among the melodic instruments, experience shows that wind sustains community singing better than strings. The excellence of the organ as an instrument for accompanying liturgical singing comes primarily and above all from the certainty and cleanness of its playing. On the other hand, it is rare that the blare of a fanfare or the full body of sound from a large string orchestra fails to predominate at the expense of the sung text or restrained celebration of the rites. The compatibility of melodic instruments with singing requires also that their design and technique should be suited to the music which is used; many melodies of the Oriental rites or of African peoples cannot be accompanied by our instruments, tuned to the tempered scale, without distortion of their exact intervals.[325]

At those moments when the liturgical action does not envisage any singing or audible praying, and when silence is not prescribed, the playing of instruments by themselves—especially of the organ—may be admitted in an accessory role. Pure music then offers a wordless and mysterious commentary on the rites, beyond the sphere of discursive intelligibility. In this case it is suitable that the supra-rational eloquence of the musical art should really impart a message and be received by the assembled faithful, not as a mere pleasure for the senses or a satisfaction for the mind, but as a way, complementary to that of the word, toward the supernatural truths.[326]

will be with difficulty attained on the supposition that the words would not be understood" (Benedict XIV, *Annus qui*, 9, in *The Liturgy*, pp. 66-67).

[324] It is a pity that in our civilization these instruments are hardly used except for profane music, and in a form which is very remote from worship. But in some of the missionary countries, such as Africa, they might well be the first to gain admission into worship. In the Ethiopian liturgy we find an example which is as eloquent as it is traditional. A recent Javanese Mass accompanied by a percussion orchestra gives a splendid illustration of this truth.

[325] It is well known what ravages have been made in the liturgical music of the Orient by Western classical harmony, and by the harmonium in certain missionary countries.

[326] R. Will draws a parallel between the role of pure music in Christian worship and the primitive charisms bestowed on certain members of the assembly whereby they expressed themselves in unknown tongues: "Religious music can be considered as an element analogous with glossalaly: a Bach fugue, a prelude by Palestrina, or even the improvisation of an organist who is both competent and pious can be felt as the outpouring of religious minds which is of an irrational character beyond expression in articulated words. But because musical understanding is not given to everyone, such musical glossalaly can never be substituted for liturgical prayer" (*Le Culte*, I, p. 232).—Pure music and glossalaly both, indeed, stand in need of interpretation, and to gain admittance into the liturgy, both ought, as St. Paul requires, to minister to "edifica-

2. That it may in no way damage the holiness of Christian worship, the playing of musical instruments has to be free from all connection with idola-trous, profane or worldly practices. In this respect there is a very great differ-ence between the patristic era and our own day, and between European countries and certain of the mission lands. Quite astonishing transformations are possible in the course of time, as in the case of the organ, which was once a theatrical instrument but is now a sacred instrument; or, to adduce a con-trary example, the zither, at one time held in great esteem, has now become an instrument for mere pleasure, a guitar for popular songs. Differences of this sort can be observed in other continents or cultures. So every distinction between classical and profane instruments is only relative and impermanent. The choices which the Church has, in fact, made during the course of her history are indicative, but they always remain subject to revision.[327] We may add that the sacred or profane character of an instrument does not depend solely on its construction but still more on the way in which it is played. Thus organ-playing is not of itself sacred.[328] What a difference there is be-tween the drum-rolls of our bands and the delicate touches of the tambourine in the Ethiopian liturgy, between the fanfares of a village brass-band and the hieratic unison of brass sustaining the song of a great crowd in a cathedral!

3. A third condition—which receives timely attention in the latest docu-ments[329]—concerns the technical standard required in the playing of instru-ments if they are worthily to serve the sacred chant or action. This question hardly arose as long as no instruments were used except those of light per-cussion demanding but slight executive ability. But the appearance of melodic instruments raised a problem: sung prayer or silent prayer can be very much disturbed if the playing of such instruments is too elementary, their technique too laborious, or their tone disagreeable. It is one of the great advantages of the organ that it so quickly attained a technical standard which did away with these inconveniences. Stringed instruments also happily reached a com-

tion." But they differ from each other in that one originates in a purely natural inspiration while the other comes from the Holy Spirit; moreover, every normal man can immediately derive some kind of benefit from the former provided it is suitable in kind, whereas the second can effect nothing except through an interpreter.

[327] To decide which instruments should be admitted, and which excluded, the *Instruction* relies on "common estimation" and on the directives of the local Ordinary (60, 68, 69, 70).

[328] The adoption of the organ as the Church's instrument par excellence has sometimes been used as a pretext for introducing into worship an organ repertoire (baroque, romantic or sym-phonic) which is quite foreign to the liturgical style and utterly out of place in the enactment of the sacred mysteries. As things are, there is a contrast in the liturgy between an almost excessive severity concerning the place of certain instruments and a surprising toleration of some forms of organ playing.

[329] "In view of the nature, sanctity and dignity of the sacred liturgy, whatever instrument is employed should normally be used in the way that is most perfect musically. Accordingly it will be better to dispense altogether with instrumental accompaniment, whether by organ alone or by other instruments, rather than to permit an unworthy performance" (IMS 60a. For the organist, see 65; cf. MSD 29).

parable or even superior ease quite early in their history, but it is only quite recently that wood-wind, and especially brass, have become capable of that flexibility, finesse, and certainty that are required. Played by competent musicians in a style suited to the occasion, these instruments are capable, beyond all doubt, of sustaining a role in support of the singing which equals, and in some ways even surpasses, that of the organ. This is something to which they could make no claim only a short time ago.[330]

The comparatively late appearance of vocal polyphony and of instruments in the liturgy leads us to conclude as follows: although the lyrical forms which constitute liturgical singing were all to be found in the tradition of those centuries which fixed the main outlines of Christian worship, and were so well developed that later centuries have added nothing of real importance to them, yet vocal polyphony and instruments have had a considerable influence on sacred music as a whole. This influence has not always been a happy one. It has caused serious alterations in forms and genres, for example in several items of the Ordinary of the Mass.[331] Still, it can be maintained that in the pieces less strictly bound up with the ritual action, such as hymnody from the nave—and *a fortiori* in extra-liturgical music—the evolution of music has had an influence on worship which is welcome. Provided that nothing impedes the ritual function of the singing, the division of roles allotted to the various agents, and the lyrical forms inscribed in the texts, the choral parts of the liturgy remain open to all the various ways in which the art of music can be of service to the rites. What happened since the Middle Ages, in differing ways in the Byzantine East and the Latin West, to the diverse genres of polyphony and various musical instruments may happen all over again in yet another way when the liturgy meets and assimilates other musical cultures which also know of several genres of singing different melodies together and the use of different sacred instruments.

[330] This holds good especially for music which is essentially monodic in type; to support this with harmonies on the organ is often treason. An oboe blends with the voices of children or of women, and a bassoon with those of men, so perfectly that they seem to melt into each other. Strings do not offer this same quality.—Others have already denounced the instrumental heresy which consists in the massive use of strings in our full orchestras (see, for example, A. Schaeffner, "Genèse des instruments de musique," in Roland–Manuel, *Histoire de la Musique*, I, pp. 110 ff.).

[331] In J. A. Jungmann, *Mass of the Roman Rite*, one can read the description of the way in which Mass used to be celebrated in the baroque era, in order to understand the extent to which the sacred rites had become overlaid by the music. Think, for instance, of the Holy Week services in which each Lamentation was turned into a concert piece: Benedict XIV in *Annus qui* makes detailed mention of these deformations and roundly condemns them (see *The Liturgy*, pp. 70ff.).

11 THE SUNG PORTIONS

OF THE ROMAN MASS

Knowing the functional laws which regulate the use of singing in Christian worship and the factors governing its musical performance, we must now determine the practical application of all these things to each sung portion of the liturgy.

This application involves two stages: the recognition of what each ritual chant implies in virtue of its function, its agents, its lyrical form, its musical genre, and its general performance; then the suitability of works of art from the past or present with regard to these characteristics. These are the matters we shall study successively in our final chapters.

The most important of celebrations, the Mass, should be our first object of study; and for us that means the Roman Mass. In considering the sung portions of the Mass, we shall not take each of them in the order in which it occurs during the celebration. Such a course would have the double disadvantage of bringing out neither the hierarchy of importance among these sung portions, nor the relationship which some of them have to others. We shall regroup them in classes according to the closeness of their connection with the sacred action. We will examine successively the readings, prayers, and hymnody. After what we have said in the preceding chapter, it should suffice to indicate summarily the characteristics of each piece.[332]

---

[332] It would be impossible to discuss the history of each item, even though a knowledge of this is often needed to understand, in the light of their evolution, the actual state of the various

A. THE READINGS

In this first class occur the following elements: the formal reading of *Holy Scripture* (Epistle, Gospel) and the specialized reading which is the responsorial *psalm* (Gradual). And we classify with them the proclamation of faith (*Credo*) and the directions given by the deacon.

a) *The Formal Readings: Epistle and Gospel*

Function. The announcement of the revealed message in the form of the solemn proclamation of a passage from Holy Scripture. A primary and essential element of Christian worship.

Agents. A minister of the sanctuary: deacon for the Gospel, subdeacon or lector for the Epistle or Lesson.

Lyrical form. Direct. But the people reply to the announcement of the Gospel with an acclamation: *Gloria tibi, Domine.*

Musical genre. Prose recitative on a melodic formula.

Performance. The melodies to be used are canonical and of obligation, whether they be those contained in the liturgical books or others preserved by local custom.[333]

b) *The Responsorial Psalm: the Gradual*

Function. Meditative [334] reading of a psalm, or of an extract from the Old Testament, after the Epistle. This is the oldest and most important of the psalms in the Mass. This constitutive element of evangelical liturgy has recourse to inspired poetry to repeat the prophetic message in lyrical form

rites. For historical information consult: J. A. Jungmann, *The Mass of the Roman Rite, Its Origins and Development*, New York, 1959; J. Froger, *Les chants de la messe aux 8°–9° siècles* (Tournai, 1950); A. G. Martimort, *L'Église en prière*. For the liturgico-musical aspect of each item, see the articles by B. Staeblein in MGG (with their bibliography); and J. Gelineau, "Fonction et signification des principaux chants de la liturgie," *Église qui chante*, 1959–1961.

[333] The formal singing of the readings in the liturgy does not happen nowadays except in Latin. The proclamation of God's word to the people in their own language, prescribed by many episcopal directives, may not at present be sung. Because the living practice of reading in a way which spontaneously becomes rhythmo-melodic whenever it is solemn, sacred, or poetic has almost died out in our culture (cf. above, note 54), this is, perhaps, no bad thing. Yet one cannot help asking whether this is a step forward or an impoverishment. Does not the proclamation of God's word lose something of its sacred character and penetrating power by not being sung? The almost universal occurrence of rhythmo-melodism in the various cultures suggests that it does perhaps contain some value which we have allowed to be lost. However, this is a trend which is not of itself irreversible. One of the characteristic aspects of the contemporary renaissance of song—whatever be its value—is revealing on this point: it consists essentially and in the first place of "saying something while singing it" (in contrast to the former romantic style in which the charm of the melody was considered as justifying all sorts of nonsenses in the words); this is something often quite close to rhythmo-melodism, which might well come into its own again among us in certain too rationalized types of speech. At any rate, in many of the mission countries the use of recitative in reading Holy Scripture in the vernacular would not only be easy, but its omission would seem abnormal.

[334] See above, chapter 6, pp. 78ff., and J. Gelineau, "Fonction et signification . . . : I. Le graduel," *Église qui chante*, 18 (1960), pp. 2–7.

directly communicable to all. It is the original fount of the Christian people's knowledge of the psalms.

Agent. Originally the verses were recited at the ambo by a specially appointed reader, the psalmist. All the people used to interpolate a short refrain between the verses. As things are now, what corresponds to the ancient refrain is a somewhat long text sung only once by the *schola* or the choir. The psalm is represented by a single verse, sung by the choir, or by several cantors.

Lyrical form. Responsorial. The psalmist alternates the verses with the people's refrain, which was normally taken from some psalm. At present there is no responsory; the Gradual presents but the simple succession AB.

Musical genre. Recitative of simple formula type for the verses; an easily memorized popular melody for the refrain. At present the refrain is in the neumatic genre suited to the choir, and the verse is highly melismatic.

Performance. In the solemn liturgy as it is now, if the Gregorian melodies are used, the Gradual cannot be anything but a time of silent meditation for the faithful; however, they are not likely to rely on listening to the text, for this is practically impossible. A performance of a psalm-tone setting comes much nearer to the authentic genre, but it does not restore the responsorial form. If it is not a solemn Mass, this form can be used.[335] Heterophonic polyphony would be quite out of place here, but homophony would be acceptable for the refrain.

c) *The Profession of Faith: the* Credo

Function. To formulate and recall the rule of faith. It is attached to the readings because of the "tradition" or "handing-over" of the Creed which the Church used to conduct originally for the catechumens, later for the baptized. In the East a Creed was inserted into the Mass about the sixth century, and then in Rome it was included on Sundays and feast days since the eleventh century. As a summary of the Christian mysteries, it brings the evangelical liturgy to a close; and as an explicit formulation of *mysterium fidei*,[336] it prepares the faithful for the eucharistic liturgy.

Agents. Of itself, it is in the form of an individual profession of faith ("I believe"); but in the Latin liturgy it is to be recited collectively after the celebrant has intoned it. The entire congregation is supposed to sing it.

Lyrical form. Traditionally direct, and by all. But alternation by two bodies of singers has become customary.

Musical genre. A statement of faith calls for some kind of recitative, free or measured, which will preserve the dogmatic formulation of the text.

Performance. The Gregorian melody which bears the title "authentic" cor-

---

[335] It would then be in order to choose several of the most interesting verses from the psalm, and to supply it with a suitable refrain.

[336] See J. Gelineau, "Fonction et signification . . . : VIII. Le Credo," *Église qui chante*, 31–32 (1961), pp. 4-7.

responds perfectly to the function of the Credo.[337] Other melodies might well be more popular.[338] Homophonic polyphony might sound better, if it is compatible with the people's part (harmonizing or alternating with their singing). Extensive developments in the form of "musical compositions" are not suited to this profession of faith, which is intended simply to be recited and not dramatized.

d) *Directions by the Deacon: the* Ite missa est

Function. Since it is the function of the deacon to "make proclamations," [339] his directions may be classified with the group of readings. Only one diaconal direction remains in the Roman Mass: the dismissal which terminates the eucharistic liturgy, from which the very name "Mass" originates. It is simply an announcement to the assembly that the office is terminated.

Agent. The deacon; if there is no deacon, then the priest-celebrant.

Lyrical form. Dialogue, for to the deacon's announcement the people reply with an acclamation: *Deo gratias.*

Musical genre. Recitative. The neumatic and even melismatic genre which later invaded the *Ite missa est* is clearly contrary to the nature of this direction, as also to that of the acclamation which answers it. It ought to retain the character proper to melodies from the sanctuary.

Performance. That this may be good, the music ought to be simple, because the deacon is not necessarily a specialist in singing the chant, and the people ought to be able to reply unanimously. The most apt melody, and probably the oldest in the Vatican *Kyriale,* is that of Mass XV.

B. THE PRAYERS

Prayers (taken in the broad sense) which occur as ritual chants in the Mass are of two kinds. The first consists in the great *eucharistic prayer* comprising Preface-Sanctus-Canon. The second is the *prayer of petition* properly so called; it occurs at different times and in different forms: the common prayer of the faithful, the litany of intercession (*Kyrie*), the litany of supplication (*Agnus Dei*), the *Pater,* and the prayers of the celebrant. Let us take a brief look at each of these.

a) *The Great Eucharistic Prayer: Preface-Sanctus-Canon*

Function. The celebration of the eucharistic sacrifice consists, together with the repetition of what our Savior did at the Last Supper, of a great prayer

---

[337] *Credo* I of the Vatican *Kyriale. Credos* I, II, V and VI are all derived from a single Greek source.

[338] This question will arise in acute form with any change in language and in culture. For it is impossible to deny that to recite a profession of the Christian faith in a form which does not ensure the direct understanding of what is professed, is something particularly contradictory.

[339] See note 126.

of thanksgiving whose unity ought to be clearly apprehended. Bridging over those prayers of the Canon which are now inaudible, there is one single movement which makes a unity stretching from the Preface—opened by the initial dialogue (*Dominus vobiscum*, etc.) and crowned, since the fifth century, by the *Sanctus*—to the concluding doxology with its final *Amen*.[340] Its purpose is to announce by means of the word, and to make present by means of the sacrament, the great mystery of our salvation accomplished in Jesus Christ. But the priest-celebrant whose office it is, as president of the assembly, to pronounce this praise, does not do it merely in his own name. Although the consecration is done by him alone, he gives thanks and makes intercession on behalf of the whole Church; with her he offers and is offered, saying in the name of all present: *Offerimus*. That is why he does not begin his noble and solemn praise (Preface) without seeking assurance that all are united with him in one mind and heart (initial dialogue); that is why his song does not end without bursting forth into a hymn (*Sanctus*) to which the entire assembly of co-celebrants, in communion with the angels, unite themselves. The memorial, the epiclesis and intercessions follow in graver tone, until at the end the thanksgiving for the New Alliance mounts up, through the Son and in the Holy Spirit, to the Father, ratified by an *Amen* from all.

Agents. There are two: the celebrant who formulates the thanksgiving, and the rest of the assembly which expresses its adherence in faith. Thus the fundamental structure, hierarchic and organic, of the liturgical community is manifested. It is therefore a serious deformation of right order if the three interventions by which the co-offerers should manifest their participation in the mystery of Christ's eucharistic action—initial dialogue, *Sanctus*, and concluding *Amen*—are taken over by a choir or cantor.[341]

Lyrical form. The eucharistic prayer is a very complex work in five sections whose variety and close mutual connection are equally remarkable. We find successively a dialogue, a direct solemn recitative (Preface), a common acclamation (*Sanctus*), a more subdued recitative (Canon),[342] and the ekphonesis and final *Amen* reminiscent of the beginning.

The *Sanctus* is a common acclamation by all the people, who associate themselves by two biblical texts with the heavenly praise of the Seraphim (Is. 6:3) and with the triumphant messianic cry of the people of God welcoming thier Savior (Ps. 117 and Matt. 21:9). Sometimes this acclamation

---

[340] We have already tried above (ch. 3, pp. 39ff., and in note 41) to sketch the wonderful lyrical movement of this song of praise. See also L. Deiss, "Le chant du Sanctus," *Église qui chante* (1957), I, pp. 5-8, and 2, pp. 9-12.

[341] On the *Sanctus* as people's song, see the historical study by J. Batteux, "Le Sanctus du peuple chrétien," *Opus Dei* (1960), pp. 140–164.

[342] Anyone who has understood that at the heart of the eucharistic prayer is situated the supreme proclamation of the mysteries of Christ who died and rose again as these are continued in the Church (supreme, because it effects what it says), cannot be indifferent to the condition to which the vicissitudes of evolution have reduced this part of the liturgy.

has been treated as the alternating song of two choirs; this has, indeed, some symbolic justification from Isaias 6:3 (the Seraphim "cried out to one another: Holy, holy, holy"). But the direct form seems more suited to the nature and function of this song.

Musical genre. The initial dialogue, Preface, and conclusion of the Canon are, in the Roman liturgy, provided with obligatory melodies: they are absolute masterpieces which remain models of functional liturgical chant.[343]

For the *Sanctus* there is also a melody which is a continuation of the recitative of the Preface (*Sanctus* XVIII) and which alone can be regarded as authentic. In every way, by its brevity and its syllabic and quasi-recitative genre, it meets the requirements of this piece. For the melody for the *Sanctus* ought to be such that everyone can sing it, and yet it should not interrupt the movement of the great eucharistic prayer.

Performance. The only practical question arises in connection with the *Sanctus*. Apart from *Sanctus* XVIII, the accepted Gregorian melodies are not well suited to their purpose.[344] Other monodic compositions may be used. Polyphony would not be out of place, provided that the chief part is left to the people, and provided also that its style runs no risk of making it stand out too much through a too violent contrast to the Preface and the recollection of the Canon. A performance reserved exclusively to a few voices would be contrary to the spirit of this piece, which is the most important of all the collective songs in the Mass. The same may be said of unduly long compositions, which would spoil the unity of the great eucharistic prayer. For the rest, a certain musical splendor supplied by polyphony and even instrumental accompaniment is no unfitting way to express the universal praise suggested by the *Sanctus* and to enhance the ringing of bells: *Pleni sunt coeli et terra gloria tua!*

b) *The Common Prayer of the Faithful* (Oratio fidelium)

Although it is no longer found in the Roman Mass, we mention here the *Oratio fidelium*, which used to have a place between the liturgy of the word and the eucharistic liturgy. Our reason for doing so is that, according to comparative liturgy, it was the most important of all the intercessory prayers, and because in theory it must still be ranked as one of the constitutive elements in the celebration of Mass. We give no description of it, for at present

---

[343] The recitative of the ferial Preface is, in its purity, of incomparable beauty. It far surpasses the *tonus solemnis*, whose ornaments seem superfluous. As regards the *tonus solemnior*, which contrasts so badly with the noble words it accompanies, the less said about that pretentious and inflated composition, the better. It is regrettable that the *tonus solemnis* is prescribed for Sundays and feast days, so that the *tonus ferialis* is in practice relegated, as far as the faithful are concerned, to funeral Masses (*New Code of Rubrics*, 515–516. The *tonus solemnior* is not even mentioned).

[344] *Sanctus* XVI suggested by IMS (25b) as a melody for universal adoption is not really well suited for its purpose; the melody is passable but the rhythm is rather vague.

it has no liturgical form.[345] However, since there may be occasion to make use of such a prayer after the sermon or during some non-solemn celebration, we may well recall that its characteristics are the same as those of the litany of intercession.[346]

c) *The (Diaconal) Litany of Intercession: the* Kyrie eleison

Function. Duplicating the liturgy's Common Prayer of the Faithful, a diaconal litany of intercession was inserted into the entrance rite of the Mass during the fifth century. The invocation *Kyrie eleison* reveals its Greek origin.[347] Having assembled in Christ's name, the community, after the entrance procession of the celebrant, feels the need to pray for the intentions of the universal Church. In ancient days they did so—as those of the Oriental rites still do—by associating themselves with the intentions proposed by the deacon, replying together: "Lord, have mercy."

Agents. In its original form the litany of intercession was carried out by two partners: the deacon who directed the prayer, and the people who replied to it. Now that the invocations have disappeared, the nine responses remain as a song from the nave. By their nature, therefore, they belong to the assembly of the faithful. Ordinarily, however, they are distributed among several groups of executants: two choirs, or *schola*–people, or soloist–*schola*–choir, etc.

Lyrical form. In theory this is binary: (A) intentions; (B) brief response. In practice, with nine responses grouped in threes (as they have been since the Frankish era), the result is an alternation. But the usual alternation between two choirs does not fit in well with the division of the text into three-times-three. This really calls for a ternary division in responsorial form, something which is also in accordance with the Gregorian melodies normally used.[348]

Musical genre. Even when deprived of the intention proposed by the deacon which should specify a motive for each invocation, the litany remains a cry of appeal and of supplication. Now it is not natural for a cry for help to spring forth in prolonged, complicated, and subtle melismata. Rather, it takes natural form in intense cries quickly repeated, not in refined, drawn-out

[345] Except perhaps that of the Solemn Prayers of Good Friday and the fourth section of the Litany of the Saints (*Te rogamus, audi nos*). See chapter 12, pp. 177ff. In consequence of the restoration in principle of the Prayer of the Faithful by the Second Vatican Council (CL 53), a definitive text for it will be worked out as part of the reforms in progress at present.

[346] See the study of the forms of this prayer given in chapter 7, pp. 94ff.

[347] Early testimony of this from the Roman liturgy is the "Prayer which Pope Gelasius ordered to be sung for the universal Church." See above, note 187, and J. Gelineau, "Fonction et signification . . . . , II. Le Kyrie eleison," *Église qui chante*, 19 (1960), pp. 4-9.

[348] Ordinarily these have a melodic theme for the first three *Kyrie*'s, a different one for the three *Christe*'s, and a return of the first theme for the last group of *Kyrie*'s, in which the final invocation is prolonged by some amplification of the formula. The mode of performance that would be most reasonable would be to have three executants or groups for each series, for example: (1) soloist, (2) choir, (3) people (and this would make the people's participation much easier).

melodies. The *Kyrie* at the beginning of the litanies of the saints offers an excellent example. We cannot deny that in some cases the sentiment of supplication can find expression in long melopoia, yet a common call for help is expressed with more sincerity, power and cohesion in short formulas, more like a cry which a man shouts out than like a song which he develops.[349]

Performance. The Gregorian repertoire offers a varied selection of melodies, several of which correspond very well with the *Kyrie's* cry of supplication.[350] Homophonic polyphony is quite suited to the litanic response. By contrast, compositions which destroy the effect of insistent repetition characteristic of this kind of prayer, or which reserve such repetition to a mere part of the assembly, are a departure from due form.

d) *The Litany of the Fraction: the* Agnus Dei

Function. In ancient times, while the sacred ministers, in imitation of the actions done by our Lord when instituting the Eucharist, were breaking the consecrated loaves for distribution to the people in Communion, the people themselves used to sing a *confractorium*, a song to accompany the fraction. From the time of Pope Sergius I (687–701), this song was the *Agnus Dei*; it is a cry of supplication to the Victim who, by His sacrifice, takes away the sin of the world. As things are at present, this chant, though still retaining its meaning, comes just after what remains of the action it was originally intended to accompany.

Agents. It is a song for the people or, in default of them, for the choir.

Lyrical form. It is in the form of a litany which has three invocations: *Agnus Dei, qui tollis peccata mundi*, and then three responses to these: *Miserere nobis (Dona nobis pacem)*.[351] The alternations between two choirs sometimes used for this piece are quite arbitrary.

Musical genre. The typical melody is given to us at the end of the Litany of the Saints and in Mass XVIII of the *Kyriale*. It is related to the other chants of the Mass, corresponds in every way with the function of this piece, and is a model of what such a chant should be. However, a setting to a neumatic recitative or to an air would not be out of place.

---

[349] As may be observed in several other instances (Gradual, long responsories, etc.), atrophy of the text is compensated for by hypertrophy of the melody: cutting out the intentions of the *Kyrie* has fostered development of the invocation; this being now isolated, a consequent cut off from its antecedent, musicians felt impelled to forge a connection between the different invocations by welding them into one continuous composition.

[350] This is true of *Kyrie* XVI, proposed by the 1958 *Instruction* for universal adoption (except for the end of the last *Kyrie*, which raises a difficulty by introducing a variant, and by its cadence in the third mode, which is too subtle for many ears). *Kyrie* XVIII is without doubt the finest example of this genre. On the modalism of this piece, see note 421.

[351] Because of the kiss of peace which now comes just after this song, the third *Miserere nobis* has been replaced, since the tenth–eleventh centuries, by *Dona nobis pacem*. The special formulary *Dona eis requiem (sempiternam)* used in Masses for the Dead dates from this same period.

Performance. The litanic structure of the texts suggests a corresponding mode of performance; most of the Gregorian settings lend themselves well to this.[352] But a polyphonic setting can be excellent, especially if it is homophonic and provides opportunity for the people to reply: *Misere nobis.*

e) *The Prayer of the Assembly before Communion: the* Pater noster

Function. In the Roman rite the *Pater noster* has appeared, for a long time, to be the sacerdotal conclusion to the Canon. But according to the findings of comparative liturgy, the Lord's Prayer is above all the most perfect preparation of the faithful for their Communion.

Agents. As things are at present, the priest sings the *Pater* at a sung Mass, the people singing only the conclusion. But in a low Mass the people may say the whole prayer.

Lyrical form. Direct enunciation by the celebrant until the final petition, which is prayed by all.[353]

Musical genre. Prose recitative, to a melodic formula.

Performance. The canonical melody of the Roman rite is a universally acknowledged masterpiece.[354]

f) *The Prayers of the Celebrant: Collect and Postcommunion*

Function. A prayer of petition formulated by the celebrant as a conclusion for the rites of entry and of Communion.[355]

Agents. Enunciated by the celebrant; ratified by the people.

Lyrical form. Direct enunciation, preceded by a dialogued greeting (*Dominus vobiscum*) and an invitation to prayer (*Oremus*), followed by a conclusion from all (*Amen*).

Musical genre. Recitative to a formula based on rhythmed prose (*cursus*).

Performance. Its melodies are obligatory, according to the books of the Roman rite, or to local custom.

C. HYMNODY

Hymnody concerns those items in the Mass which, from the musical point of view, are the most important, even though from the ritual point of view

[352] Most of the settings in the *Kyriale* (fourteen out of the twenty) provide an invariable melody for the response. Some of them (XVIII, I, V, VI, VII) also use the same melody for each of the initial invocations. These, which render possible an indefinite number of repetitions, are probably the oldest. Others have a variant at the beginning of the second invocation; in several instances the entire second *Agnus Dei* is quite different from the others.

[353] The Mozarabic liturgy used a responsorial form: the people interjected an *Amen* after each of the petitions.

[354] The collective recitation of the Lord's Prayer, at the present time merely spoken, really calls for the rhythmo-melodic form in all the languages and cultures which would permit of this. It would thereby gain enormously in ease of performance, in beauty, and in dignity.

[355] Originally the Secret also was a sung prayer; its subject matter is not the people, but the offered gifts. This perhaps explains why it is not preceded by a greeting.

they are the least essential. These pieces fall into two groups: *processional psalmodic hymnody*, which comprises the antiphons for the Introit, Offertory and Communion (and with these we classify the *Alleluia* before the Gospel); and *free hymnody*, which includes the *Gloria* and the Sequences.

a) *The Song of the Entrance Procession:* Antiphona ad Introitum

Function. To accompany and solemnize by psalmody (since the fifth century?) the entrance of the celebrant and his ministers; to involve the community in prayer by turning their minds and hearts toward the mysteries about to be celebrated.

Agents. By its nature this psalmody is the concern of the whole assembly: verses to be recited by a psalmist and refrain to be sung by all. But if the people do not in fact sing the refrain, this is supplied by the choir to which the people listen.

Lyrical form. Antiphonal, that is, psalmody sung in the antiphonal manner. The form comprises at least two elements: (a) psalm verses sung by a soloist, intended to be listened to; the psalm as a whole is represented at least by its first verse [356] and the doxology; (b) an intervenient refrain sung by two choirs. As things are now, this refrain consists of a text, psalmodic or not, which is rather long and is reserved to the choir; it is sung at least at the beginning and at the end of the piece. There is no trace now of any alternation between two choirs.

It is impossible to say whether this long verse is original in the Roman Mass.[357] The oldest antiphonaries, in fact, give a different *versus ad repetendum* taken from the psalm. It is probable that this brief psalmodic text was the genuine interpolated refrain of a psalmody which later became enclosed between the more developed antiphon and its repetition.

Musical genre. For the verses, a simple recitative according to accepted formulas; for the long refrain, a developed melody, neumatic in style, closely connected with the text and expressing the meaning of its words. We do not know how the *versus ad repetendum* was sung, but because this was the affair of all the people, we can deduce that it must have been syllabic. The contrast between the sobriety of the verses and the relative splendor of the refrain explains why interest became concentrated on the latter rather than on the former—of which only the number of verses required to fill up the time taken by the procession were sung.

Performance. The Introit readily offers scope for the art of music, as is

---

[356] Or, if the first verse of the psalm was used as a refrain, by the second verse.—The *Instruction* of 1958 suggests that other useful verses might be brought back into use.

[357] When the Introit was first introduced into the Roman liturgy, was it a psalm? Did it have, from its very beginning, a long refrain reserved to the choir? a short refrain for the people? or both? and was the refrain sung alternately by two choirs, as the authentic form of antiphonal singing would suggest? (cf. note 202 above). We cannot answer any of these questions with certainty. Cf. the additional note 202a.

proved by the Gregorian melodies themselves. Everything should conspire to produce a sense of festivity in the community: emphasis on the text chosen for use as an antiphon, melodic or polyphonic developments by the choir with, if possible, an interpolated refrain by the people and even judicious accompaniment by instruments. The verses of the psalm, because of their solo performance and recitative genre, will always remain a distinct element within the composition; a simple psalm-tone or a *faux-bourdon* would suit them well enough, but not heterophonic polyphony nor an air in the strict sense of that word.[358]

b) *The Song of the Offertory Procession:* Antiphona ad Offertorium

Function. To accompany and solemnize, by the aid of psalmody, the procession in which the faithful presented their offerings,[359] for "God loves the cheerful giver" (2 Cor. 9:7). Nowadays this procession does not take place except on rare occasions,[360] but its accompanying song has survived. It is now performed during the actions and prayers whereby the priest makes ready for the sacrifice.

Agents. According to evidence originating from Africa and from Milan, this psalmody was the concern of the entire assembly (verses by a psalmist, refrain by the people) until the fourth or fifth century. But from the time when it was adopted in Rome it seems to have become an antiphon executed by the choir.

Lyrical form. Antiphonal. The verses by the soloist, which have now disappeared, are still to be found (though not very plentifully) in the old manuscripts. The refrain which survives, whether psalmodic or not, is a rather long text; repetitions of text sometimes found in it may be a trace of the former alternation by two choirs, which is an element characteristic of antiphonal psalmody.[361] On the other hand, there is no evidence of any *versus ad repetendum.*

Musical genre. This remains somewhat free because of the lack of ritual precision of this song. It might be a Gregorian or a polyphonic antiphon, or a restored form of psalmody with a people's refrain; even instrumental interludes could be admitted. If some form of procession is restored—whether an Offertory procession in which the faithful bring up their gifts, or one in which the clergy carry these to the altar—then a more precise adaptation

[358] Apart from the solemn celebration of the Mass, it is not self-evident that the Introit song must always consist of psalmody. Provided that it suits the mystery of the day, a hymn or chant, which often allows a greater measure of participation by the faithful, may well fulfill the same function of accompanying the entrance procession.

[359] Not, as in the East, the "Great Entry," wherein the gifts are brought up by the clergy; this is something totally different from what is described in the *Ordines Romani.*

[360] Papal Masses of canonization, ordination Masses, and funeral Masses with "offertory."

[361] See note 202.

of the singing to the function will be required.[362] In any case, a period of silence before the Preface is both desirable and traditional.[363]

c) Song of the Communion Procession: Antiphona ad Communionem

Function. This song is the most ancient and the most important of the processional songs of the Mass. It is intended to accompany and solemnize the Communion of the faithful. More than at any other point in the Mass, the singing here should express the fraternal charity which unites the communicants and the paschal joy which fills their hearts. In the beginning, hymns were used for this purpose, but later on the inspired psalms (especially Psalm 33) replaced them. During the period when the faithful hardly ever communicated, this song was relegated to the time of the ablutions, but in our own day its eucharistic and communal importance is again being recognized.

Agents. All those who receive Communion; they should meditate on the verses sung for them by the psalmist, reply to him with a simple and contemplative refrain, and listen to the antiphon by the choir.

Lyrical form. Beyond doubt it used to be responsorial, but in the Roman rite it was made to resemble the songs for the Introit and Offertory. In our books there is nothing left of it except the old "long verse" of the choir. The text of this is sometimes drawn from the psalms, sometimes from the Gospel of the day, sometimes from a different source. But in manuscripts of the eighth century we find, as for the Introit, a mention of the psalm (executed by the psalmist) and of a *versus ad repetendum*, which appears to have taken the place of the true refrain (sung antiphonally by two choirs?). Because the ornate antiphon of the choir could not normally fulfill this role, it was probably used to begin and to end the whole piece. Just as the Introit psalm was brought to a conclusion by the *Gloria Patri* and a final repetition of the *versus*, so also the same was done here when the distribution of Communion came to an end. The restoration of the psalmody is nowadays encouraged.[364]

Musical genre. Just as for the Introit, the verses of the soloist ought to consist of a simple and easily audible recitative. In the Gregorian repertoire the antiphon of the choir is in neumatic style, usually quite unassuming; it follows the words and expresses the meaning of the text. If the *versus ad repetendum* was used as a refrain, its melody must have been simpler still.

Performance. The singing for the Communion calls for a certain recol-

---

[362] If the faithful again come up to present their gifts, as has been requested in certain mission countries, then it would be desirable that they sing a responsorial psalm, hymn or chant. If a sacred minister is to carry up the *oblata*, such as the hosts to be consecrated, then some chant analogous to those used in the East would be needed.

[363] The commentators of the Middle Ages insist on this (e.g., Innocent III; PL 217, 832). The usefulness of such a pause is more than ever apparent: after the sustained attention required by the liturgy of the word, a time of silence is needed so that this attention can become renewed and intensified when the time comes for the great eucharistic prayer.

[364] IMS 27.

lection in the spirit of intimate union and joy. If the verses of the psalm are to aid the meditations of the communicants, both the role of the soloist and the recitative style are indispensable. And if there is to be a refrain for the people, it must be easy enough to be sung by them as they approach the holy table and meaningful enough to lead them to contemplate the sacred mystery. For the opening antiphon of the choir the Gregorian melody is preeminently suitable; but the judicious use of polyphony would be acceptable also. If the distribution of Communion lasts a long time, so that uninterrupted singing would become tiresome, it is a good plan to include some interludes by the organ.[365]

d) *The Song before the Gospel: the Alleluia and Tract*

Function. Although it occurs as an intervenient chant during the office of the readings, we classify the *Alleluia* as processional hymnody because, in the Roman rite, it wears the aspect of a joyous paschal acclamation accompanying the solemn Gospel procession and the coming of the Savior in the form of His word, rather than that of the meditative reading of a psalm. The Tract, which replaces it in the important Masses of penitential seasons, is, on the other hand, nearer to psalmody properly so called.

Agents. In principle, the acclamations of the assembly, sometimes supplied by the choir, reply to the soloist who intones the *Alleluia* and sings the verse.

The Tract, however, contains no response; though it was undoubtedly sung by a soloist in former times, it is now usually taken over by the choir.

Lyrical form. Responsorial (aA'bA'). The *Alleluia* is its refrain; and a verse, which may or may not be taken from a psalm, goes with it.[366] The Tract is direct psalmody of certain chosen verses, often performed by two alternating choirs.

Musical genre. In the Gregorian melodies the *Alleluia* undergoes an important melismatic development known as the *iubilus*; the verse of the soloist which is added to this is also highly ornate. The exultant character of this paschal acclamation sufficiently explains why it has undergone such a melodic ornamentation. But from the time when this development reached

---

[365] Apart from the solemn liturgy, it is quite in order to use well adapted hymns, of which ancient tradition offers many beautiful examples (Greek, Celtic, Milanese), or similar chants.

[366] The history of the Oriental rites shows that this chant used to contain several verses or even entire psalms (cf. *The Armenian Lectionary of Jerusalem*). In any case, it was originally alleluiatic psalmody. But in the Roman rite little remains of this chant except its connection with the Gospel which follows. It is an acclamation, to which a verse is conjoined. In some of the eighth-century antiphonaries, some of the Masses lack any specified verse; this was taken at choice from an *ad libitum* collection. The lack of any connection between the *Alleluia* and the verse is shown also by the fact that only the comparatively late compositions manifest any melodic unity between the acclamation and the ornate verse. Moreover it may well be questioned whether, in more remote times, the Roman liturgy always included an *Alleluia* after the Gradual. The description of the Mass given at the beginning of the *Hadrianum* says: *gradale* (sic) *seu alleluia*—which points rather to a single *psalmus responsorius* which might be alleluiatic on certain days.

a certain degree of complexity, it has become impossible for the acclamation to be repeated except by the choir. We may well doubt whether this state of affairs is original.[367]

The Tract borrows the formulary melodic structure of psalmody, but in an ornamented form.

Performance. The *Alleluia*, which is deprived of its full meaning if there is not in fact a Gospel procession, should retain its festive attraction. It would be difficult to find any music which rivals in beauty certain of the Gregorian *iubili*. If sung by a choir, these do not offer any special difficulty; but if the acclamation is to be repeated by the people, there must be a very careful choice, or else simpler melodies must be adopted. According to the Western concept of the *Alleluia*, there would be no place here for polyphony. In any case, the text of the verse should ever remain clearly intelligible.

The Tract may be sung according to the ornate Gregorian melody or according to a *faux-bourdon*. But in every case it should be possible to hear distinctly the inspired words of the psalm which is being sung.

e) *The Great Doxology: the* Gloria in excelsis

Function. Although at first this was a hymn of morning praise, this very ancient and venerable Christian hymn gradually found its way into the entrance rite of the Roman Mass on feast days, as a praise of the divine glory and a prayer to the Lord Jesus. It complements the supplication of the *Kyrie* by the sentiments of thanksgiving essential to Christian prayer.

Agents. It is a hymn of the community intoned by the celebrant (formerly a privilege of a bishop, who turned toward the people) and continued by all present. In later days clerics and cantors alone became responsible for singing it.

Lyrical form. Artistic prose, allied to biblical poetry, employing binary or ternary parallelism in short phrases, freely grouped or interconnected. Of its nature it calls for the direct form, yet would not exclude alternations. In the monodic genre, performance by two alternating choirs has become the general practice.

Musical genre. Beyond doubt the most ancient and typical melody is that given for the *Gloria* of Mass XV in the Vatican *Kyriale*:[368] it is a syllabic

---

[367] There is explicit evidence, from the fifth century in Syria, that the people did in fact repeat the *Alleluia* in the Mass. This would have been possible only with a simple melody. Sometimes the melismata of our Gregorian *Alleluias* have been likened to the jubilant vocalizations referred to in sundry texts by St. Augustine and others (see above, ch. 1, p. 26 and note 20); cf. Th. Gérold, *Les Pères de l'Église . . .*, p. 120, in order to prove how ancient they are. But that is too hasty a comparison. Even if they be prompted by the same spirit, one cannot explain ninth-century music by texts from the fourth and fifth centuries, especially if one notes that the texts do not make any explicit mention of the word *Alleluia*.

[368] This should be compared with the melody of the ordinary Ambrosian *Gloria*, which is more recitative in style. The Instruction of 1958 proposed, with very good reason, that *Gloria* XV should be adopted for universal use. On this piece, consult *Église qui chante*, 26 (1960), pp. 3–9.

recitative of the formulary type repeating the same pattern eighteen times. The other Gregorian settings, which are airs according to their genre, are more concerned to bring out the text; nevertheless they hardly depart from the syllabic style. This was preserved also in the earliest polyphonic compositions of the fifteenth century. The kind of music which best suits this piece is something in the nature of a popular melody.

Performance. The *Gloria* should be a lively and joyous praise, a confident and adoring supplication from the disciples of Christ. The Gregorian melodies offer plenty of choice, though they are not equally popular. Homophonic polyphony, of which there is an interesting repertoire, is well suited to the character of this piece, especially if it provides opportunity for the entire assembly to sing. Heterophony, on the other hand, runs the risk of changing somewhat radically the function of this hymn within the celebration.

f) *The Sequence*

Function. The Sequence was introduced into the Mass indirectly by way of tropes of the alleluiatic *iubilus* (ninth century) as a development of the intervenient chants in the office of readings. It became very popular during the Middle Ages. Once the constitution of the *Antiphonarium Missae* was complete, lyricism found at this point of the Mass a suitable place for its effusions, which proliferated for several centuries. The Roman liturgy has preserved only five Sequences.

Agents. Although these songs were very popular, it seems that in practice there were sung chiefly by clerics and cantors.

Lyrical form. A typical Sequence is made up of pseudo-verses, often rhymed, grouped in small strophes which answer each other, two by two, according to the principle of isosyllabism (more or less tonic rhythm), and permitting two choirs to sing the same melody one after the other.[369]

Musical genre. Typically an air in measured rhythm with a basic beat or rhythmic mode.

Performance. There seems to be no reason why these compositions—which are of but secondary interest in the Mass—should not be sung to the original music. But in that case their authentic rhythm ought to be restored.[370]

In spite of the seeming monotony of the preceding nomenclature, one cannot help being struck by the great variety of songs which find a place in the Roman Mass. Among the fifteen pieces which it includes, there are hardly two which are alike. Each one stands out according to the way in which it occurs in the celebration and the specific form which results from this. Such diversity, fully respected by the more authentic of the traditional

---

[369] See ch. 7, p. 108.

[370] The square notes of our liturgical books make it impossible for us to guess the length of the notes in the authentic, often metric, rhythm of these pieces.

melodies, shows not only fidelity to the liturgy but also artistic richness. In the course of history there have been attempts to treat all these pieces according to a single genre, or to bind them together in one "great musical composition"; such attempts, in spite of their apparent formal unity, always risk replacing the logic of the rites by some particular esthetic. The unity of a single

	RITE	FUNCTION	CLASS	AGENT
ENTRANCE RITE	Introit	Processional song of entrance	Psalmodic hymnody	[Psalmist-people] (choir)
	Kyrie	Prayer of intercession	Litany	[Deacon]-people (choir)
	Gloria	Doxology	Free hymnody	People-(choir)
	Collect	Concluding prayer	Prayer	Celebrant-people
LIT. OF THE WORD	Epistle	Reading	Reading	Sacred minister
	Gradual	Psalmodic reading	Pure psalmody	[Psalmist-people] (choir)
	Alleluia	Acclamation for Gospel procession	(Psalmodic hymnody)	[Psalmist-people] (choir)
	Gospel	Reading	Reading	Deacon
	Credo	Profession of faith	(Hymnody)	People-(choir)
EUCHARISTIC LITURGY	Offertory	Processional song of offertory	Psalmodic hymnody	[Psalmist-people] (choir)
	[Secret]	Prayer over the gifts	Prayer	[Celebrant]
	Preface	Thanksgiving	Prayer of praise	Cel.-people-cel.
	Sanctus	Acclamation	Free hymnody	The assembly
	[Canon]	Great Eucharistic prayer		[Celebrant] Conclusion: people.
	Pater	The Lord's Prayer	Prayer	[Assembly] (Celebrant)
	Agnus Dei	Song to accompany fraction	Litany	Cantor-people (Choir)
	Communion	Processional song of communion	Psalmody (psalmodic hymnody)	[Psalmist-people] (Choir)
	Postcommunion	Concluding prayer	Prayer of supplication	Celebrant-people
	Ite missa est	Monition for dismissal		Deacon-people

Square brackets show the authentic form of the rite, which is not being observed in the liturgy as at present celebrated. The parentheses show that the present practice has been modified. When the word "Gregorian" is italicized, this indicates that the ritual melody is of obligation.

whole has never been compromised by the diversity of styles and genres of its parts, provided that these were themselves authentic. The riches of the mystery revealed to us by the eucharistic rites are so inexhaustible that the signs intended to impart them can never be other than multiform, as regards both words and music.

FORM	GENRE	REPERTOIRE AND PRACTICE	
		High Mass	Low Mass
Antiphonal	Ant: air (ornamented) Verse: Psalmodic recitative	Gregorian or otherwise	Psalm or hymn
Responsorial	Melodic recitative or otherwise	Gregorian or otherwise	Prayer of intercession
Direct (or alternating)	Melodic recitative or air	Gregorian or otherwise	Short hymn
Dialogue and direct	Pure recitative	*Gregorian*	—
Direct	Pure recitative	*Gregorian*	—
[Responsorial]	℟: air (ornamented) ℣: Recit. (ornamented)	Gregorian	Responsorial psalm
Responsorial	Air (ornamented)	Gregorian	—
Direct	Pure recitative	*Gregorian*	
Direct (alternating)	Melodic recitative or air	Gregorian or otherwise	—
Antiphonal	Ant: air (ornamented) Verse: (recit. ornamented)	Gregorian or polyphonic	(Hymn) or prayer of intercession —
[Direct]	[Recitative]	—	—
Dialogue and direct	Recitative	*Gregorian*	—
Direct	Melodic recitative or air	Gregorian or otherwise	Gregorian or otherwise
[Direct]	[Recitative]		—
Direct	Recitative	*Gregorian*	—
Responsorial	Melodic recitative or air	Gregorian or otherwise	Gregorian or otherwise
[Responsorial] (Antiphonal)	Ant: air (ornamented) Verse: Psalmodic recitative	Gregorian or otherwise	Psalm or hymn
Dialogue and direct	Pure recitative	*Gregorian*	—
Dialogue	Melodic recitative	Gregorian	

12 OTHER SONGS

OF CHRISTIAN WORSHIP

The celebration of the Eucharist, the summit of Christian worship, is surrounded by a great number of other ceremonies, some strictly liturgical and others not, which call for singing to a greater or lesser extent. In the most important of them (the liturgy of feast days, solemn Divine Office, funerals, processions of various kinds), almost all the texts are sung. In others, singing is mingled with spoken texts (sacraments, blessings, *pia exercitia*, etc.).

It would be impossible to do for these what we have attempted to do for the Mass, namely, to consider and analyze separately all the ritual chants from each ceremony of the Pontifical, Breviary or Ritual. Many of them have functions and forms analogous to some of the sung parts of the Mass. But many are different, and for this reason we must give them some attention. To study them we shall begin by regrouping them into classes: litanic prayers, psalmody, psalmodic hymnody, free hymnody. Nevertheless, the singing which is strictly liturgical does not by any means cover the entire field of religious singing. There are other pieces, which we may group together as hymns, that are of value to the faithful. The main functions and forms of these will be our second subject of study.

A. VARIOUS ITEMS OF LITURGICAL SINGING

The sung items which can be classified as *readings* in the strict sense (lessons, lives of saints, homilies, *capitula* in the Breviary; prophecies, lessons, readings of the Passion during Holy Week) do not call for any discussion different from that which we gave to items of this class occurring in the Mass.

a) Among items classified as *prayers*, prefaces of consecration (ordinations, Paschal Vigil, etc.) or of blessing (*praeconium paschale*) are analogues of the great eucharistic prayer. And collects are analogues of those in the Mass. But there are other kinds of community prayer, not found in the Mass, which deserve mention.

1. The *Solemn Prayers* of Good Friday are the most venerable item of this type. In a developed lyrical form [371] they furnish the best extant example of community prayer bringing the service of the word to a climax.

2. The *preces* which the Divine Office retains for some of the Hours in penitential seasons are another kind of developed community prayer leading up to the concluding prayer of the celebrant.[372] On a very simple recitative, a series of versicles in binary form, which are sometimes psalm-phrases and sometimes ecclesial intentions, is sung in alternation between a soloist and the assembly, the whole being concluded with the *Pater noster*.

3. The *Litanies of the Saints* sung at the Paschal Vigil, on Rogation Days, at ordinations and on other similar occasions, at present appear in the Roman rite as a complex whole comprising, after the opening *Kyrie eleison*, a series of invocations of the saints (*Ora pro nobis*), penitential petitions (*Libera nos, Domine*), intercessions for the Church (*Te rogamus, audi nos*) and the *Agnus Dei*; then a psalm, some verses in the form of *preces* and a series of collects. The history of the text of this important prayer is but little known. The long list of saints is doubtless the result of a late development, but the second part has preserved a very ancient type of penitential prayer, while the third recalls the old *Oratio fidelium* both by its content and its form.[373]

These litanies have a twofold function: (a) collective prayer of *supplication*—in accordance with the Greek etymology of that word—chiefly penitential in character; (b) processional singing. The word *litania* is often understood as a synonym for a "procession with singing." [374] Clergy and people take an equal part in this, generally under the direction of one or several cantors or of a choir. The form is, in fact, typically responsorial; it includes, after the variable invocation of the soloist, a common petition expressed in a repeated formula: *Ora pro nobis*; *Libera nos, Domine*; *Te rogamus, audi nos*. Some ancient documents inform us that on certain occasions the litanies comprised five or seven repetitions, perhaps by different choirs; but apart from the opening invocations (*Kyrie . . ., Christe . . .*) and the *Agnus Dei* at the end, we do not know the texts which were thus repeated.[375] But we must call

---

[371] See above, ch. 7, p. 95.

[372] Like the *Kyrie eleison* retained in the Hours of the monastic Office.

[373] Diaconal litanies give the intentions in the form of invitations, whereas here the petitions are in direct form, more reminiscent of a priestly prayer of intercession.

[374] In the *Ordines Romani* almost every movement from place to place seems to be accompanied by a litany (Cf. H. Schmidt, *Hebdomada sancta* [Rome, 1957], pp. 861–866).

[375] Doubtless the initial *Kyrie* and final *Agnus* were thus repeated; there may well have been repetitions also of the invocations to the saints, a section which, in the Gelasian text, contains

attention to this mode of performance because it corresponds so perfectly with the very nature of a litany.

As regards musical genre, it is a recitative formula that is called for. We may well ask whether it did not originally have a measured rhythm; for measured rhythm is particuarly well suited to the genius of responsorial singing when it has short responses occurring at close intervals.[376] We find, in fact, that the genre "air" has become very popular in recent centuries for modern litanies, especially the Litany of Loreto.

b) Psalmody in the strict sense contributes the greater part of liturgical singing outside the Mass. It appears with differing functions and forms.

1. The main form is responsorial psalmody after a reading, corresponding to the *psalmus responsorius* (Gradual) of the liturgy of the word in the Mass. The chief witnesses to this are the *responsories* which follow the Old Testament readings in the office of Good Friday (Psalm 139 and the Canticle of Habacuc) and in the Paschal Vigil (Canticles of Moses and of Isaias).[377] These pieces have undergone the same changes as the Gradual: from being a modulated reading by the psalmist from the ambo with a refrain by the people, they have become ornate melodies for the choir on just a few verses.[378]

More typical are the *short responsories* which follow the *capitulum* in monastic Lauds and Vespers and in the Roman Little Hours. In spite of the fact that, from a certain period, non-psalmodic texts have been used for some of the feasts and commons, the function of this psalmody remains clear enough. The same may be said of its abbreviated responsorial form (one verse and the *Gloria Patri* with the *responsio a latere*). The formulary and syllabic kind of melody used both for the refrain and for the verses are the purest extant witness of the musical genre which is proper to responsorial psalmody.[379]

The *long responsories* which follow the readings at Matins are, in principle, analogous pieces. Originally these were genuine responsorial psalmody; but with the elaboration of new texts and variations of the melodies they have now become psalmodic hymnody.

only a few names. But we can hardly imagine repetitions of this kind in the section which resembles the *Oratio fidelium*.

[376] Many African chants provide a living witness of this. The employment of "number" in chants of this kind gives them an astonishing power.

[377] Until the restoration of the Holy Week liturgy by Pius XII, these pieces used to bear the unfortunate name of "tract." Their title *responsorium* has been restored, but not their responsorial form.

[378] In Rome, however, the canticles of the Paschal Vigil seem to have retained their correct name for a long time (even if the people did not have any part in them), as is proved by the documents of the "Roman chant." Cf. H. Huglo, "Notes historiques à propos du décret sur la Vigile pascale," *Revue grégorienne,* 1952, p. 131.

[379] We have already pointed out (note 142) the relationship between many of these melodies and the oldest Latin psalmodic refrains which survive in the Office.

2. Responsorial psalmody in the strict sense is used, secondly, as an accompaniment to certain rites, especially in processions. Its psalmodic refrain enables the people easily to take part in the singing. It is found in a restored form during the procession on Palm Sunday (Psalms 23 and 46), during that of Candlemas (Canticle of Simeon) and in the rite of the dedication of a church. It seems to have held an important place in days gone by during Rogation and other processions. It is found also during the adoration of the Cross on Good Friday (Psalm 118 with the antiphon *Ecce lignum*). But in many of these instances it has been changed into the direct or alternating forms,[380] or even into that of a long processional responsory.

3. Alternating psalmody by two choirs forms the largest part of the Divine Office. Its function is to be the opening prayer of the Hours, leading up to the series of fundamental elements: reading, singing (responsory), prayer. This initial psalmodic section was greatly developed under the influence of monasticism. In the ancient morning and evening parochial offices we find only a few carefully chosen psalms or biblical canticles, and these always in the responsorial form.[381] It was the ascetics and the monks who caused the offices of the Hours to be preceded by continuous extracts from the psalter recited in its entirety.[382] For a long time the purely antiphonal form was used (verses by one or two soloists, brief refrains alternated by the two choirs of the assembly). Psalms were normally grouped in threes and concluded by the doxology. About the seventh century some intervenient pseudo-refrains were inserted, with long texts and ornate melodies (troparia, stichera in the East; our antiphons in the West); the performance of these compromised the original structure of the antiphon. In the West the antiphon finally was sung only at the beginning and at the end of the psalm. Then the verses, having now become consecutive, were sung collectively by two alternating choirs.[383] The simple recitative formula was retained for the verses, perhaps even becoming simplified and systematized for the purpose. The antiphons, on the other hand, are frequently of the neumatic genre. Later still came the *faux-bourdon*, generally alternating with plain chant. The use, fortunately not continued, of polyphonic antiphons, as also the replacement of these by organ interludes, is still further removed from antiphonal psalmody. It is

---

[380] As we may see in the case of Psalm 69 of the Rogations and other processions of the Roman Ritual.

[381] Such as Psalm 62 for the morning office in Antioch (according to Chrysostom), the three biblical canticles of the Saturday night vigil (according to Etheria), or Psalm 140 for the *Lucernarium* (evening office) in nearly all the rites.

[382] Nevertheless each psalm (or psalm-section) was always followed by a prayer, silent or in collect form.

[383] The history of the way in which psalms came to be recited collectively by two alternating choirs has not yet been written. It would seem that the spread of this practice was much later than some people think, and that even until in the Middle Ages psalm verses were still recited by soloists. The adoption of collective recitation can first be substantiated by Cluny, and the practice, then doubtless new, was hotly discussed.

only in the invitatory at Matins (Psalms 94) that antiphonal psalmody has been preserved, though without alternation between two choirs.

c) Two kinds of pieces originating from psalmodic hymnody, both degenerate forms of responsorial and antiphonal psalmody, are found in the liturgy, especially in that of processions. They are the *great responsory* and the *anthem*; the latter, in turn, has several forms according as it diverges more or less from psalmody.

1. As in the case of the long responsories of Matins, the responsorial psalmody for processions evolved toward the creation of large-scale musical compositions such as those found, for instance, at Candlemas (*Obtulerunt*) and on Palm Sunday (*Ingrediente*). They have kept the name of responsory. The old books contain numerous examples. The responsories at funerals (*Subvenite, Libera me*) belong to the same group. The texts are only rarely from the psalms. The form remains responsorial, but normally employs the *responsio a latere*. The musical genre is neumatic in type, but may include melismatic elements. In the response proper, the melody usually follows the words and meaning of the text. The verses, by contrast, often have the structure of a typical psalmodic formula but somewhat developed. As a consequence of the melodic genre of these pieces, the performance of the verses is reserved, as is fitting, to soloists, but that of the refrain requires a *schola* or a trained choir. Finally it should be noted that the text can be heard only with difficulty. Many of these pieces have given rise to polyphonic compositions. Though polyphony is hardly practicable in a procession, in other respects it is reasonably well suited to the actual characteristics of the responsory.

2. The word *antiphona* has undergone an evolution rather like that of the word *responsorium*, but even more complex. Originally it meant an entire psalm (or even a section of three psalms) sung with a refrain for two choirs; it ended by meaning, in a rather vague way, a whole series of pieces ultimately derived from antiphonal psalmody.[384]

The most important category is that of the *processional anthems* of the Mass, which we studied apropos of the Introit. This abridged psalmody, reduced to a single verse but enriched by a long refrain, occurs also in other analogous rites: *Exsurge Domine* at the beginning of penitential processions (Rogations, etc.); *Exaudi nos* of Ash Wednesday; *Crucem tuam* of the adoration of the Cross on Good Friday; and all the anthems of the *Mandatum*.[385] The analysis of these pieces is like that for the processional chants of the Mass.

When detached from all psalmody and considered as an item on its own, the refrain provides what we now call an *anthem*. Like the Oriental troparion, to which it corresponds, the anthem consists of a single strophe in unitary form. Its text is sometimes from the psalms, sometimes from the

---

[384] For the vocabulary connected with antiphony, see note 197.

[385] Observe that many of these make use of verses not taken from the psalms.

Bible, and sometimes ecclesiastical in origin. Nevertheless, some of these pieces reveal their psalmodic origin by a kind of detachable coda. This coda, in the form of an acclamation or short prayer, is doubtless a trace of an ancient refrain sung by the people.[386] In most cases the composition is entirely free, either because it is made up of a patchwork or because it displays continuous invention. Its genre, less ornate than in the responsories, is syllabic or neumatic. Given the variety of functions which these anthems have to fulfill in the Office, processions and diverse rites, as well as the rather indefinite nature of these functions, there may be considerable liberty as regards their performance.

3. The *Improperia* for the adoration of the Cross on Good Friday are best classified as psalmodic hymnody because of the typically psalmodic forms they have preserved. They are made up of two quite distinct parts: the great *Improperia* (*Popule meus*) consisting of three verses and the *Trisagion*, which is used as a refrain; and the little *Improperia* beginning with the verses *Ego. . . .*[387] With three verses of the great *Improperia*, alternated by the soloists of the two choirs, the *Trisagion* has been combined as a refrain. No doubt it is its bilingual nature which has preserved for this refrain its pure antiphony. In each of the three acclamations the first choir sings in Greek, and the second replies in Latin to the same melody. Although the verses of the little *Improperia* are sung alternately by the soloists of the two choirs, the actual performance of this section is derived from the responsorial form with a common refrain: *Popule meus*. The verses of one part employ a neumatic formula, while those of the other part use a syllabic formula. The structure of the melody is psalmodic, although the texts are prophetic in origin. This ancient piece, on account of the elements which it contains and the way in which these are arranged, is one of the most typical examples of Christian song.

d) Free hymnody, hardly represented at all in the Roman Mass, is developed to a far greater extent in the rest of the liturgy.

1. Pride of place must be given to that venerable hymn which the manuscripts call "Praise of the Holy Trinity," the *Te Deum*. As it stands now, the piece is a compilation of verses grouped into three sections clearly distinct in their content, rhythm and melody. The first part (vv. 1-13), in rhythmic

---

[386] The phenomenon which is quite common in the East (for example, in the old Byzantine troparia of Psalm 50) is well exemplified in the Palm Sunday anthems ending in *Hosanna in excelsis*. Compare these with the anthems *Quando natus est, Rubum quem viderat, Germinavit radix Iesse* (of Oriental inspiration) for Vespers of January 1, and also the *Salvator mundi* (reconstructed from Hartker) for bringing the Blessed Sacrament from the altar of repose before the Communion service on Good Friday.

[387] The *Trisagion*, Greek by origin but used in the Gallican liturgy, first appears by itself about the ninth century in the Antiphonary of Corbie; thereafter it is found together with the three verses of the great *Improperia* in the Antiphonary of Senlis and the Romano-German Pontifical. The little *Improperia* appeared later (eleventh century) but carry a long tradition. See H Schmidt, *Hebdomada sancta*, pp. 793 ff., and H. Hucke, *ibid*, pp. 940 ff.

prose and traditional formulas, expresses, in union with the angels, saints and the entire Church, the praises of God the Father; a Trinitarian doxology concludes it. The second part, composed according to the laws of the *cursus*, is in memory of the redemptive work of the Word-made-flesh, and ends with the petition: *Te ergo quaesumus* (vv. 14-20). The third is a prayer of supplication in the form of versicles (of the type *preces*), some from the psalms and some ecclesiastical. The three parts may well be of different origins and different epochs; the fact that they have been grouped together depends on the use to which this polyvalent hymn of thanksgiving and of supplication has been put.[388] In the monastic rules of the sixth century it appears as a hymn for Sunday Matins, and it has remained ever since at the end of our Matins for Sundays and feast days. But it is also used as a solemn act of thanksgiving, especially at ordinations and consecrations (kings, abbots, virgins). By its very nature it is evidently a song for all the assembly. Like the *Gloria*, it borrows the form of a noble and cadenced prose, divided into verses normally consisting of two phrases. According to the traditional melody, it calls for a quasi-syllabic recitative constructed on the principle of the psalmodic formula: a recitative line with an intonation, mediation, and cadence.[389] It is nowadays performed by two alternating choirs, but there is no reason for this apart from practical considerations. The melody is related to the most ancient stratum of Western chant (Roman Preface, *Gloria* XV, etc.). It is a model of what ecclesiastical and liturgical music should be.

2. The strictly poetic productions of the Church included in the general term "hymn" form an enormous body of literature.[390] The Roman liturgy, which has always shown itself somewhat reserved toward hymns and accepted them at a comparatively late date, has retained only a few of the best known pieces.

The sphere in which hymns find their main employment is in the Divine Office. In the Roman Office as it is now, there is a hymn for each of the Hours. Sometimes it occurs at the beginning (as in Matins and the Little Hours) as an anticipation of the psalmody to express the meaning of the Hour or the mystery of the day which is being celebrated; sometimes it comes after the *capitulum* (as in Lauds and Vespers) as a lyrical development of the second

---

[388] In spite of the considerable amount of work devoted to the study of this hymn, the problems of its history have by no means been cleared up. Most authorities today, following Dom Morin, prefer to attribute it to Nicetas of Remesiana (ca. 400) on the evidence of a family of Celtic manuscripts. But, because it has the nature of a patchwork, there can be little doubt that it has earlier connections, and its present form might well be dated later.

[389] The "solemn tone" is only an amplification of the "simple tone," which is purer and more typical. This has three binary formulas corresponding with the three parts of the hymn, each having two reciting notes followed by their mediant and cadential groups. Formula A: DOH-*lah* without intonation: LAH-*soh*. Formula B: DOH-*lah* (with intonation on *soh*); *lah*-ME. Formula C: FAH-*doh* (with intonation); SOH-*me*. The third part resumes formula B.

[390] The collection of Latin hymns from the Middle Ages made by G. Dreves and Cl. Blume, though not exhaustive, by itself fills fifty-five volumes (Leipzig, 1886–1922); and this is without mention of hymns from other rites.

item in the series reading-song-prayer.[391] St. Ambrose, usually considered the Father of Western hymnody, is said to have introduced ecclesiastical poetry into the vigils as a popular element intended to add a less austere note to the psalmody.

The hymn is to psalmody what decoration is to architecture or what preaching is to the reading of Holy Scripture. It seeks to render the mystery more immediately eloquent and familiar. That is why hymns have always borrowed the poetico-musical forms in vogue at the times and places when they were composed: metric, tonic or syllabic, rhymed or unrhymed. It is probable that the rhythm of their performance likewise conformed to the customs of contemporary poetry.[392] The Ambrosian melodies intended for the people were syllabic, and hardly ever exceed a fifth in range. Later melodies, written for the chorus of clerics, though retaining their choral character, seem some what labored. In any case, throughout the entire Middle Ages there were to be heard authentically popular metrical melodies in which the people could really take their part, sometimes by means of verses in their mother tongue,

3. There is a category of hymns which should be mentioned separately because of their function and their special form. These are the *versus*. This type of hymn may be a product of Byzantine influence on the Carolingian renewal of liturgy and letters. The Roman liturgy has preserved three examples: the *Gloria laus* of Theodulf of Orleans, the *Pange lingua* of Good Friday, and the *O Redemptor, sume carnem* at the veneration of the holy oils on Maundy Thursday. All three are processional hymns, and their prosody is metrical. Finally, and most important, each has a refrain intended to be sung by everyone, in between the strophes entrusted to soloists. The *versus* demonstrates the permanence of responsorial singing in hymnody.

B. ON THE THRESHOLD OF LITURGY: HYMNS

The items contained in the official books, which alone are entitled to be called liturgy, form the pre-eminent and exemplary, but not the exclusive, treasury of Christian song. The Church has always surrounded the essential

[391] In these two of the greater Hours the monastic Office has retained the *responsorium* after the *capitulum*; and in them we can better appreciate how the hymnody is a prolongation of the responsorial psalmody which follows the reading. Compare with the proses and sequences in the intervenient chants of the Mass, where hymnody fulfills the same role.

[392] It can hardly be doubted that the Ambrosian hymns were metrical, not only as regards the principle of line-construction, but also as regards their melody. (It was, in fact, the melody which caused them to be metrical rather than prosody hardly appreciated by the people.) Later on isosyllabism came to prevail and the rhythm became equalized, even though it remained measured with subdivisions of the basic time for ornamental notes. Finally the ornaments themselves were multiplied, each note was treated as a beat, and so the performance turned into free rhythm. This is the explanation advanced by H. Sesini (*Poesia e musica nella latinita christiana dal III al X secolo* [Turin, 1949], p. 89), and it seems quite satisfying. This does not exclude a return to measured time for certain pieces, for example with the rhythmic modes of the thirteenth century.—See Plate III, p. 127, for an example of an Ambrosian hymn.

rites of her worship with a number of secondary elements which help the people to understand and assimilate the former. The liturgy as we have it now has adopted into its ceremonies a great many of these complementary signs, borrowed from diverse cultures and epochs, to convey more explicitly in ceremonial language the meaning of the simple sacramental actions. We are wont to do the same kind of thing in speech; we are not content merely to pronounce words in isolation, but we put them into sentences or clothe them in a speech which renders their meaning more precise. These adventitious, and yet necessary, elements are by their nature changeable, while the rites themselves remain essentially the same.[393] It was the Council of Trent which first reserved to the Holy See the power of determining the liturgical rites. For the period prior to that council it is often difficult to draw any hard and fast line between what we now call the liturgical and the extra-liturgical. And so quite a number of the popular religious songs of the Middle Ages, such as proses, litanies and hymns which were inserted into the official worship itself and even held a very important place in the religious life of those times, have left little or no trace in a liturgy which is supposed to bridge the centuries. Today, when public worship has recourse to such singing, it seems to us non-liturgical, even though it may at times accompany, precede or follow a liturgical action.[394] Nevertheless, the functions which singing of this kind must fulfill are analogous to those of the sung items of the liturgy; evangelization, participation in sacramental rites, and union with the never-ending praise of the Church. And the conditions which follow from these functions, even though less rigid, are entirely similar as regards agents, lyrical forms and musical genres. Hence, it will not be a waste of time to examine here the main kinds of religious singing which are included in the modern and generic French term *cantique*,[395] as far as these can be useful or necessary in the life of a Christian community.

a) The first role of the *cantique* is that of evangelization. Singing is an admirable way of making known the "good news" and of aiding the assimilation of Christian doctrine. By means of number and cadence, the word which imparts the message becomes more penetrating and pleasing. By the melos which accompanies it, the word softens the hearts and charms the minds which it is to impregnate. By the repetition of rhythmo-melodic sentences it becomes engraved on the memory. Thus it acquires practical value for Christian living and motivating power for Christian action.[396]

---

[393] "All these transformations testify that the Church is vigorously alive; that in the course of the ages there has been development in the language which she uses to express to her divine Bridegroom her own faith and inexhaustible love and that of her people. It is a proof of her skill as a teacher, always inculcating and increasing in the faithful the 'sense of Christ' " (MD 47).

[394] See ch. 4, pp. 63ff.

[395] We do not seem to have any exactly parallel term in the English language. "Hymn" is too narrow, for *"cantique"* includes sung prose as well as sung poetry (Tr.).

[396] "The melodies of these hymns (which are mostly in the language of the people) can be committed to memory with little or no difficulty. Along with the melodies, the words and

The use of singing in the spread of the gospel is an unbroken tradition of the Church's missionary and catechetical apostolate. And it is no less significant that heretics also have never failed to use it to spread their doctrines.[397] It was partly to counteract Bardesan's gnostic psalms that St. Ephrem, sometimes adopting the very rhythms and melodies of his predecessor, composed in the Syrian language that summary of lyrical instructions known as his *madrâshê*.[398] And it was as a reply to the Arians that St. John Chrysostom, newly elected bishop of Constantinople, imitated their antiphonal singing by organizing processions and vigils at which the people sang the inspired psalms.[399] By his *Faêd Fiada* St. Patrick, apostle of the Irish, made Christ known to the sailors on their ships. St. Adalbert of Prague composed for the Moravians the famous *Boga Rodziska*, which became the national song of Poland. In the immense work of re-evangelizing the ignorant masses undertaken during the Counter Reformation, as well as among missionaries to pagan lands, singing played an important part. Père Michel Coyssard, at the beginning of the seventeenth century, justified its value in his treatise on sacred music, and he also composed an entire catechism in hymn form.[400] St. Grignon de Montfort wrote his *cantiques* for the purpose of prolonging the effect of his parochial missions, and he used popular airs for them because, he said, "the devil does not need to have all the good tunes just for himself alone." No matter what we may think of his productions, there can be no doubt about his missionary intentions.[401]

What kind of sung items are there which correspond in practice with this prime function of evangelization?

1. First of all come the inspired hymns: psalms and biblical canticles. More

ideas of these hymns impress themselves on men's minds, are often repeated and perfectly understood. If children learn such sacred music at an early age, they are singularly helped by it to know, appreciate and remember the truths of our faith. This musical aid is no small blessing to the catechist" (MSD 16).

[397] It is worth pointing out that those who condemn vernacular singing on the grounds that it can be used to spread heresy are forgetting that the vernacular is a *conditio sine qua non* for all evangelization, and that the best defense against error is an even clearer proposition of the truth.

[398] See Plate III, p. 127.

[399] The Fathers often expatiated on the catechetical value of singing—a fact which proves the importance they attached to it. From many possible quotations on the subject we select the following short passage from St. Ambrose: "In the psalms both doctrine and grace are conjoined: you sing for the pleasure of it, but you receive instruction; commandments taught with violence are not retained; but what you have learned in an agreeable manner will not disappear once it has been well impressed on your mind" (*Enar. in Ps.* 1; PL 14, 925–926).

[400] M. Coyssard, *Traité du profit que toute personne tire de chanter en la doctrine chrétienne* (Lyons, 1606). This treatise serves as a preface to a collection, many times re-edited, of pieces "to be sung before and after catechism lessons." On the compositions of this period see A. Gastoué, *Le cantique populaire en France* (Lyons, 1924), ch. 6.

[401] We should recall also the evangelization of the American Negroes, for whom the "Negro Spiritual" was the means whereby the message of the Bible entered into every sphere of their lives. Nowadays, in Africa, the attempts which are being made to enable Bible stories to be sung to native music are of the greatest interest for the spread of the gospel and Christian culture.

than any merely human compositions they transmit revelation because they are God's word. As a lyrical resumé of the entire history of salvation, of prophetical preaching and sentences of Wisdom, they are the key to biblical language. The mysteries of our Savior are expressed prophetically by their imagery and phrases in a specially excellent way. It is impossible for the faithful to acquire any deep knowledge of Scripture or to participate fully in the Church's liturgical prayer unless they become familiar with a certain number of psalms by singing them in their own tongue. Just as the preaching at catechetical reunions, convert classes, missionary gatherings, bible vigils, etc., ought to be based on the reading of Holy Scripture, so also the meditative singing, and the prayer of praise which enable the "good news" to be inwardly grasped, ought to be based on the inspired psalms and canticles, And thus the word of God is received and given back, is heard and answered. To achieve this end, an exact and faithful translation has to be used, one, moreover, which respects not only the meaning of the words and imagery of the text, but also its poetic literary genre and most especially its rhythmo-melodic character.[402] The lyrical forms to be adopted are those consecrated by tradition: first and above all the responsorial form, which gives pride of place to the inspired word recited by the psalmist and the response to it made by the assembly; then, as opportunities may occur, antiphonal and alternating forms, according as stress is to be laid on the refrain or on the verses. The musical genre chosen should confer upon the word the maximum of power and intelligibility. The melody must hide behind the words which it supports; it must never engulf them nor monopolize attention for itself, for then it would be betraying its role.

2. Corresponding to the prophetic songs of the Old Testament are those which sing of fulfillment in the New. Every Sunday at the beginning of Mass, Christians of the Byzantine rite sing the Beatitudes. How could the baptized, who often know other texts by heart, be ignorant of the summary of the New Law which our Lord Himself formulated for us in harmonious sentences? In every language the disciples of Christ ought to be able to sing the Beatitudes by heart.

There are other texts in the New Testament, especially the *Magnificat* and certain hymns from St. Paul or from the Apocalypse, which deserve to win a place among items sung by the faithful. We might also include some

---

[402] The poetic rhythm of the psalms, which make use of parallelism and of tonic prosody, is so fundamental that it has been transferred, *mutatis mutandis*, into other languages. The version of the psalms in the *Bible de Jerusalem*, 2nd edition, 1953, has attempted to give full value to the rhythmo-melodism proper to the literary genre of the psalms, and it has been imitated in many countries. The restoration of a recitative which is free, yet also measured, provides psalmody with a basis that is both religious and popular. See *La Maison Dieu*, 33 (1953), and *Église qui Chante*, 34-35 (1961).

Translator's note: The English version of the psalms according to these principles is published by The Grail, 58 Sloane St. London S.W.1. It can be obtained from the Gregorian Institute of America, 2132 Jefferson Ave., Toledo 2, Ohio.

passages of the Gospel, like the parables, whose oral structure suggests rhythmo-melodism. The task of memorizing and assimilating these sacred texts is made much easier by singing them; this might be done by using the responsorial form, which is fundamental and universal,[403] or by direct recitative, whether individual or collective.

3. The Church's teaching, although based on Holy Scripture, has from the very earliest times found expression in dogmatic formulations, summaries of doctrine—the creeds. Such formulas, which were intended to be memorized, can be learned and assimilated more easily if they are cast in lyrical form. In the tradition of the *cantique*, quite a number of songs are to be found which express the contents of the Creed or of the commandments. There are others which set forth, in didactic strophes, the contents of a catechism lesson. In our modern civilization, based on the written rather than the spoken word, songs of this kind have fallen into disfavor. Yet pedagogy and pastoral missiology are agreed in maintaining the human and spiritual value of this kind of instruction wherein the fixed formula, rhythm and melody are used to convey the doctrine.[404] As in recitative, the melody employed here has the object, not so much of expressing the meaning of the words, as of giving to them a style which is more vocal, more human, more spiritual.

b) The participation in the ceremonies of Christian worship of those faithful who have been converted and instructed requires the aid of a whole series of songs intended to prolong the effect of those which are strictly liturgical completing them and, in some cases, even supplying for them.

1. The Roman Ritual provides for little or no singing in the administration of most of the sacraments and sacramentals, apart from the funeral rites. This is rather surprising when one considers the customs in use among the Oriental churches, which give an important place to psalms and hymns. It would seem most fitting that the sacraments and the principal acts of Christian life and death should be surrounded with songs which express the mysteries of these events for those who take part in them. Pastoral liturgy

---

[403] We have heard African Christians doing this; a cantor improvised a recitative, and the assembly punctuated it with a doxology or a phrase of supplication summing up the meaning of the parable.

[404] Modern catechetical pedagogy, while very rightly insisting on the personal and conscious assimilation of what is to be taught, has tended to neglect or depreciate the value of learning formulas by heart. The value of the social and ecclesial background in assimilating the word of faith is today being discovered anew. But the literary formulation of our catechism answers is often amorphous and devoid of rhythm; would not the answers gain very much if they were inspired by the tradition of rhythmo-melodism?

We may also ask how it is possible to ensure any stable Christian culture among the enormous number of illiterate people who still make up the majority of the human race, except by having recourse to the art of speech. An old woman from Calabria who had emigrated without knowing anything except her native dialect was able to recite to me a compendium of Christian doctrine and of the mysteries of Christ in the melopoeia of her homeland. It was practically the only knowledge of her faith which she possessed; yet all the essentials were there.

cannot afford to neglect the needs which are making themselves felt here, for example in the mission countries.[404a]

For reception into the catechumenate, for the celebration of baptism, of confirmation, of marriage and some parts of the funeral rites, it would be suitable in many cases that singing, carefuly adapted to the meaning and progress of the ceremonies, should express and underline the rites. As there is no tradition about this in the West, the hymns used in the Oriental liturgies could well serve as examples.

2. In the everyday Christian worship it is above all in the celebration of the Mass that a repertoire of suitable songs is most needed. No doubt it is desirable that a fitting form of celebration should permit the adoption, for all parochial Masses, of a solemn rite in which all the singing should be strictly liturgical. But, in fact, the number of *missae lectae*, even on Sundays, is far greater than that of the *missae in cantu*. As long as this state of affairs continues,[404b] it is of vital importance to ensure the best possible "active and intelligent" participation of the faithful in the eucharistic sacrifice. One of the chief means to this end is singing.

Singing which is designed to "accompany the sacred action" is both authorized and commended by the Church "on condition that it be well adapted to the various parts of the sacrifice." [405] This means that, like the liturgical chants themselves, they must correspond with the functional laws which justify them.

Among the most important pieces is the *responsorial psalm* exemplified by the Gradual. For the faithful this has an importance in the liturgy of the word very like that of the Epistle and the Gospel.

Because it is a priestly prayer, the great eucharistic prayer does not provide any scope for the exterior participation of the people except in the dialogue at the beginning of the Preface, the *Sanctus*, and the concluding *Amen*. Yet the Syrian, Maronite and Coptic liturgies all provide us with examples of a troparion of remembrance and of intercession sung by the people after the consecration. Addressed to Christ Himself, this chant expresses marvellously well one of the essential aspects of the Eucharist, and associates the people with it actively.[406] Almost as important are the *communal prayers of intercession* which the liturgy supposes at the *Kyrie eleison* and needs before the Offertory.[406a] If they have the form of a diaconal litany, these prayers can

[404a] The Second Vatican Council's Constitution on the Sacred Liturgy opens up plentiful opportunities for such things. Cf. CL 40, 65, 77, 79, 81.

[404b] There are grounds for hoping that the measures taken by the Second Vatican Council will render possible developments which will favor the sung Mass.

[405] MSD 30; cf. IMS 33. On the pastoral application of this principle, consult for each item in the Mass J. Gelineau, "Fonction et signification . . . ," *Église qui chante*, 1959–1961.

[406] The words are as follows: "We recall Thy death, we proclaim Thy resurrection, we await Thy return, O Savior; have mercy on us."

[406a] Cf. CL 53. And see footnote 184.

help the faithful to take their part in the sacrifice of propitiation offered for the whole Church and for themselves.

Of secondary, but by no means negligible, importance are the *processionals.* The Mass itself opens with such a chant. A corresponding chant for the people might consist of an antiphonal psalm with a refrain chosen for the day, or else of a hymn suited to the feast or season. The most suitable form for an opening hymn[406b] is one which has a chorus (verses by a choir, chorus by the people). As regards musical genre, the air is welcome, for an entrance hymn lends itself to a certain melodic development.

There may perhaps be a procession in which the faithful bring up their gifts in kind, or else one in which the elements to be consecrated are brought up to the altar. Here singing can be most useful, in the first case to emphasize the spirit of joy and generosity of the givers, in the second, to express reverence for the Victim who is already represented by the sacred gifts placed upon the altar.[407] The lyrical form and musical genre best suited to this chant are analoguous to those of the entrance chant, but have greater liberty. If there is no procession, there does not seem to be any real need for singing at the Offertory of a low Mass.

On the other hand, every time a number of people receive Communion together, this calls for singing which expresses the mystery of fraternal unity and paschal joy. We have already pointed out that responsorial singing on such occasions can foster meditation on the words sung by the soloist and also communal prayer in a simple refrain. It might well be a psalm such as the traditional Psalm 33, with the refrain: "Taste and see how good is the Lord"; or it might be a hymn, of which liturgical traditions provide some excellent examples.[408]

3. There is one kind of ceremony especially which calls for singing by the people, and that is the *procession.* When the entire community goes in procession from one place to another on some festive or penitential occasion, the procession is always accompanied by singing.[409] Traditionally the main form of it is a responsorial psalm with a refrain for the people; but there are also litanies, collective prayer par excellence; finally there are hymns, preferably those with a refrain. Whenever there is a procession that can be

---

[406b] See the additional note 202a, which modifies this statement.

[407] Liturgical tradition does not furnish any examples of Offertory hymns in the strict sense to accompany the offerings of the faithful, except in the rather general form of the psalmodic or scriptural texts of the Roman "offertories." By contrast, the Oriental liturgies have admirable hymns, such as the *Cherubikon* of the Byzantine liturgy, to accompany the bringing up of the sacred gifts.

[408] Quite a number of ancient hymns (3rd–4th century?) have come down to us, having been edited by H. Borgia, *Frammenti eucaristici antichissimi* (Grottaferrata, 1932). See A. Hamman, *Prières des premiers chrétiens* (Paris, 1951), pp. 202 ff. Compare also certain Ambrosian and Celtic *transitoria.*

[409] See *La Maison Dieu*, 43 (1955), *"Les Processions,"* especially pp. 74–93; and *Église qui chante*, 6-7 (1958), "Procession-Pèlerinage."

classified as a *pium exercitium*, it can be suitably accompanied by a responsorial psalm, a litany or a hymn.

c) Whenever a group of people want to dedicate some particular time of
the day to God, they find the most natural way to do so is to sing together.
Community singing intended for this purpose has acquired canonical form
in the Hours of the Divine Office. Originally the Church's morning and
evening hours of prayer were celebrated by the entire local community;[409a] but
in the course of time the Divine Office came to be mainly a clerical and monastic prayer with the Hours increased in number and complexity. The piety
of the faithful had to find expression in other forms: devotion to the Real
Presence, benedictions with the Blessed Sacrament, devotions attached to
particular months, novenas in honor of our Lord, of his Mother, or of the
saints, etc. In spite of this, there does fortunately linger in some places a tradition of public prayers for the morning and evening.[410] And for most of these
gatherings singing is necessary.

1. To be in line with the Church's own prayer, all these *pia exercitia*[410a]
should be based on the elements which are fundamental to Christian worship: readings, singing, prayer. In our view, then, they should always contain Scripture readings, preceded or followed by responsorial psalmody;[411]
there should be prayers of intercession in the form of the diaconal litany;
there should be acclamations, which are so often used in the liturgy. And
because *pia exercitia* are intended, above all, to be the prayer of the people,
hymnody also should be largely represented.

2. Beyond doubt it is one of the main tasks of the *cantique* to celebrate
in noble and simple poetic language all the many riches of our faith: the
coming and birth of our Savior, His life and work, His words and miracles,
His sufferings and death, His resurrection and ascension, the descent of the
Holy Spirit and His action within the Church, the merits and glory of the
Blessed Virgin and of the saints, the participation of each and every baptized
Christian in the mysteries of the Church, and the expectation of the second
coming of Christ. If these mysteries are to be celebrated in song, and thus

---

[409a] Cf. CL 84 and 100, which call fo rthe renewal of this participation by the faithful.

[410] The spreading practice of assistance at Mass during the week, facilitated even more by
the introduction of evening Masses, has diminished the frequency of *pia exercitia* in many places.
The question may well be raised whether the prayer of praise has not thereby been too much
curtailed; does not the exclusive celebration of the Mass lack something if there be no preliminary meetings for catechesis, or meetings for prayer like those of the Divine Office, in order to
prolong its effects? In many mission communities which cannot have the Mass owing to lack
of priests, services of this kind are extremely important for preserving the Christian life of the
community. Hence we may be permitted to hope for the restoration of parochial-type prayers
something like those used of old for the Saturday night vigils, or, above all, like those of the
Lucernarium (evening office), elements of which are to be found in the Vespers of nearly all
the Eastern rites. (An example: J. Gelineau, *Lucernaire* [Lyons, 1959].)

[410a] As also the "Bible services" mentioned in CL 35 § 4.

[411] Certainly not an uninterrupted series of alternating psalms on the model of the present
Hours of the Breviary—such a concatenation is not traditional and its multiplication is a monastic
phenomenon—but one or two chosen psalms with definite forms and functions.

impressed on the minds of the faithful, hymns must be written for this express purpose. The Oriental offices abound in troparia which can hardly be surpassed as models for the kind of hymn required. There are so many treasures contained in the Church's cycle of seasons and saints' days; all nations should be enabled to sing of these in their own tongue, so that the grace proper to each feast and season may be brought to every member of the faithful.

The forms that can be used are various. One might draw on psalmodic hymnody, adding onto each psalm-verse a stich (free strophe) which applies and displays its prophetic meaning. Or one might adopt strophic hymnody, with or without a refrain. The musical genre for this would be an air which would reconcile, in a perfect rhythmic, metric and syntactical union between music and text, the primacy of the sung word and a form of melody as well defined as possible. The idiom of both words and music would be that which the particular culture acknowledges as sacred, beautiful and popular.[412]

3. The role of religious singing extends far beyond public worship. It has a part to play in spiritual recreation, and in building up, proclaiming and spreading the faith. In these spheres it has the utmost freedom in its inspiration and forms. Here, however, we are not discussing religious singing that is to be classified merely as "religious music."

> Singing awakens in the soul an ardent desire for the content of what is sung; it calms the passions aroused by the flesh; it drives away the evil thoughts suggested to us by invisible enemies; it waters the soul that it may become fertile and bring forth divers good fruits; to those who strive piously it gives strength to bear heavy trials; for all pious persons it is a remedy against the evils of this earthly life. The apostle Paul calls the canticle the "sword of the spirit," because it provides a weapon for those who virtuously fight against the invisible spirits; for the word of God, taking possession of the spirit when sung or spoken, has power to drive away the demons. All this gives the soul power to perfect itself in all the virtues, and it is given to pious persons by the songs of the Church.—Diodorus of Tarsus (?).[413]

[412] "If religious hymns are to benefit and be of use to the Christian people, they must be in complete accord with the teaching of the Catholic faith, setting it out properly and explaining it. Their vocabulary must be simple, their tunes easy. They must be unpretentious, and not just a meaningless stream of words. They must be marked with a religious dignity and seriousness, however short and easy they may be" (MSD 30; cf. IMS 51–53).

[413] *Questions et réponses aux Orthodoxes,* quoted by Th. Gérold, *Les Pères de l'Église . . .* p. 102.

13 CATEGORIES AND WORKS

When it is known what conditions each sung item has to fulfill within Christian worship, then—but only then—it becomes possible to judge whether any particular musical work is or is not fitted for use in divine service. The criteria which derive from the functional role of singing in the liturgical action, and which must be applied to particular works or general categories of music, may be reduced to four:

1) The *canonical* criterion, according to which a melody is obligatory, recommended, permitted, tolerated, or excluded.

2) Th *ritual* criterion, according to which a melody must conform to the person or persons appointed to sing it, to the literary text and its specific form, and to the musical genre which results from this.

3) The *pastoral* criterion, according to which a melody must correspond to the living musical idiom and religious sentiment of the community which is at worship.

4) The *esthetic* criterion, according to which its musical performance is judged to be beautiful, artistic and a worthy sign of the sacred.

The first two criteria are objective, since they depend on the Church and on the very nature of her public worship. The last two are relative to culture and admit of a considerable margin for subjective opinions.

These four criteria have to be applied simultaneously. Someone who judges, for example, only according to the esthetic criterion might choose some masterpiece of art which does not correspond at all with any definite ritual function. On the other hand, someone who takes no notice of any but the ceremonial and rubrical aspects runs the risk of neglecting that edification which active and intelligent participation in the liturgy ought to bring to those who are celebrating it. And conversely, someone who is concerned with nothing but pastoral efficacy and practicability can hardly be sure of doing what the Church wants in the way she wants it.

Indeed, it is not possible to make a discerning choice for each occasion and for each sung item by the application of any one single criterion. Life and history, then custom and law, have picked out and grouped musical works into categories to which simplified criteria can be applied in a general manner. Thus it is that recent documents distinguish several categories of musical works and divide them according to a hierarchical arrangement: (a) Gregorian chant; (b) sacred polyphony; (c) modern sacred music; (d) sacred music for the organ; (e) hymnody; (f) religious music.[414] This classification is doubly interesting in that it shows the Church's preferences (the reasons for which it will be instructive to seek), and provides a simple and certain practical rule.

And yet this subdivision is insufficient. Resting mainly on a historical stratification,[415] it is of value chiefly for each group considered as a whole. But it passes no judgment on the qualities of each particular piece within any group. It is possible, for instance, for some particular modern composition to be better suited to the functional laws of the liturgy than some piece of Gregorian chant. Therefore we have to examine these different categories, and apply the essential criteria in a more detailed way to the works which they contain.

A. GREGORIAN CHANT

It was not until the ninth century that the name "Gregorian" was given to the chant of the Roman liturgy. The men of those days wanted to endow the chants with the prestige and authority attaching to the name of Pope Gregory the Great (590–604).[416] Later on this kind of music was often called "ecclesiastical chant," and later still it was called "plain chant." Those who undertook the restoration of the chant about the end of the nineteenth cen-

---

[414] IMS 4. See chapter 4, pp. 59ff.

[415] Apart from organ literature and "religious music," these classes of composition have been enumerated in the historical order of their appearance: Gregorian, classical polyphony, modern music, popular religious music (which envisages chiefly those of the present pastoral renewal according to the degree in which they ought, as it is said, to be suited to the various parts of the Mass).

[416] See above all the letter of Leo IV (middle of the ninth century) to Honoratus. The prologue of the Antiphonary: *Gregorius praesul . . . composuit hunc libellum musicae artis,* appeared at the end of the eighth century. References prior to that time speak only of *cantus romanus* or of *cantilena romana.* Cf. H. Hucke, "Die Einführung des gregorianischen Gesang in Frankreich," *Römische Quartalschrift,* 49 (1954), pp. 173–187. On plain chant, see note 238.

tury did again what those of the ninth century had done—they revived and consecrated the term "Gregorian."

How can we define "Gregorian chant?" We cannot do it etymologically according to the relationship which it is supposed to have with St. Gregory, for we know nothing of the personal work of composition done by this great pope.[417] Some melodies originated before his time; most of them date from after his day. Nor can we define Gregorian chant historically by saying that it is the most ancient song of the Roman Church, since it contains some items that are very late, even some contemporary neo-Gregorian works. To define it according to a certain melodic technique, plain chant or free rhythm, would be a *petitio principii*; for the various ways in which it has been sung during the course of the ages do not settle the musical nature or the authentic interpretation of these pieces. It would be even more arbitrary to attribute to Gregorian chant some particular and unique esthetic quality. Ultimately, therefore, we are reduced to a definition which is merely practical and canonical: Gregorian chant is the chant of the Roman Church.[417a] It consists of those melodies which the Roman Church has retained in the books approved by the Holy See and which are proposed, sometimes as of obligation, sometimes as recommended and sufficient, for the execution of the ritual texts.[418]

The following are the qualities attributed to this *corpus musicae*: "It is the chant proper to the Roman Church, the only chant she has inherited from the ancient fathers, which she has jealously guarded for centuries in her liturgical codices, which she directly proposes to the faithful as her own . . . as the supreme model for sacred music" (Pius X); it "may almost be called the patrimony of the Church"; its excellence consists mainly in "the intimate union of the melody with the sacred text"; in liturgical actions it should be preferred, other things being equal, to other kinds of sacred music; hence it is to be "carefully preserved" and "the Christian people should be induced to take part in it frequently" (Pius XII). It possesses in the highest degree those qualities of holiness, true art and universality which are needed by the chant of the Church. It is liturgical par excellence.

But these qualities are not to be found always and to an equal degree in all parts of the Gregorian corpus. Notable differences are to be found between one part and another. These are to be explained by the variety of the milieux and times when they were composed. They appear in the diversity of idioms

[417] The liturgical work of Gregory I, which is certain, has to be distinguished from his musical work. Apart from a few allusions or comparisons of a musical nature (few and of no particular significance) found here and there in his writings, the only known intervention by Gregory I in the musical sphere is restrictive. It was the decree of the Roman synod of 595 by which the performance of "psalms and other readings" was reserved to deacons. (See note 140.)

[417a] It would be better in the future to use the more exact phrase of CL 116: "the chant specially suited to the Roman liturgy."

[418] "The only authentic Gregorian chant is that which is contained in the 'typical' Vatican editions or has the approval of the Sacred Congregation of Rites for use in a particular church or religious community" (IMS 59; cf. 5 and 16).

and styles; and they influence the greater or less functional value of each chant. Therefore, even at the risk of being misunderstood, we must distinguish several strata or species of composition.[419] Although researches in this field are not very advanced, we can at least set up a few fairly reliable signposts, even though some precisions or corrections may have to be added later.

a) The most fundamental stratum of the Roman liturgical chant is made up of the recitatives of readings and prayers, the verses of psalms, the acclamations and dialogues, and some of the most ancient of the hymns. All the tones used for the Gospel and for Lessons, the Prefaces and the *Pater*, the collects and litanies, for some psalms, for *Sanctus* XVIII, *Te Deum* and *Gloria* XV form the main part of it. All these melodies, of the formulary type, are perfectly suited to the words of the rites. They are extremely simple, and form the kernel of Christian song.

This group of chants is, moreover, allied to the Jewish "cantillations" of the Scriptures.[420] We may presume that, in spite of differences in oral and written traditions, many of these formulas have roots in the very origins of the liturgy. It is in recitatives that the music of the various Christian liturgies show the most notable resemblances.[421] These chants have never grown old; their functional congruity remains perfect and their restrained beauty is perceptible to all, both sacred minister and people. When their use is obligatory, far from occasioning difficulties, they usually provide the surest basis for community singing. Even if it may prove necessary to change the language of some of them, their musical genre, apart from the modifications

---

[419] The fact that we are wont to find all the pieces called "Gregorian" assembled together in our *Liber Usualis*, that we see them all written in the same special notation, that we interpret them according to a single technique held to be *the* interpretation of Gregorian, and the very efforts that are made to promote *the* Gregorian chant considered as a whole have all contributed to obscure contrast and abolish all perspective. We may end by forgetting, for example, that *Gloria* XV and *Gloria* VIII—so near to each other in our books—are beyond doubt twice as far apart in time as are William de Machaut (1300–1377) and Debussy (1862–1918).

This confused way of viewing the entire field empties of all sense the contradictory statements one sometimes hears: "Gregorian is so simple; Gregorian is very difficult; Gregorian is universal; Gregorian is Western music from the Middle Ages; Gregorian is popular; Gregorian is esoteric; Gregorian is always the ideal liturgical chant; Gregorian is impracticable for some parts of the liturgy in parishes." Senseless also are controversies about *the* interpretation of *the* Gregorian chant, as if the matter discussed were one single homogeneous kind of music.

One may and should speak of *the* Gregorian chant on the canonical and practical plane. But on the historical, liturgical, esthetic and pastoral planes—each of them different and distinct— it is absolutely necessary to make clear which piece or class of pieces one is discussing and from which viewpoint they are being discussed.

[420] The Jewish musicologist E. Werner has pointed out a number of close similarities between the music of the synagogue and Gregorian chant (following Gastoué and Idelsohn). The examples he quotes do not put the matter beyond discussion, but his thesis merits consideration (*The Sacred Bridge* [New York: Columbia University Press, 1959]).

[421] One might show, for instance, that the recitative in the mode of *te* (the Roman tone called "irregular") is to be found in all rites (see Plate IV: The Mode of *Te* in Christian Music, p. 213). The shape *me-soh-lah-soh-(fah)-me* is also a fundamental Western troparion (Roman Preface, Mozarabic *Pater, Gloria, XV, Te Deum,* etc.).

that may be required, should never be changed, nor should their traditional formulas be abandoned.

b) Another signpost is found in the refrains which, from about the fourth to the fifth centuries, were the part which the people took in the old responsorial and antiphonal forms of psalmody. It is impossible, by external criticism, to assign this or that piece of Gregorian to this epoch. But from the indications about psalmody furnished by the writings of those days, we can assemble a whole series of Gregorian antiphons typified by: *Notum fecit Dominus, Laetentur caeli, Illumina Domine*. These are short refrains on psalmodic texts, popular and of syllabic genre, composed on the principle of the "timbre," or melodic motif, adaptable at will to a whole series of different texts. These three characteristics (psalm text, syllabic genre, melodic motif) all point clearly to the early date and originality of this stratum of liturgical chant.[422] No examples of it survive today except the antiphons preserved in Matins of festal Offices (Christmas, Epiphany, Ascension, and some of the oldest vigils), and in the psalter of the ferial Office. The people know them no longer. But their youthful alertness, their flavor of popular singing, and their perfect functional adaptation to responsorial psalmody still exercise their charm. Do the *versus ad repetendum* of the antiphons for the Introit and Communion of the Mass originate from this group? We do not know. But several short responsories are directly connected with it.

c) When responsorial and antiphonal psalmody developed into the forms now found in our responsories, Graduals and anthems, we come to a new stratum of more elaborate melodies. This found its typical and definitive form in the *Antiphonarium Missae*, which seems to have been fixed about the ninth century in some school of singers within the Frankish empire (Metz?). From there, if one can believe in the travels of the old manuscripts, it became diffused gradually throughout all the West.[423] For the first time in the history of the Church, a musical repertoire as such, recognized as superb, obtained an authoritative status equal to that of the texts themselves. The practical art of the cantor, who re-created the word by singing it in a way handed down by tradition, suffered eclipse behind an achievement of fine art, musi-

---

[422] (1) The psalmodic nature of the refrain is characteristic of fifth-century responsorial psalmody. Later on other biblical texts were used, and still later ecclesiastical texts. (2) The sixth century began the decline of the active participation of the people in liturgical singing, especially in psalmody. It would then be natural for the melodes and cantors of the seventh-eighth centuries to compose and use more ornate pieces. (3) It seems that the more rudimentary principle of composition known as "timbre" was succeeded by the more complex principle known as "centonization" (fitting together passages taken from other compositions). On the subject of the melodies, see above, notes 142 and 195.

[423] Some local traditions were preserved for a while in Gaul and in Spain, in Aquilea and Benevento, and especially in some of the Roman basilicas where the ancient chant called "Roman" was kept, even though it continued to evolve melodically until the thirteenth century. Only the Milanese tradition of the chant resisted this expansion, though the fixation of the Ambrosian melodies seems, at least in part, to have come later than that of "Gregorian." On these questions still under dispute, see J. Hourlier, *Études grégoriennes* (Solesmes, 1959), III, pp. 187–192.

cally defined and fixed. For this repertoire of melodies, one of the most astonishing in the whole known field of music, is a work of the highest quality. It was created by specialists in vocal technique and was intended for elite singers so highly trained expressly to perform it that one might call it *bel canto*, even though, at that time, the term had not yet been invented.[424] What is so admirable—especially in pieces of the neumatic style (Introits, Communions)—is the close symbiosis of words, melos and number. This music, which has grown out of the text, carries the text to its lyrical perfection without in any way fettering its melodic invention. Rightness of expression, modal homogeneity and variety, firmness of sonorous design and liberty of rhythm all contribute to produce an impression of singular perfection.

This group, the most typical of Gregorian chant, comprises the pieces of the Proper of the Mass, ornate responsories, and the majority of the antiphons. Yet it is not completely homogeneous. To begin with, we have to set aside melismatic verses for soloists which occur in the Graduals and Offertories; these are a particular genre of composition. Then there are many antiphons in the Office which are more syllabic than neumatic; these may well originate from the former strata. And there are other pieces, of later and differing provenance, from the Alleluia *Veni Sancte Spiritus* of Robert the Pious (d. 1031) to the responsory *Media vita* from Saint Gall, which exemplify notably diverse styles.

From the liturgical point of view, this repertoire is strongly marked with the stamp of the milieu which created it. The Romano-Frankish epoch from whence it dates made changes in a number of the rites which were only imperfectly understood at that time.[425] The active and intelligent participation of the faithful in the basic rites then became more and more reduced. In the singing they were replaced by cantors or clerics whose powerful trained voices could now be heard from the ambo, the rood-screen or the choir. We have already pointed out that melodic ornamentation reduced or even suppressed the psalmody in the responsories after the readings and in the processional chants.

Judged solely as Christian art, this category of chants possesses an immortal beauty; but judged according to the functional laws of liturgy implying the active and intelligent participation of the people, it is far from satisfactory. Even when the psalmodic verses have survived, it is very difficult to hear their text because of all the melismata. The refrains from the psalms are far too difficult for the people to sing. A large number of the melodies are so complex and subtle that most parochial choirs find them utterly beyond their

[424] Our present interpretation of Gregorian chant—justified by the fact that the choirs which have to perform it are often made up of amateur singers and large groups—can give us only a feeble idea of the vocal virtuosity it implies: repercussions of notes, tremolos, glissandi, liquescences, notes barely touched or else dwelt on, lengthening or shortening of values, etc. The existence of all these can be demonstrated from paleography.

[425] J. A. Jungmann, *The Mass of the Roman Rite*, I, (New York: 1955).

performing skill. In consequence, the average parish choir attempting to sing these chants cannot but deform them and deprive them of all their beauty. For all these reasons we have to conclude that this repertoire of Gregorian chant does not provide music fitted for the needs of the average community celebrating the liturgy. Finally, from the esthetic point of view we have to say that these chants have considerable limitations. Unlike the first two traditional strata mentioned above, a great many of them are "dated"; they display an artistic magnificence and a musical expressionism that belongs solely to their own era; the particular form of religious sentiment characteristic of that time appears in them far more clearly than many people care to admit, even though the way we interpret them nowadays waters them down considerably.

In this twentieth century many of the faithful are seeking a more direct approach to God's word; they want to celebrate the sacred mysteries in ways that are simpler, more restrained, more "evangelical." Surely their ideals are just as worthy of respect and attention as are those of others who seek satisfaction in these musical splendors, even though they have been carefully preserved, maternally dispensed and duly approved by the Church.

d) We must consider separately those pieces for the Ordinary of the Mass which have been assembled in the *Kyriale*. Of itself, this collection contains melodies from every epoch, of every genre and style. But what connection is there between *Kyrie* XVI or XVIII (genuine litanic invocations) and the melismatic *Kyrie* II; between the formulary recitative of *Gloria* XV and the Florentine air in ternary rhythm which is *Gloria* VIII; between *Sanctus* XVIII, organically one with the Preface recitative in melody and style, and *Sanctus* IX, a lied in modern tonality; between authentic *Credo* I and plagal *Credo* IV? It is not the mere age of a piece or even its musical style that determines its value, but its accordance with the functional laws of the liturgy. From this point of view, the chants contained in the Vatican *Kyriale* are of very unequal value. Once we admit that the pieces of the Ordinary are, by their intrinsic nature, congregational items, then we have to recognize also that most of the accepted melodies were written for a choir rather than for the assembly, and that they call for the remarks we have already made on the subject of the Romano-Frankish Gregorian chants. However, there are just a few of them which do correspond admirably with the requirements of worship and can be considered as examples which set the norm for the Roman liturgy.[426]

e) Of quite a different nature is the group of pieces, whether poetic or not, which includes the hymns, proses and sequences. This category, popular by nature and spread over a period of from six to ten centuries, has followed

<hr/>

[426] On the other hand, there do exist within tradition quite a number of other similar compositions, such as certain old Gallican *Kyries*, the Ambrosian ferial *Gloria*, and so on, which might well be put forth in the official books. This desire was expressed as a formal proposition at the Fourth International Congress of Church Music held in Cologne in 1961. A certain

the fluctuations of the poetico-musical taste and religious sentiment of the times. Even though some hymns have undergone moderate neumatic development, most of their melodies have remained simple. One must admit, however, that their musical interest is not great. Indeed, for the people of today, these hymns do not form that immediate lyrical element, that homely singing and affective prayer which caused their composition throughout the centuries. The reasons for this breach are the evolution of musical taste, the distance which grew between Latin and the people's own languages, the abandonment of the authentic rhythms,[427] and the very nature of this category, which is unstable and peripheral.[428] Nevertheless, custom has kept alive among the faithful a small number of these liturgical compositions.

f) Finally we must mention those modern adaptations which have been provided for use in new offices. It would seem that the sung parts of the Office and Mass of a new feast may not appear in the official books unless clothed with a "Gregorian" musical grament.[429] Now the principle of imitation is admissible in art provided that it is used in genuine composition, not in the production of a pastiche. But if a technique is employed which belongs to a dead and gone era, something which is no longer a living tradition, a mere pastiche is the almost inevitable result. A policy of this kind runs the risk of identifying liturgical art with some particular style that has now become merely academic.[430] In fact, these new "compositions" do not bring anything new to the corpus of Gregorian chant, and they call for no further remarks.[431]

B. "SACRED POLYPHONY" AND "MODERN SACRED MUSIC"

There are numerous and varied categories which historians of music employ to list and to classify compositions from the artistic point of view: by

number of examples have been collected by B. Staeblein, "Kyrie," "Gloria," "Litanies," etc., in MGG).

[427] Until a few decades ago it was possible to hear our people in country places singing some of the hymns or proses (such as *Veni Sancte Spiritus*) to a measured rhythm that was more or less traditional. But when performance according to equal notes was imposed, the participation of the people disappeared. Even so, it is very doubtful whether an archeologically inspired restoration of the authentic rhythms would ever restore life to this art.

[428] The function proper to hymns has, as we might expect, been partially taken over now by popular religious singing (vernacular hymns).

[429] "Should it happen that new settings are required for new feasts, these must be composed by true experts in Gregorian chant. They ought to be in accordance with the laws of the original Gregorian chant, and worthy rivals of the older compositions both in excellence and in unworldliness" (MDS 21).

[430] Just as during the last century it seemed inconceivable that anyone could build a church unless it were Romanesque or Gothic. In some countries modern religious architecture has happily broken free from such academicism, which can never produce anything except stillborn works.

[431] The diversity of the musical genre represented in the Gregorian corpus raises the difficult question of their rhythmic nature. There is still a great deal of uncertainty about the authentic rhythm of the different parts of the liturgical repertoire. We can but erect a few signposts.

It seems certain that many of the hymns belonged to the measured genre (because of their poetic meter) or to the orchestic genre (because of the symmetrical elements essential to

epochs, schools, styles, genres and forms. And they apply these categories to monodic or polyphonic works composed during the Middle Ages for the liturgical texts which are not included in the Gregorian corpus, and also to all those which composers have never ceased and do not now cease to write for use in worship. These distinctions overlap only partially and indirectly the classification according to function, which is that of the liturgy. Can these other classifications be justified?

a) The *Instruction* of 1958 distinguishes, in contrast to extra-liturgical religious music, two genres: "sacred polyphony" and "modern sacred music" (6-7). The first category holds up the style of the Palestrinian school as the ideal. But it includes also the works, whether earlier or later than the sixteenth century, which have a direct or indirect connection with Gregorian themes and which are to be sung *a cappella*. The second includes works of more recent styles insofar as they are "destined for liturgical use."

This distinction contains two important positive elements. First, it brings out the excellence of classical sacred polyphony typified by Palestrina on account of its essentially vocal character and its connections with the Gregorian tradition.[432] And secondly it states that good liturgical music is not

them, and their range), whereas the prosaic recitatives (readings and prayers) are of the spontaneous genre. There are reasons for thinking also that many syllabic chants, like certain antiphons, are of the purely measured genre: one indivisible note (short) combines with itself to make a long note.

But is neumatic chant also measured? One might say yes because of the *aequalitas canendi* which it requires, and which is usually interpreted by treating each simple note as an indivisible unit of duration. But we still do not know the degree of uniformity or strictness wherewith this principle of indivisible units is to be applied. Moreover, both the legitimacy and interest of incommensurable values (lengthenings which are not proportional), sometimes introduced nowadays to interpret what are called "rhythmic signs" in the manuscripts, have to be proved. Should we not rather admit our inability to determine their exact value? Because if the manuscripts have been so faithful and so exact in transcribing these differences (otherwise "nuances") that we cannot doubt their existence, this can only be because they were specifically defined in their performance. The idea of these things being *ad libitum* or variable contradicts the facts of paleography. For if there are specific written signs, clearly differing from each other and yet constant, it follows that these must correspond with musical phenomena equally specific and objective. *Rubato*, by hypothesis, does not need any such specific and elaborate system of signs. This is confirmed in practice by choirs when they sing: whenever there is to be some lengthening —*a fortiori* when several consecutive notes are to be lengthened—the singers have no standard of reference wherewith to preserve the unity of their movement and the choir becomes ragged, unless it is somehow possible to determine objectively the value of the lengthening. This "woolliness" is often engendered by the horizontal episemata of the "rhythmic editions."

On the other hand, it remains an open question as to whether there is, in neumatic chant, any such thing as a unit of duration larger than the basic indivisible unit—that is to say, whether there are structures of orchestic type mentioned by the old theoreticians, such as the "foot"; perhaps this term is used as an analogy to explain something rather than as a technical datum of the music. We must also take into account the fact that during the ninth century some chants could be accompanied by a "beat" and by percussion instruments (see p. 152 and note 309).

Finally, to what degree is melismatic chant partially related to that kind of spontaneous rhythm which a soloist, ornamenting an original recitative, could allow himself to employ?

[432] "Classical polyphony agrees admirably with Gregorian chant, the supreme model of all sacred music, and hence it has been found worthy of a place side by side with the Gregorian chant in the more solemn functions of the Church, such as those of the pontifical chapel" (TLS 4; cf. MSD 26).

solely a phenomenon of the past, but that the door is wide open to the art of our own days.[433] But because the distinction is half historical and half technical, it is not of much use for judging the value of works which are Gregorian.

We observe, to begin with, that it does not include monodic music, which has never ceased to flourish since the *Kyrie* of St. Hildegarde, through the many plainsong compositions of the seventeenth century (of which the Masses by Du Mont are a living witness), down to those of recent years. These works ought to be considered, for they can play a more important role in the cultural life of the faithful than compositions which are musically of greater worth. They should be judged in each case according to the functional and pastoral needs of the liturgy.

In the second place, the line of demarcation between religious music and liturgical music remains somewhat vague. Beyond doubt all those works which alter the ritual texts in any way, such as by substitution, suppression or addition, or by undue postposition or repetition, cannot be reckoned as liturgical art; [434] the same must be said of those which obscure the text by separating its syllables too much, by mixing up the different voices, or by drowning them under the sound of instruments; [435] and those which substitute other lyrical forms for the authentic forms of the items.[436] But we must also exclude those of such inordinate length that they interrupt or deform the due unfolding of the rites;[437] those not worth considering because devoid of true art; works which seem pretentious and, by their difficulties, exceed the capacities of those expected to sing them;[438] those too reminiscent of worldly music; those which arouse curiosity or disconcert their hearers by their novelty—in a word, everything which seems to be aimed at the worship of art rather than at the worship of the mysteries of Jesus Christ.[439]

The first series of criteria is objective. But the second is relative to the artistic and religious sentiment of the diverse epochs, and to the sensitivity of different communities to richness or sobriety of musical expression, to its worldly overtones and its archaic, classical or modern character. It depends also on the manner in which the Church desires to celebrate her worship. For a long time more importance was attached to the surroundings of the rites than to the rites themselves; in our own day the rites are recovering their due primacy. So it comes about that a number of works which were composed expressly for use in the liturgy, such as certain Masses with

[433] "Modern music is also admitted in the Church, since it furnishes compositions of such excellence, sobriety and gravity that they are in no way unworthy of the liturgical functions" (TLS 5; cf. MD 188; MSD 27-20).

[434] TLS 8-9.

[435] TLS 9 and 16; MSD 27; IMS 48. For previous documents, see above, ch. 10, pp. 142ff.

[436] TLS 10-11.

[437] MSD 27.

[438] MSD 27; IMS 18.

[439] TLS 5; MSD 9-12.

orchestra, certain lessons at Tenebrae or symphonic psalms, should now be considered as "religious music." The same applies to a considerable number of motets (*Ave verum, Ave Maria, Panis angelicus, Salve Regina, etc.*) which appear in the literature as autonomous pieces of music having no direct connection with any given ritual function. To an ever-increasing extent they are now out of place in strictly liturgical celebrations.

In the light of the rules and principles laid down by St. Pius X, and thanks to a liturgical sense that is becoming more refined in consequence of contemporary reforms, it is now possible to make a more discerning choice of works.[440] Quite a number of pieces which, till Pius X's time, were commonly used in the liturgy itself rightly seem to be incompatible now with the restored rites.[441] How can we make an even better choice?

It is not sufficient to cut up history into epochs, or styles into genres, in which the works would be classed as more or less liturgical. Among the intoxications of the *Ars nova* and the contrapuntal virtuosities of the fifteenth century there can be found some works, e.g., certain homophonic *Glorias,* which are marvellously functional.[442] On the other hand, during the very period of Palestrinian classics, not all the Masses are of equal liturgical value. In the wave of the dramatic style or the heart of the romantic, so often far removed from the spirit of the liturgy, some works were written with good proportions and taste. In our own day we witness the publication of concert pieces written on liturgical texts as well as genuine liturgical music. There is no evading the task, in each particular case, of confronting the music in question with the various functional laws of liturgical singing explained above.[442a]

b) There is one particular genre, however, which merits our attention because of its importance. We refer to the "Mass" which brings together in one single composition several of the pieces normally borrowed from the Ordinary of the Mass. First appearing in the fourteenth century, reaching its apogee in the second half of the sixteenth, this genre is still very much in favor with composers and with choirs.

The desire to confer a certain musical unity upon the different items of a

[440] The *Instruction* also points to consultation of the diocesan commission for sacred music (e.g., 48) which should consist of "men who are skilled in both the theory and practice of the various kinds of sacred music" (188).

[441] The greater or less incompatibility of some ancient work with the liturgical worship of today casts no aspersions on its "religious" value, as has been pointed out by N. Dufourcq apropos of classical French music ("La musique religieuse française de ses origines à nos jours," *Revue musicale*, 222 [1953–1954], p. 109).

[442] The best known pieces from this rich, but incompletely edited, period are not always the most liturgical pieces. Hence the invitation to research among such works, and to publish them (IMS 49), on condition that they profit not only erudition and archeology, but also the musical life of communities.

[442a] The Constitution of Vatican II makes mention, after Gregorian chant, of "other kinds of sacred music, especially polyphony" (CL 116), but in connection with this refers to art. 30, which lays stress on the necessity of active participation in the singing by the people.

single office is, in itself, quite legitimate. Some liturgical recitatives, indeed, give us examples of this. But it can be done only on condition that the laws proper to the composition of a single musical work do not supersede, or even conflict with, those proper to the liturgy. When musicians discovered in the sung items of the Mass an ideal field for the exercise of their vocal skill, there was already a great risk of succumbing to the logic of the musical art by integrating into them the procedural techniques of thematic, imitative and cyclic composition. The landslide became almost inevitable, even with artists who had a great respect for the holiness of the rites, when the only understanding of these which they now had was somewhat obscure. Each of the five pieces in the Ordinary of the Mass has a function all its own; this difference of function ought to find expression in well differentiated lyrical forms and in musical genres suited to each; but in most of the classical Masses all this is blurred. They are more like five symmetrical movements of a single choral composition than five specific actions of a celebrating community: the litany of the *Kyrie*, the hymn of the *Gloria*, the proclamation of faith in the *Credo*, the unanimous acclamation of the *Sanctus*, the litanic supplication of the *Agnus Dei*. Sometimes the *Gloria* or the *Agnus Dei* of a Mass fits well enough into a festive celebration, but most of the *Credos*, because of their length, compromise the harmonious progress of a Mass. A *Sanctus* which prevents the participation of the people in the great eucharistic prayer is a serious curtailment of their role, and *Kyries* which do not sound like cries of appeal deprive the assembly of an important element in its Catholic prayer.

We might say, in the words attributed to Palestrina, that if the compositions do not suit the worship, the fault does not lie in music but in the way in which it is used. No doubt it is possible for polyphony and instrumental music to contribute something of value to the celebration of Mass; but the works which demonstrate this are still exceedingly few. If composers will allot to the different singers their own proper role,[442b] and will respect the original form of each piece by setting it in an idiom perfectly suited to its function, then the way is still open to them to provide us, not with further "musical Masses," but with "music to which the Mass may be sung."[443]

[442b] Cf. CL 121.

[443] Contrary to the customs at present in vogue, polyphony would make its most valuable contribution if it were used only for the processional items of the Proper of the Mass; for, as its early history shows, it springs forth naturally from the purpose and spirit of these pieces.

An Introit, for example, might be composed thus: (1) the long opening antiphon in homophonic polyphony sung by the choir; (2) the psalm verses in *faux-bourdon* by a few voices; (3) a *versus ad repetendum* put in by the people, and perhaps accompanied homophonically by the choir; (4) with the organ leading up to and accompanying the whole, and instruments sustaining the *versus ad repetendum* of the people. Some pieces of the Ordinary might integrate polyphony into their structure, either by alternating with the people's unison or by accompanying them homophonically. Thus the threefold repetitions of the *Kyrie* might well give rise to the following kind of sequence: (1) solo or unison by the choir; (2) unison by the people; (3) polyphony by the choir. Or again: (1) solo, (2) choir, (3) people and choir together.

C. HYMNODY

According to present laws, popular religious singing, or hymnody, is extra-liturgical because it does not normally employ the Latin language.[444] But for all that, it is not just simply "religious music" since it may, under certain conditions, accompany liturgical actions.[445]

a) The history of this category helps us to understand the present state of affairs. Even though it was possible, during the Middle Ages, to mix strophes or couplets in the vernacular with some of the liturgical chants, the sixteenth-century reform of the rites introduced a legal distinction which excluded from the liturgy in the strict sense all singing that was not Latin. And so attempts had to be made to provide the people with two kinds of hymn to sing: one kind, of a catechetical type, was to instruct them in Christian doctrine; the other, for prayer in common, translated or paraphrased a great many of the psalms and liturgical hymns. This remarkable effort was to be seen in every Christian country and also in the mission lands. Nevertheless, with the anti-Protestant and anti-Gallican controversies in Europe, and the quarrelling about rites in the mission field, discipline was again tightened, and Rome forbade even the translation of liturgical texts. The catechetical hymn was able to continue its progress, especially among the people, even though its content had lost some of its dogmatic power. But the devotional hymn, more and more cut off from scriptural and liturgical sources, became ever more insipid. It was subjected in turn to the influences of philosophic rationalism and then of romantic sentimentalism.

A short while ago the liturgical movement, having brought forth fruit among the elite, began to be concerned with ordinary people. Then it was found, especially in the Latin countries,[446] that there existed no repertoire of hymns capable of expressing the contents of the rites and mysteries in which the people were to be brought to participate. What is needed in a hymn these days is not just an individualistic renewal of the spirit or expression of piety; and it is something more than the fulfillment of its traditional catechetical function. A hymn is expected to fulfill a role analogous to that of liturgical singing, so that the people can be actively and consciously associated with the rites by means of acclamations, litanic prayers, psalms, troparia and hymns which express the sacraments and mysteries of Christ.[446a]

We are faced, then, with a completely new situation. We must not be surprised that in this sphere, unlike that of liturgical chants, the past has little or nothing of use to offer us. It is very rare that the texts of bygone days correspond exactly with present needs. Their content is often of little value, and their inspiration insufficiently biblical, liturgical and theological. And if we exhume the beautiful translations of psalms and hymns made in

[444] MSD 30; IMS 9, 19, 51.
[445] MSD 31; IMS *ibid.* See ch. 4, pp. 63ff.
[446] German-speaking countries have preserved their *Kirchenlieder*, which are of high quality.
[446a] Cf. CL 30.

former centuries, we find that their linguistic style is now too out-of-date to be used. Fortunately it is much easier to preserve good popular tunes from the past. If they are well suited to the genius of a particular nation and have remained a living tradition, and if their lyrical form accords with the needs of what is to be sung, we can quite often make use of them with new texts, or draw on them for inspiration in composing something new.[447]

b) Contrary to what is frequently held, the real essence of a *cantique*, if it is to be judged according to its function in worship, does not reside in its music but in its words. All the great promoters of popular singing, e.g., Ephrem, Ambrose, Romanos, Cesarius, etc., have left a name in the Church, not for their melodies (which simply correspond with the musical culture of their own days), but for their literary work. In spite of the diversity of languages used, the content of Christian hymnody is a real treasure of the Church. Both her message and her prayer find their due place in it. We can easily understand why the *Instruction* says that "hymnody is much to be praised and encouraged."[448] A great creative effort is called for.

In the melodies for the hymns the particular lyrical genius of each people should find expression. Sometimes, in the more fundamental and traditional types of song (psalms, litanies, acclamations) it will spontaneously come near the common and quasi-universal character of liturgical recitatives. At other times, in the freer forms of hymnody, specific qualities will be accentuated.[449] It is particularly desirable that in mission countries native compositions should be encouraged rather than the imported tunes of European hymns, for they can suit the musical idiom of the country and the poetry which belongs to the language concerned.[450]

[447] The *Instruction* (53), following MSD 32, commends making "collections of hymns and religious folk-songs, including those of former days, which have been handed down in writing or by *viva voce* tradition." In many European countries this has been done. But we have to admit that this work has produced very limited results. Most of the texts cannot be used because of linguistic evolution or poverty of content. The music, too, is frequently no longer in accordance with present-day sensibilities among the people or with the prosodic requirements of a language which has now changed. Thus, in France nearly all the *cantiques* earlier than the seventeenth century have been swept away by the successive waves of operatic airs, romantic ballads, etc. Just a few traces of them can be found in the Breton and Basque *cantiques*, some of which have been used again, and in the old French Christmas carols. But any tunes from the Middle Ages which it has been possible to refurbish are nearly all sophisticated, rather than popular, melodies whose rhythm is strange or uncertain. The Protestants, on their side, have kept alive until today an entire popular sacred repertoire of sixteenth-century melodies in the form of the Huguenot psalms. But the rhythm of those psalms, which accords with the declamatory art of the French language in the sixteenth century, now confronts librettists with difficulties that are almost insurmountable (especially because of the long note which begins each verse and the regular binary scansion). From traditions of this kind it is often better to retain the characteristic spirit rather than the letter.

[448] IMS 51, CL 118.

[449] "As hymns are more adapted to the mentality and temperament of individual countries, they differ very much according to local and national characteristics" (MSD 30; cf. IMS 9).

[450] See MSD 34, and the letter of Cardinal Constantini to the Third International Congress of Sacred Music (*Actes du 3ᵉ Congrès international de Musique sacrée* [Paris, 1959], pp. 523–525):

D. ORGAN MUSIC

Both in fact and in law, the organ, during the period between the ninth and the twentieth centuries, has gradually won for itself an increasingly important place in the Roman liturgy. The Council of Trent merely mentions the use of the organ; the *Ceremoniale Episcoporum* recognizes it; Pius X "permits" it; Pius XI said it was "fully according to the mind of the Church"; Pius XII praises it.[451]

a) The organ was somewhat rare during the Middle Ages, but became more common from about the end of the fifteenth century; its role became more precisely determined during the centuries which followed. At first it was considered an instrument for feast days only; later it was used every Sunday except during Advent and Lent. Closely connected with liturgical singing, it came to be associated with polyphony, probably in order to sustain or supply for a voice, to introduce pieces to be sung, or to supply them by reducing vocal works to the keyboard. Musical scores have preserved some examples of this. The main function of the organ in the sixteenth and seventeenth centuries was to alternate with the choir of singers, after the manner of a second choir, in the psalms, hymn and *Magnificat* of Vespers, as also in the chants of the Ordinary of the Mass (except the *Credo*). The rule was that the entire plainsong melody had to be executed in full. But then, after reproducing vocal works and experimenting with passages and chords of a genuinely instrumental nature, the organ gave rise to the first specific forms of organ music: *ricercare, toccata, prelude*, etc., which were put in after the *Asperges* or the Epistle (sometimes replacing the Gradual and Alleluia), during the Offertory, at the elevation, at the Postcommunion. These short pieces, often inspired by the liturgical melodies and punctuated with frequent cadences so that they could be shortened, remained very functional and seem to have been well suited to the liturgy of those days.[452]

With the advent of symphonic music, the organ acquired a new and direct role in the singing itself. This was developed chiefly in the evangelical churches, but to some extent also in Catholic worship, by the *continuo* which accompanied motets or other liturgical chants. The independent forms of

"It seems evident to me that in making Christ known to these distant peoples, it is not necessary—it is even illogical and dangerous—to take to them Western music in the liturgy." Cf. CL 119: "In certain parts of the world, especially in the mission lands, there are nations which have their own musical traditions, and these play a great part in their religious and social life. For this reason, due importance is to be attached to their music, and a suitable place is to be given to it, not only in forming their attitude towards religion, but also in adapting worship to their native genius. . . . "

[451] "The organ rightly holds the first place among instruments allowed in church. It is eminently suited for sacred music and ceremonies, and gives a wonderful brilliance and a magnificence all its own to the Church's worship. Its grandeur and sweetness deeply move men's souls, fill them with an almost heavenly joy, and lift up their thoughts to God and the things of heaven" (MSD 28). Cf. CL 120.

[452] Cf. L. Tagliavini, "Le rôle liturgique de l'organiste des origines à l'époque classique," *Actes du 3ᵉ Congrès international de Musique sacrée* (Paris, 1959), pp. 367–372.

organ music, for their own part, also became more definite: prelude, fugue, canzona, toccata, all used as a framework or as punctuations for the liturgical action.

But during the course of the eighteenth century, organ-playing gradually made itself independent of the liturgical action both in its style and in its function. The nineteenth century still produced some religious and artistic works, but these preserved hardly a trace of any concern for adaptation to worship or even of any real organ technique. A new and very important element appeared: a generalization of the function of accompaniment. Toward the middle of the century, organists began to accompany Gregorian chant and to use their instruments as substitutes, in musical works, for orchestras, which were too expensive.[453]

Happily the renewal of Gregorian chant and of interest in the liturgy of our own days has prompted the publication of a literature much nearer to the melodies in use and showing more concern for the true role of the organ in worship. At the beginning of our century such literature was sparse, but it became more plentiful later on.

b) From all this repertoire stretching over four centuries, what ought to be retained, and in what order of preference? Before deciding this we must remind ourselves of the true function of the organ in worship.

To begin with, organ-playing is subject to the same general laws as all the rest of Christian music. It must be free from all profane overtones, worldly vanity, unwonted peculiarities, striving for mere esthetics, but also from artistic mediocrity, whether in the work played or in the manner of its performance. For all these things would make organ-playing alien to the celebration of the mysteries.[454] It must also respect all the functional laws of worship. "The playing of the organ at liturgical functions or other devotions should be carefully adapted to the spirit of the liturgical season or day, to the nature of the rites and devotions, and to each of their parts" (IMS 66).

To assess more precisely the role of the instrument it will be useful to distinguish five different functions:

1. *To accompany the singing.* It is when accompanying the sung portions of the rites that the organ is most closely integrated into the liturgical action. But this accompaniment must be subject to several conditions. In the first place, it must sustain the singing and never drown it out (TLS 16). In the second place, an accompaniment is not legitimate unless it is truly a help to the singers and if the nature of the musical work calls for it or permits it.

---

[453] See J. Bonfils, "Note historique sur le rôle de l'orgue dans la liturgie catholique," *Église qui Chante*, 16 (1959), pp. 7–8; and "Le rôle de l'organiste," *Musique et Liturgie*, 82–83 (1961), pp. 70–75.

[454] See TLS 18; DC 8: "It is necessary to avoid that mixture of the profane with the sacred which, through the fault partly of organ-builders and partly of certain performers who are partial to the singularities of modern music, may result eventually in diverting this magnificent instrument from the purpose for which it is intended."

If not, accompaniment is superfluous or undesirable. In truth, the more music subserves the word—and thus the more purely vocal it is—the more it is in accordance with the spirit of the liturgy. On the other hand, art which is purely monodic—such as Gregorian chant—is frequently not capable of harmonization (which is foreign to its own nature) except at the cost of suffering a profound change in its character.[455] This would not apply to more recent melodies to which harmonies are a natural complement, nor, of course, to original compositions which have been written with accompaniment. Finally, we should note that the artistic quality of the accompaniment should be such as to promote sung prayer by its discreet support; and it should not be a distraction on account of clumsy playing which easily attracts attention. Faults in accompaniment are more intolerable than in singing, and they are less excusable; for accompaniment, unlike singing, is not of obligation.

The accompaniment may be improvised or written. In the latter form it may be merely sketched out, or it could be a figured bass or an original score. None of these, however, would be, strictly speaking, a repertoire of organ music.

2. *To alternate with the singing.* In the days when the organ was responsible for supplying the alternate verses of the psalms, hymns, or pieces from the Ordinary of the Mass by playing the liturgical melody (whether the singers recited the corresponding text at the same time or not), it used to fulfill a genuine liturgical function of substitution. Quite an important part of the repertoire of classical organ music owes its origin to this function. But a custom like this, though codified very precisely in the *Ceremoniale Episcoporum* (I, 28), was, in fact, a serious alteration in the liturgical celebration; modern reforms could not do other than apply remedies. So today, in the solemn liturgy, all the sung items must be actually performed (IMS 21). The organ repertoire that was composed for the purpose of "supplying" for the voices can no longer be used for that purpose.

3. *To provide preludes and postludes to the singing.* It belongs to the organ to introduce singing by a prelude (as at the Introit), to lengthen a sung item by a postlude (as at the Offertory), and to punctuate it by interludes (as for a long Communion when uninterrupted singing would become tedious). In this role, organ-playing enters again intimately into the ritual

---

[455] In the days when Gregorian chant was accompanied by castanets (see p. 152), the freedom of its melos was not thereby fettered in any way. In the classical era it was supported by two "serpents." The sound of these instruments used to blend perfectly with men's voices (in those days the music concerned was "plainchant"). But when Adrien La Fage (1805–1862) hit on the idea of harmonizing plain chant, modalism had to be forced onto the Procrustean bed of equal temperament, and rhythm had to hobble along on the crutches of heavy chords. The restoration of Gregorian chant has suffered from this common custom. All that has been done amounts to an attempt to lighten the accompaniment and make it resemble modalism. From the musical point of view, the problem of accompanying Gregorian chant on an organ is quite insoluble. When it appears that some choirs cannot do without it (though often they really could do so) and that the faithful cannot be deprived of it, then it would be better not to seek continual harmonization.

action itself, for it is but a sort of commentary on, or amplification of, the singing. It supplies ornament or embellishment, which is its proper function.

That it may always correspond fully with the action and the singing and avoid the risk of becoming a solo performance, such organ-playing must not take the form of long interventions which might seem to divide the ceremony into sections or even interrupt it completely (TLS 17). For these spells of organ music are not themselves a rite, as is the singing; their purpose is but to increase the solemnity of the rite. Hence they should lead up to it, or originate from it, preferably by developing its melodic themes or at least by preserving its modality and spirit—in any case without introducing an alien or contrasted effect.

Any suitable kind of music, whether ancient or modern, may be used here. But no written piece can be so effective as regards its adaptation to function as an improvisation which is inspired by the music actually being sung, which flows forth from the very act of the celebration, expresses its spirit, fits into its progress, and takes shape according to its due proportions.[456] Together with accompaniment, improvisation is pre-eminently the art—the practical art—of the liturgical organist.[457]

4. *To take the place of singing.* Replacement of singing is, strictly speaking, impossible in solemn liturgy; but there is a kind of lyrical replacement (in a broad sense) which falls to the lot of the organ in the non-solemn forms of liturgy wherein there is no or little singing. Thus, at a low Mass the organ might be used to evoke the processional chants of the Introit, Offertory or Communion by means of pieces suitable in length, style and spirit. For such purposes improvisation is fully admissible, but often it is easier to use some written work because it is quite independent of all liturgical singing.

5. *To surround the ceremonies with music.* It is a happy privilege of the organ that it can help the assembly to achieve a spirit of recollection, can invite it to praise God, can suggest to it quiet meditation or joyful thanksgiving. This it does by filling the holy place with living beauty before or after the sacred function. For such preludes and postludes written pieces can easily be employed. Here and there the quiet playing of the organ is considered acceptable during the silence of the Canon, preferably as a sequel to the *Sanctus.*[458] Here improvisation is normally better than a written piece.

---

[456] As G. Litaize remarks, written music "is not always fitted for use in the course of a liturgical function: the length of one piece, the too worldly character of another, often preclude their use; and the unity of the 'context' of a celebration nearly always rules out the employment of written music" (Paper on "Liturgical Improvisation," Zweiter internationaler Kongress für katholische Kirchenmusik [Vienna, 1955], p. 241).

[457] The technique of improvisation is an indispensable ingredient in the training of organists, even though it is the most difficult and delicate aspect of their art. "As it is very often necessary at liturgical functions for organists to improvise music that will be in keeping with the various parts of the ceremony, they must have knowledge and practical experience of the canons of organ-playing and those of sacred music in general" (IMS 65).

[458] Organ-playing is forbidden between the consecration and the *Pater* of a low Mass except "where there is such a custom" (IMS 29c).

At *pia exercitia* the organ has the same functions as at the liturgy; its role therefore should be judged in a way that is analogous. The organ has a much more important part to play in sacred concerts devoted to religious music; but here there is no longer a question of worship in the strict sense.

Of the five functions just enumerated, not one is essential to worship. The organ is "an ornament" which the liturgy can always dispense with, and which it does forego at certain times as a sign of penitence.[459] That is why the repertoire proper to the organ cannot really be called liturgical music in the strict sense. It is "associated with the liturgical rites" (DC 8), and when it is played apart from the singing it is called "sacred music for the organ" (IMS 8). But it brings most valuable help to the liturgical celebration—practical help when it accompanies the singing, religious help when it interprets the sacred mysteries by the audible signs of music.

c) Since the main contributions of the organ to worship consist in accompanying the singing and in improvisations which this inspires, it follows that the playing of compositions written for the organ (and these are what is meant by "sacred music for the organ"[460]) has but a secondary rank. It is easy to understand that there is always a certain amount of difficulty in inserting an extraneous piece into the sequence of the ritual actions. An organ piece should not appear as something alien or as a tidbit imported into a celebration. This is the principle which should govern the choice of repertoire.

Many of the compositions of the sixteenth–seventeenth centuries, created within and for the Roman liturgy, still find their natural place in it now, provided that they retain a sufficient musical interest for contemporary taste. Often inspired by themes borrowed from the liturgical chants, written in a polyphonic style which suits the organ, these short pieces (which can often be linked together or abbreviated) make good preludes, interludes or postludes for singing; they can even take the place of singing at low Mass. Some of the old verses originally intended to alternate with the singing can be used today for similar purposes. It is important, however, to make sure that these ancient pieces are, as far as possible, performed only in their authentic liturgical and musical context.[461]

A fortiori, it is preferable to make use of the literature which contemporary organists have written directly for the liturgy, inspired by Gregorian melodies and adapted to the precise needs of the celebration: Introit preludes, Offertory postludes, Communion interludes, etc.

The sacred music of the evangelical form of worship raises a question. It

---

[459] IMS 8off.

[460] "Sacred music for the organ is that which has been written for the organ alone. From the period when the pipe organ became sufficiently developed to warrant such compositions, this type of music has been much cultivated by great masters; and, provided it fulfills the conditions required for sacred music, it can be of no small assistance in enhancing the solemnity of liturgical functions." (IMS 8).

[461] "Too often we play these pieces detached from the surroundings in which they came to birth and in which they ought to live" L. Tagliavini, *op. cit.*, p. 372.

contains great masterpieces of sacred music for the organ, such as the works of Bach; but it is most usually based on the themes of Protestant chorales, and thus introduces into the liturgy, by its melodies and the religious sentiment which created them, a world of music which is alien. Now one should avoid that which is alien. And yet we should note that quite a few of the Reformation chorales are themselves based on traditional liturgical themes (*Victimae paschali*, *Veni Creator*, etc.); and, on the other hand, a certain number of these chorales have now been adopted by us. Provided that they are carefully chosen and well placed, many of the "choral preludes" make excellent pieces, especially when used to supply for the absence of singing, or to precede or follow sacred functions. Works of pure music (preludes and fugues), although they can find no suitable place except before or after services, are always fitted for the praise of the one true God.

An entire literature which is genuinely organistic grew up during the nineteenth and twentieth centuries (the chorales of Franck, the symphonies of Widor and Vierne, etc.), and this constitutes a musical category of its own. Although some of these works bear the imprint of an authentically religious spirit, they were really conceived for their own sake. Normally they could not be introduced into a liturgical action for which they were never destined. We should add that there are other pieces, written in former days expressly for use in worship, whose composers lacked a sufficiently enlightened liturgical culture; these can hardly be retained nowadays in the liturgy.[462] As Maurice Emmanuel once said, the task of the organist is not to play *during a service*, but to *play the service*.[463]

THE MODE OF "TE" IN CHRISTIAN MUSIC

The musicologist who works through the traditional repertoires of the Christian liturgies cannot help being struck by the occurrence in all rites of a characteristic type of melody, especially frequent in the recitatives. Its tonic is on *te*, and it usually forms its cadence by using the semitone above (*doh*), which plays the part of a quasi-dominant. Often restricted to three or four notes of the scale, it rarely goes higher than *re* or lower than *soh*. When it does touch the fifth degree (*fah*), the fifth is diminished, which prevents its assimilation to the mode of *me*, otherwise so common.

The harvest of examples seems infinite. We reproduce here just one example from each liturgical tradition.

1) The occurrence of this mode in several of those Jewish traditions which are regarded as the most conservative is interesting with regard to the connections existing between Christian recitative and the Jewish cantillation of the Bible. Opposite we give an extract from a Yemenite *ḳedushah* (accord-

---

[462] Present-day customs still display a reprehensible complacency as regards this extra-liturgical category of music.

[463] Quoted by A. Bonnet, "Musique d'orgue et chant grégorien," *Congresso internationale di musica sacra* (Rome, 1950; Tournai, 1952), p. 344.

ing to A. Z. Idelsohn, *Hebräisch-oriental Melodienschatz* [Jerusalem-Leip-zig–Vienna, 1914–1922], I, p. 62). Perhaps more characteristic still would be the recitative from Proverbs 31:10-16 (the valiant woman) given by J. Parisot in "Note sur les récitatifs israëlites orientaux," *Tribune de Saint-Gervais* (1902), pp. 357-358; even then he pointed out its likeness to a series of Greek and Latin melodies in the mode of *te*.

2) The prayer at the beginning of the offices and of the Mass according to the tradition of Mosul (according to J. Parisot, *Rapport sur une mission scientifique en Turquie d'Asie* [Paris, 1899], no. 302; cf. nos. 303, 306, 307; the *Pater*, no. 311; and the psalm tones, nos. 314, 315, etc.).

3) An evening troparion for Psalm 133 on the fifth Wednesday in Lent (see J. Jeannin, *Mélodies liturgiques syiennes,* [Paris, 1928], II, no. 651).

4) Chant for the priest's prayer at the beginning of the Coptic Mass, quoted by J. Dupoux, "Les chants de la messe," *Tribune de Saint-Gervais* (1903), p. 162, according to L. Badet; compare this with the deacon's direction before the anaphora (*ibid.*, p. 167) and the recitative for the Epistle (p. 170).

5) Armenian deacon's direction according to the usage of Calcutta. J. Du-poux, who quotes it (*ibid.*, p. 167), compares with it a version from Venice which is in the same mode. See also the chant for the Preface (p. 234).

6) This ordinary *Alleluia* from the Liturgy of St. John Chrysostom is found with variants among the Syrians (see J. Dupoux, *op. cit.*, 1904, p. 232) and among the Russians. A recitative for the *synapti* of Vespers, brought back by A. Gastoué ("Grecs et latins," *Tribune de Saint-Gervais* [1897], pp. 42–43), furnishes an example of a very pure recitative in the mode *te*, where the response *Kyrie eleison* strongly resembles the one we quote in (8), and also the Gregorian *Kyrie* XVIII. — The formula for the psaltic *aanes*, transcribed *te-doh-lah-te* by Chrysantes, corresponds with the mode *te*. One cannot but recall also the upper (descending) tetrachord of the old Dorian scale: *me-ray-doh-te*.

7) According to G. Prado, *Manual de Liturgia Hispano-Visigótica o Mozárabe* (Madrid, 1927), p. 303. Compare with the *preces*, p. 297.

8) According to I. Angles, in *The New Oxford History of Music* (Oxford, 1955), II, p. 76.

9) Milanese antiphonary: ferial Vespers for Tuesday. One recognizes the "irregular" tone, given on Plate II (p. 99), which is well represented in the Milanese antiphonary. The syllabic cadence of this tone (*te-doh-lah-doh-te*) is also found in one of the common tones of Milanese psalmody.

10) Comparable with this recitative are the one for the *Ite missa est* from Ordinary XV, and several of the *Kyries* (especially XVIII, which is very characteristic of the mode of *te*). See also the third tone in its restored (monastic) form with termination b, on *te*. Compare with Psalm 46: *Alleluia (ter) omnes gentes* (*Variae preces*, Solesmes, 1901, p. 153), the solemn psalmody of which provides one of the most beautiful examples in this mode. Finally, see the antiphons and short responsories, Plate II, p. 99.

1. Yemenite *Kedushah*:

Ka doš ... mi - me - Ko - mo -

2. Chaldean Recitative:

Awun ... qaddiš, qaddišat awun dwaš-māyā ... el-ā-lam 'almin amin.

3. Syrian *M'irono*:

'et 'iru wqumu bnay nuhrō wšabbahunoyhi lmoryo lhaw ... dnepruq beryoteh.

4. Coptic Entrance Prayer:

Ten shephemot ent - totK ... nem hetve hob niven : nem ehem hob ni-vem

5. Armenian Deacon's Direction:

Asduzo ierghebakēstzuk .

6. *Alleluia* from the Byzantine Mass:

Al-li-lu-ī - a , al-li-lu - i - a .

7. Mozarabic Acclamation:

In nomine D.N.J. Christi ℟ Deo gra - ti-as .

8. Gallican *Kyrie*:

Kyri-e ele-i-son, Chris-te e-le-i-son ... Miserere no - bis.

9. Ambrosian Antiphon:

Qui-a fe-cit mi-hi magna qui po-tens est . Magnificat _ e.o.u.a.e.

10. Roman Epistle:

Lectio...

14   CONCLUSION

THE TASK OF THE COMPOSER

In the true worship which applies salvation in Jesus Christ, music is a sign of the mystery only in the very act of its ritual execution. And it is only the believer, taking part in the liturgy of the Church as she sings to her Bridegroom, who transcends the evanescent phenomenon of number and the transient harmony of melos to enter into the history of salvation and the communion of the Spirit.

A question may now arise in the mind of the musician: If liturgy is essentially a practical art and if ritual music consists, not in sounds which are written down, but in a living dialogue between God and His people, what—in these conditions—becomes of the composer's role? How can he be a servant of worship if singers and performers are the only true agents therein?

Every composer knows already that his work cannot live except by the activity of the interpreter to whom he hands it over and who, in his own way, creates or re-creates it. In like manner he will easily understand that, if he is not himself *hic et nunc* an agent in the celebration, the service which he renders to the liturgy is not a directly liturgical act. Of itself, the composer's work is not a ritual action.

Worship, however, cannot do without musical compositions. If the faithful are to sing together, they must have a definite repertoire common to them all and suited to them. It is for men of art to provide a vehicle in the realm of sound for the prayer of the believers and to give to the Church herself, as it were, her musical bodily form. This is the sublime, and yet formidable, task of the composer.

This task may be considered as an ecclesial ministry.[463a] In a broad sense and

---

[463a] Cf. CL 121: "Composers, filled with the Christian spirit, should feel that their vocation is to cultivate sacred music and increase its store of treasures."

according to the etymology of the word, it is a "liturgy," that is, a sacred service rendered to the visible Body of Jesus Christ in order that its supplication and praise may ascend to the Father. The purpose of the composer's work is not merely to advance the art of music nor to give esthetic satisfaction to a few initiates; still less is it the personal glory of the composer. It is a *diakonia* of the Church—a service rendered to the assembled community of the faithful in order to foster their prayer.[463b] In the broad sense it shares in the nature of the priesthood, which constructs the bridge of mediation, both visible and invisible, between God and men, so that they may receive His grace and render to Him their worship.

No one will deny the glory which surrounds the purpose of this task, so wonderfully performed by the anonymous singers who, for centuries, provided the Latin liturgy with recitatives for the Preface or *Te Deum*, or by the Byzantine monks who painted the icons for their rite. But we may well ask whether this high purpose has not been obscured during the course of centuries by a number of human preoccupations which caused its pursuit to be less pure. Do we not find it difficult to divest ourselves of certain imperatives which have gradually imposed themselves upon secular art but are not consistent with liturgical art?

a) The very act of artistic creation evokes a concern for the work of art itself; this is a sign of the integrity of the creator, and is usually a prerequisite for the quality of what he creates. The artist is, first and foremost, an artisan, a good workman, a master of his craft, who demands that a work be done well, as perfectly as possible, in a good and true style. It is a striving after perfection which is intrinsic to creative work.

But there is another concern, more extrinsic, which can come to light and may involve a lowering, more or less perceived and accepted, of the ideal. The artist becomes concerned, not only that his work shall be as beautiful and perfect as created beauty permits and as the splendor of the divine realities demands, but also that his work be appreciated and acclaimed. Interest is diverted from that which art signifies to that which it produces. The ideal becomes the "masterpiece" acknowledged as such, the "creation" to be praised and applauded. This is a descent from the pursuit of the art (which simply makes a beautiful thing) to the pursuit of a thing (which seeks primarily to appear beautiful). What is appreciated above all is the richness of the materials used, the variety of the means employed, the skill exhibited by the artist.

This worship of the acknowledged masterpiece runs counter to the spirit of the liturgy; it diverts practical and functional art, destined to subserve the

---

[463b] *Ibid.*: "Let them produce compositions which have the qualities proper to genuine sacred music. And they must not confine themselves to composing works which can be sung only by large choirs, but should provide also for the needs of small choirs and for the active participation of the entire assembly of the faithful."

mystery, to a pursuit of a hypostatized beauty which is but mythical, rational
or worldly. For fear of being looked down on by esthetes or technicians,
through anxiety not to be thought naive or ignorant, the composer will hardly
dare to restrict his use of means to that economy which alone will permit
the divine realities to be seen through worship. Not content with the few
notes which would suffice for a recitative to support the sacred words, he feels
constrained to wrap them up in superfluous melismata or to bury them in
sophisticated harmonies. Disdaining simple monody, which alone enables a
crowd to express itself easily and prayerfully, he is interested only in pieces
which need a trained choir to interpret them.

No one can produce work which is truly liturgical in spirit unless he has
meditated on the Beatitudes, unless he appreciates the richness of evangelical poverty, unless he understands that the supernatural glory of Christmas
is that of a *kenosis* and that the brightness of Easter shines forth from the
Cross. The richness of liturgical art is not that of the senses, nor of the intelligence, but that of charity.

b) In every act of artistic creation it is a man who is expressing himself.
But that which he expresses is something infinitely greater than his own self;
in true art all persons other than the artist can recognize something of themselves. A work of beauty speaks a universal language in which every man
can express himself. The artist is the spokesman of the vague desires and
obscure visions to be found in the heart of every man.

Over against this social and universal conception of the artist's role, our
modern age in the West has enthroned the individual, the man of genius,
who is to impart to his contemporaries his own personal message. Beyond
doubt, art has thereby gained in personal overtones, in psychological refinement, in diversity of style and idiom. But it is to be feared that liturgical art
has lost one of its essential qualities.

In the celebration of Christian worship it is Christ who is expressing Himself in His visible Body, the Church. The message which art should transmit
is not that of any individual man, no matter how great his genius or profound his mind. It is first of all the "good news" which Jesus the Messiah proclaims to the ears of men; it is secondly the cry of appeal or of praise which
all believers utter for that salvation which they await from the Lord who
has saved them.

The composer puts his art at the disposal of the community that it may
cry for help or render thanks, just as the singer lends his voice so that the
word of God may be heard. It is not his place, by claiming a sincerity which
is but psychological, to provide the community with "his" music, nor to
propose "his" sentiments, nor to impose "his" idiom. Just as the painter
of icons, following the canons of tradition and seeking universal truth,
would represent Christ, the Virgin, and the saints with their traditional in-
signia so that they could be recognized by all, so also the composer should

provide, for the community of the faithful, music in which they can spontaneously express their faith. The truth that he will seek in his art, the sincerity that he will strive for in himself are not his own but those of the faith. It matters not at all whether his style is new or old provided it is recognized and adopted. It matters not at all whether the music is by a famous composer or by an unknown writer provided it becomes the music of the Church. And the composer need not fear that his personality or his style will suffer from this if he realizes that both the one and the other exist only for and in the community.

c) The worship of the masterpiece or of individual expression often betrays itself by a feature characteristic of modern Western art: a striving for originality. How many there are who would feel that they have lost face if someone said to them: "Your work is written as So-and-So might have done it" or: "This composition reminds me of such-and-such a work." The carvers of the old cathedrals and the psalmists of ancient days would not have been disturbed by such remarks! Among the Greeks the invention of the *nomoi* was held to be a revelation from the gods, and the task of the musician was to employ them according to the rules of the art.[464] Originality is not a criterion either of beauty or of artistic quality. On the contrary, creative imitation is a constant law of art. To it history owes most of its revivals.

In liturgical music creative imitation is of special value. The Church lives from a tradition whose principle is the Spirit of Pentecost, but which expresses itself visibly in signs whose permanence is a condition of their being understood. The Church has created for herself her own mode of expression, which, though relative as regards the historic forms it has assumed, is not itself separable from her life. Her personality is visible therein. From the way in which the Church expresses herself one learns what she is and what she tends to become. That is why she attaches such great value to the traditional forms in which she has expressed her true worship: the Western and Eastern rites; the formulas of prayer; Gregorian, Syrian, Byzantine chants, etc. When she feels the need to adapt or renew these forms, it is never done by means of a breach with tradition.

[464] "The ancients used to view the act of musical composition from a standpoint very different from ours. Whereas in our day the composer seeks above all to be *original*, imagining for himself his motifs with their harmonies and their instrumentation, those Romans and Greeks who wrote melodies (and, after them, the writers of liturgical chants) normally worked on traditional themes from which they drew new chants by way of amplification. From very early times a theme of this nature was called a *nomos*—law, rule, or model. Just as in architecture, composition in music consisted in producing new works out of materials taken from the common domain. This mode of procedure is not limited to the ancient Greeks; it can be found wherever homophonic music reached up to the concept of modal unity, to the recognition of a fundamental harmony. Analogous to the *nomos* of the Greeks, the *sâman* of the Vedic priests and the *râga* of modern Hindus form a simple melodic scheme serving as a groundwork of an indefinite number of chants; each one of them is the common element in a distinct group of melodies" (F. A. Gevaert, *La mélopée antique dans le chant de l'Église latine* [Ghent, 1895], p. 123).

What member of the Church is there who believes himself so penetrated with her spirit that he could claim to give her an absolutely original language that could express her authentically? The musicians of the Church have always loved to go back to traditional themes taken from the liturgical chants in order to draw their inspiration from them. There are dozens of Gregorian antiphons which have been shaped from a few melodic formulas taken up again in all sorts of ways. The Latins have adapted many of the Greek chants, and the choral art of the Renaissance used many airs borrowed from plain chant. This is where novelty can enter in: by employing in a new idiom, with different rhythms or with the aid of an instrument, music which is itself timeless. It is very naive to think that imitation is incompatible with the sincerity of the artist or with the quality of his work of art. The genuine Church composer feels at ease in the world of tradition without any diminution of his facility for invention or of his power to appreciate contemporary forms of art.

Between the celebration of worship and artistic activity there exists a tension which is both inevitable and salutary. Art seeks that which is most beautiful; the liturgy seeks that which is most holy. Although holiness and beauty may fuse at the highest plane, art is concerned immediately with visible signs of the sacred, whereas liturgy maintains the transcendence of the invisible. The delights of beautiful forms inevitably take possession of man's senses, and sometimes become an obstacle to the prayer of his spirit. St. Augustine both experienced and spoke of this temptation. It is inevitable that a composer finds more satisfaction in working for the cultured rather than for the simple people. Attention to sensible forms is a prerequisite for progress in art, and yet a certain detachment from these is required for progress of faith. Nevertheless, faith cannot dispense with signs any more than art can content itself with the things of the visible world.

From this tension there ought to result a living equilibrium which is prompted by the Holy Spirit but controlled by the Church. Pius XII, in a passage of *Musicae sacrae*,[465] has reminded us that there is a necessary relation between the faith and the creative activity of any artist who intends to serve the Church:

> The artist who has no religious faith or whose thoughts and way of life are far removed from God cannot lay claim to a religious art. His soul lacks the power of seeing what God's majesty demands, what His worship requires. Works of art that have no religious inspiration may perhaps proclaim an artist of experience and of some technical ability. But they cannot express religion and faith in a way that is becoming to God's house and its holiness and thus worthy of being admitted by the Church into her worship. For it is

[465] MSD 11-12.

the Church, the guardian of the religious way of life, that must decide what is worthy or unworthy.

But the artist whose faith is firm and whose way of life is worthy of a Christian has the love of God as his motive power and puts to reverent use the artistic ability he received from his Creator. And so he will try by every means in his power to express and to put before men the truths he holds and the religion he practices . . . His artistic work is like an act of religious worship for the artist, while it moves and inspires others to profess their faith and practice their religion.

When reading this text, couched in terms that are rhetorical rather than strictly theological, and wherein certain words—such as the adjective "religious"—are somewhat imprecise, we have to be on our guard against all misunderstandings. We may not conclude from it (for this would be contrary to facts) that an artist is incapable of all religious art if he lacks the fullness of Christian faith and morals. A non-Christian can have a well-developed sense of the sacred; a sinful member of the Church can correctly express her faith. But the former, even though capable of art which is religious, cannot (apart from exceptions) transmit that which is specific to the Christian revelation. His art, "religious" in a broad sense, cannot *a priori* be called Christian (even if it adumbrates or integrates some Christian values), still less "liturgical," since liturgical art has the specific function of signifying the mysteries of Christ. The latter could make some claim to do this. But since artistic creation is for any normal man an act which engages him totally, personally and socially, it is only right and fitting that some experience of the life of grace should be the background of his art, and that a spiritual sensitivity marked by the love of Christ should be manifested in what the faith holds and expresses.

In a word, the artist who would serve Christian worship ought to possess in a high degree, in addition to mastery of his art, an understanding of the mind of the Church. This is a point developed by Msgr. Johannes Wagner when commenting on this same text:[466]

> The religious artist who wishes to produce liturgical art today must have profoundly grasped what the *civitas Dei* assembled in hierarchical order really is, and what the full meaning of active participation is. Not only must he himself have piety, but he must know how to raise his voice with priest and assembled community to praise God in common worship, and actively to cooperate in celebrating the sacred liturgy. Otherwise little may be expected from him in the way of liturgical art. St. Augustine needed but a brief word to

[466] "Liturgical Art and the Care of Souls," a paper read at the First International Congress of Pastoral Liturgy, Assisi-Rome, Sept. 18–22, 1956. Quoted from *The Assisi Papers* (Collegeville, Minn.: The Liturgical Press, 1957), pp. 72–73.

the Christians of his time in order to give expression to Christian freedom while at the same time inculcating Christian duty: "*Ama et fac quod vis*—Love, and do what you will."

May God enable our own generation to raise up great artists animated with the liturgical spirit who will say "I am here" to devote themselves to works of art. Beyond doubt these are called for by "the awakening of the Church in men's souls" (Guardini), by the liturgical reforms which the Popes have introduced, and above all by the great directive concerning active participation of the people. We may indeed hope to witness the emergence of a great and new liturgical art. It should be enough to quote to such artists a phrase which, like that of St. Augustine, expresses both liberty and solidarity: "*Vivas cum Ecclesia et fac quod vis*—Live with the Church and do what you will."

The letter "n" preceding a reference number refers to footnotes.